D1526686

Blueprints for Battle

FOREIGN MILITARY STUDIES

History is replete with examples of notable military campaigns and exceptional military leaders and theorists. Military professionals and students of the art and science of war cannot afford to ignore these sources of knowledge or limit their studies to the history of the U.S. armed forces. This series features original works, translations, and reprints of classics outside the American canon that promote a deeper understanding of international military theory and practice.

SERIES EDITOR: Roger Cirillo

An AUSA Book

BLUEPRINTS FOR BATTLE

Planning for War in Central Europe, 1948–1968

Edited by
Jan Hoffenaar and Dieter Krüger

English translation edited by
Major General David T. Zabecki, AUS (Ret.)

UNIVERSITY PRESS OF KENTUCKY

Published by special arrangement with Militärgeschichtliches Forschungsamt
[Military History Research Institute, MGFA], Potsdam, Germany

Published by the University Press of Kentucky
Scholarly publisher for the Commonwealth,
serving Bellarmine University, Berea College, Centre College of Kentucky, Eastern
Kentucky University, The Filson Historical Society, Georgetown College, Kentucky
Historical Society, Kentucky State University, Morehead State University, Murray State
University, Northern Kentucky University, Transylvania University, University
of Kentucky, University of Louisville, and Western Kentucky University.

Editorial and Sales Offices: The University Press of Kentucky
663 South Limestone Street, Lexington, Kentucky 40508-4008
www.kentuckypress.com

16 15 14 13 12   5 4 3 2 1

Library of Congress Cataloging-in-Publication Data

Blueprints for battle : planning for war in central Europe, 1948–1968 / edited by Jan
Hoffenaar and Dieter Krüger ; English translation edited by David T. Zabecki.
    p. cm. — (Foreign military studies)
  Includes bibliographical references and index.
  ISBN 978-0-8131-3651-6 (hbk. : alk. paper) — ISBN 978-0-8131-3652-3 (pdf) —
ISBN 978-0-8131-3982-1 (epub)
  1. Military planning—Europe—History—20th century. 2. Military planning—
United States—History—20th century. 3. Military planning—Soviet Union—
History—20th century. 4. North Atlantic Treaty Organization—History—20th
century. 5. Warsaw Treaty Organization—History. 6. Military history, Modern—20th
century. 7. Cold war. 8. Europe—Defenses. I. Hoffenaar, J. II. Krüger, Dieter.
III. Zabecki, David T. IV. Germany. Militärgeschichtliches Forschungsamt.
  U155.E85B54 2012
  355.02094'09045—dc23   2012015258

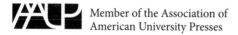

Contents

Foreword

In November 1986 I was working at the Ruppertsweiler Underground Facility during a North Atlantic Treaty Organization (NATO) exercise. Affectionately known as "RUF," the huge subterranean complex in the German state of Rhineland-Pfalz near the French border was the wartime command post of NATO's Central Army Group (CENTAG). At the time, CENTAG consisted of two U.S. Army corps, two Bundeswehr corps, and a Canadian brigade. I was working in the Intelligence (G-2) Cell, which was in a large, rectangular room deep in the bowels of the earth. One of the long walls of the room was covered by a 1:250,000 scale map of Central and Eastern Europe, depicting CENTAG's area of operations, area of responsibility, and area of interest. The map itself was covered with Plexiglas, on which the relevant tactical information could be written as the exercise unfolded. Computers had not yet taken over such functions.

The day before the exercise was scheduled to start, several of us were setting up the G-2 room, checking communications, and making sure all the necessary log books and reference files were in order. The Bundeswehr Feldwebel (staff sergeant) who was in charge of the map-posting detail walked up to the eastern half of the map with a grease pencil in his hand. In the sector of what was then East Germany he crossed out the name of Karl-Marx-Stadt and wrote in "Chemnitz." Moving into Poland, he crossed out Wroclaw and wrote in "Breslau." And then he crossed out Gdansk and wrote in "Danzig." Finally he turned around and looked at the rest of us and said, "Now we're ready to start."

That German noncommissioned officer's actions, of course, were in no way representative of the policy of NATO, or of the Federal Republic of Germany. Rather, it was a typical example of grim soldier humor. Soldiers tend to be pessimistic, and what strikes them as funny runs toward the black. It is an occupational hazard. That Feldwebel's attempt at a joke really expressed the broad frustration over what seemed to be the practical impossibility of ever altering the status quo of the Cold War, or leastwise, not altering it for the better. By 1986 the Cold War had been going on for as long as most of us in that room had been alive, and there was no likelihood that we would ever see any significant changes during the remainder of our lives. Personally, I had been involved in the Cold War for eighteen years at that point, starting from when I worked in the Fire Direction Center of a nuclear-capable 8-inch artillery unit in 1968. In August of that year I was with my unit in Grafenwöhr right opposite the border with Czechoslovakia as the forces of the Warsaw Pact moved into that country to suppress the Prague Spring movement. For a couple of days it looked like World War III was going to start then and there.

There was no way we ever could have foreseen it at the end of 1986, but a scant three years later the Berlin Wall fell, on 9 November 1989. Eleven months later the German Democratic Republic ceased to exist when it merged with the Federal Republic of Germany on 3 October 1990. The following year on 1 July the Warsaw Pact was disbanded, and six months later on 26 December 1991 the Soviet Union itself was disestablished. Along the way, Karl-Marx-Stadt did resume its old name of Chemnitz in 1990. Even more remarkably, the following year Russia's Leningrad resumed its old name of Saint Petersburg. Not all of the Feldwebel's predictions came true, however. Gdansk and Wroclaw still go by their Polish names, but in 1999 Poland itself became a member of NATO—something my Polish-born grandparents would have loved to have seen. Yet everything that happened with seemingly blinding speed during that ten-year period would have been thought of as sheer fantasy by those of us in the CENTAG bunker in 1986. That's what made the Feldwebel's cynical little joke so ironic.

Almost from one minute to the next, what had for so long seemed a frozen political-strategic environment that would endure forever dissolved. The Cold War was over. In the immediate euphoria that followed, it then seemed that the era of global conflict had come to an end, and some theorists even speculated about "The End of History." That rose-colored aura did not last long, of course. Today, twenty years after the end of the Cold War, there are still festering hostilities and tensions throughout the world, and in many ways the world is less stable today than it was at the height of the Cold War. But the stakes and the risks are much different now. At least the world's two nuclear superpowers are not trying to stare each other down, each with its finger on the nuclear trigger of Armageddon. Whatever conflicts may erupt in the near future, Central Europe most likely will not be the objective over which such conflicts may be fought, nor is it likely to be the central battleground.

The Cold War was not completely cold, of course. There were many hot flare-ups around the periphery—Korea, Vietnam (twice), Afghanistan, and the proxy wars in the Middle East. But Central Europe, and specifically the territory of the two Germanys, would have been the battleground on which any direct clash between NATO and the Warsaw Pact would have taken place. Would such a conflict have remained limited to just Europe? Or would it have escalated into a thermonuclear global conflagration? We may never know for sure, and historians will continue to debate that question for many years to come.

A more intriguing question is why that clash never happened. Was it just pure luck? Or did mutual deterrence actually work? Throughout the Cold War it was an article of faith among most peace activists that the presence of nuclear weapons and massive military forces on either side of the Inner-German Border made war more likely and unnecessarily increased the risk of some sort of accidental flash point. On the other hand, the French philosopher and modern interpreter of Clausewitz, Raymond Aron, noted in his book *Peace and War: A Theory of International Relations* (1961), "The direct contact of the armies tends to forestall incidents, accidents, and misunderstandings: it was in the void created by the retreat of the American troops [in the late 1940s] that the North Korean aggression occurred. A military void is more dangerous than a presence."[1]

The Cold War was only about fifteen years old when Aron wrote those lines. Looking back on the history of the Cold War in Europe's Central Sector from today's perspective, it seems like Aron had it right. But in the twenty years that followed the end of the Cold War there was a dearth of critical scholarship examining what was the central event of the second half of the twentieth century. Fortunately, that has begun to change in recent years, with historians on both sides of the Atlantic and on both sides of what was once the Iron Curtain devoting more and more attention to the Cold War. This book, the combined effort of German, Russian, British, American, and Dutch scholars, is a significant contribution to that process.

This volume is the first in a new series from a partnership between the Militärgeschichtliches Forschungsamt (MGFA) and the Association of the United States Army (AUSA). MGFA, or the Military History Research Institute, is the official history organization of the Federal Republic of Germany's Bundeswehr. Its mission is to conduct fundamental research in the field of military history, focusing on the era of the two world wars and the military history of the Federal Republic of Germany and the German Democratic Republic. MGFA also maintains the essential foundation for history education throughout the Bundeswehr. The mission of AUSA includes fostering public understanding of the U.S. Army's role in national security and providing professional education programs, especially through its Institute of Land Warfare. In coordination with the University Press of Kentucky, the MGFA-AUSA partnership sponsors and promotes the translation and publication in English of selected MGFA books, which are internationally recognized for their depth and quality of scholarship. This initiative will make these important works accessible to a broader range of English readers.

D. T. Z.

Notes

1. Raymond Aron, *Peace and War: A Theory of International Relations* (London, 2003 [1961]), 503.

Preface

Cold War and Virtual Warfare in Central Europe, 1950–1968

Research on the Cold War as an epoch-making phenomenon of the twentieth century began long before the era ended. Before the events of 1989–1990, reflections on the Cold War's origins and impact were an integral part of the Cold War itself. Consequently, scholars initially focused on who bore the responsibility for the conflict. Deliberations later centered on the issue of whether the Cold War was the result of ideology or power politics.[1] Today, two decades after it ended, historians widely agree that the Cold War had in principle been a global ideological conflict.[2] Ideological and material structures were subject to a process of dialectical transformation perceived in the hearts and minds of the people as an epochal process of learning, which in the end helped to preserve peace. Capitalist democracy, as the inheritance of the American Declaration of Independence of 1776 and the French Revolution of 1789, claimed universal importance, just as bureaucratic Communism did as the totalitarian continuation of the European labor movement of the nineteenth century.

Under the flags of their respective models of society, the two superpowers on the flanks of the formerly European-centered international political system established blocs of states. The immediate reason for this was probably less the basic intention of one side to set up a zone of influence than each side's concern about having to preempt any imperial aspirations on the part of the other. The leading powers tried to maintain the internal coherence of their blocs and to extend their boundaries. Thus, the ideological antagonism took the form of a worldwide power conflict. As such, it interfered with and shaped the cultural, economic, and political clashes of interest between and within all states worldwide. Traditional power conflicts between states—for example, between Russia and Western Europe or between France and Great Britain—were transformed without yet disappearing.[3] Consequently, the new characteristic of the "New Cold War" that had been conjured up (against the background of the Georgian-Russian conflict over South Ossetia and the issue of American missile defense installations in summer 2008) was actually that of the old one. It was the conflict for control between two world powers, along with the Europeans' concern about the overshadowing colossus on their eastern flank, with its opaque political system and its extensive Asian hinterland.

The Soviet Union secured its bureaucratic regime with an army that was superior to any other in Europe and a secret police that was mostly unscrupulous. In accordance with their totalitarian characters, the Communist-ruled states did not countenance a social sphere beyond their governmental party rule. Everything was political; every social phenomenon either was controlled by the party or tended to be subversive. This was perceived by the elites in Europe and America as a threat to their own societies, which were relatively free from governmental interference; to their economic structures, which were based on private property; and to the associated pluralism of interests and views of the world. For the Communists, the United States was hardly less of a threat given America's economic superiority and its standing as a nuclear-armed sea power that had formed a number of military alliances on their opposite coasts.

What was perceived as "encirclement" by the Soviet Union was understood to be "containment" by the United States and its allies. The intent was to foil the alleged or actual aspirations of the Soviets to incorporate states into their sphere of influence through a combination of military pressure and internal subversion by Communist movements. The foreign relations of the Western states, on the other hand, were not monopolized by the political apparatus. Instead, they were shaped by businesses, associations, political parties, and networks of people who were relatively independent of the state apparatus. Those various elements regularly had differing and even conflicting interests. Consequently, the aggregate economic and cultural relations that were not under direct state control also secured the influence of the United States. This paved the way for peaceful penetration by entertainment, culture, and economics, which the Communists considered a particularly insidious challenge.

Of course, Washington rarely hesitated to use its clandestine services whenever there was the threat of change to the capitalist social order in key geopolitical zones or areas of influence. Overthrows were mostly perceived as a Communist-inspired export of the social revolution, which removed the leverage for exerting Western economic and cultural influence. Communist foreign policy, on the other hand, was the domain of the party state that as a matter of principle allowed neither external nor internal opposition.[4] Whereas relations within the North Atlantic alliance were democratic, those within the Warsaw Pact were more autocratic, as proved by the Soviet Union's repeated military interventions in its sphere of influence.[5] In contrast, the United States often carried out covert actions in coordination with indigenous groups.[6] Western societies widely believed that the alliance was protecting the emerging welfare states in Western Europe from violent attack. The alliance restricted Soviet influence and consequently challenged Soviet dominance in Eastern Europe, because the prosperity, culture, and lifestyle of the Americans fascinated the Europeans, including those countries under Communist rule.

The asymmetric character of the Cold War is plain to see in hindsight.[7] The majority of the Western states enjoyed the advantages of democracy, which basically delimits business and society from political rule. The free thinking, competition of ideas and interests, and technological advantage this encourages lead to a consumer society. The Communist model of society, on the other hand, lost its persuasive power because of the at-first gradual and later rapid loss of economic significance of the Soviet Union and its allies. Even the militarization of the societies and the oppression by the secret police, which grew more and more subtle as time went on, could not stop this process. On the contrary, investments in the armaments and the security complex accelerated the decline in the production of consumer and civilian capital goods.

Deeper insight into this asymmetry underlies the former antagonism between "classical" and "revisionist" Cold War historians.[8] Some had assumed the Cold War's origins were based in the aggressive totalitarianism of the Soviet Union, whereas others had thought it was to be found in the economic imperialism of the United States. In the end, the decisive factor was the "soft power" of the West—an element occasionally underestimated by Western strategists.[9] The summary chapter by Gregory W. Pedlow in this volume, however, is a reminder that not only the Eastern societies but also those in the West ran the risk of being militarized. After all, it was probably the most important American military leader, Dwight D. Eisenhower, who as president raised the warning flag about the military-industrial complex that called prosperity and freedom into question.

From the second Berlin crisis (1958–1961) and the Cuban missile crisis (1962) at the latest, it was obvious that an armed conflict between the superpowers involved the risk of human civilization being exterminated. Consequently, a nuclear regime comprising the Nuclear Test Ban Treaty and the Treaty on the Non-Proliferation of Nuclear Weapons was established between the two superpowers in the 1960s.[10] This regime, however, was unable to prevent permanently the emergence of new nuclear powers. In the course of the decolonizations of the 1950s, the competition between the two systems had extended into the so-called Third World. Nevertheless, Europe, Germany, and Berlin remained the theaters of a potential all-out military conflict. As the conflict played out, however, it was actually waged only in the form of proxy or colonial wars in the Asian and African periphery.[11] The events on the periphery did not, of course, gain so much influence as to change the basic course of the competition between the systems. In Europe, the conflict remained permanently cold. And at least after the erection of the Berlin Wall in 1961, the physical boundary between the systems in Europe became a "frozen front," as Richard J. Aldrich puts it in his contribution to this volume.

Nevertheless, all the parties continued to see preparations for a possible military conflict as a key prerequisite for their security. On the one hand, arms limitation became an integral part of military strategy. On the other, peaceful coexistence and détente had been elements of the confrontational security policy of the military alliances and their leading powers since at least 1967. Soviet premier Nikita Khrushchev was convinced that Communism would prevail as a form of society as long as the Soviet Union was able to prevent the opponent from forcibly eliminating existing and future socialist states through military force. Instead, we now know that the West's economic and technological lead increased as long as it could maintain its internal coherence while both appropriately and credibly deterring the Warsaw Pact from launching a preventive military strike.

The Cold War was the result of a mutual perception, a discourse between and within the two camps in which many views were voiced. The subsequent institutional consequences derived from this perception and discourse. The comparative perspective was thus laid down at the very beginning.[12] After the end of the Cold War, historical research on the period gained momentum, thanks to increased access to the relevant records. Internet portals operated by the Swiss Federal Institute of Technology Zurich (Parallel History Project on Cooperative Security) and the Woodrow Wilson International Center in Washington (Cold War International History Project) were instrumental in the process of digitizing documents and making available bibliographies and papers.[13]

Those who understand the Cold War as a mutual process will endeavor to be fair to both sides. This does not by any means turn the Cold War into a demiurge that can be made responsible for all the atrocities and crimes committed during its epoch. The former Cold War actors cannot escape the historical and moral assessments of their deeds by pointing to their alleged logic and inevitability, just as they can little elude the accusations of their victims. Only two decades after it ended, however, the Cold War seems as far away as ancient times, as Pedlow notes in his conclusion to this volume.

Despite the surprising speed at which it has become history (compared to World War II), the ideological positions adopted during the Cold War will reverberate for a long time as that conflict undergoes future historical reappraisal.[14] The term "New Cold War" coined by journalists is more confusing than enlightening from the historian's point of view, but above all it makes clear that the Cold War is not by any account forgotten. Consequently, the "losers" of the actual Cold War are under pressure to justify themselves, whereas the "winners" are faced with the problem of appropriately exploring their opponents' room for maneuver at that time.

When researching the military strategies and operational planning of the alliances, contemporary and military historians are confronted with a rather strange situation.[15] The higher-level politics of the transatlantic Western alliance, NATO's strategy debate, even its history as an international organization and the relationship between European integration and Atlantic security, are well documented.[16] NATO has posted its important strategy documents on the Internet, including those detailing the changes in the parameters of military strategy during the 1950s and 1960s—from the initial Peripheral Strategy, to Massive Retaliation, to Flexible Response.[17]

In contrast, little research has been done on the operational planning of the alliance, that is, the conversion of the military strategy into emergency plans by SHAPE (Supreme Headquarters Allied Powers Europe) and its major subordinate commands, army groups, and air fleets. Apparently the historical documents of these commands—namely their emergency defense plans, general defense plans, and atomic strike plans—have either gone missing or are difficult to access.[18] The reasons for this are explained by Robert Evans at the start of his chapter in this volume. The headquarters of the British Army of the Rhine (BAOR) continuously destroyed their classified operational records as soon as they were revised or rescinded. This situation might find favor with some German historians in particular, among whom an aversion to the trade of the soldier is rather common. In the introduction to his chapter, however, Helmut Hammerich correctly insists that the battle history of the Cold War—that is, the operational planning of the alliances—should be just as much a part of the period's historiography as its political, economic, and cultural history. The operational history of the Cold War, therefore, is the central focal point of this volume.

The situation is different for the Warsaw Pact, as Torsten Diedrich explains in his chapter. Available informative accounts are dedicated to strategic and operational questions.[19] Moreover, former member states of the Warsaw Pact that now belong to NATO have made parts of their relevant record holdings accessible or have even published them.[20] Russia, however, has so far kept the strategic documents of the General Staff of the Warsaw Pact under lock and key. It is possible to draw conclusions about the Pact's strategy from the available military and security policy records of that alliance's former member states. Nevertheless, a high degree of uncertainty remains, especially since the armed forces of the Warsaw Pact evidently went to great lengths to make it almost impossible to draw from its exercise records precise conclusions about the Pact's real strategic-operational concepts. Subordinate headquarters were informed about the general concepts only to the degree deemed absolutely necessary for them to accomplish their assigned tasks. A result of Moscow's secrecy mania is the persisting focus on the United States and NATO, if only in the field of "big strategy," which John L. Gaddis noted as a characteristic of the early Cold War research more than a decade ago.[21]

So far, research on the two military alliances has been dominated by a perspective that focuses primarily or exclusively on the one camp.[22] This conforms to the parameters of the Cold War itself but is also the product of more mundane factors, such as the lack of language proficiency or access to sources. For years, however, contemporary witnesses and historians from the states of the two former camps and from neutral countries have met to exchange views on the strategic and operational plans of the Cold War period.[23] This, of course, does not yet reach the level of a problem-oriented comparative approach to the two alliances.[24] Such an approach would have to encompass comparing the intentions and problems of the alliances and the solutions they reached. The comparison would allow for conclusions to be drawn about the character of the alliances and their member states, as well as about their respective societies and political systems. As Lawrence S. Kaplan writes in his chapter, the perceptions the alliances had of the threat were the result of the simultaneous perception of the external adversary and internal tensions. A comparative approach, however, requires an adequate foundation of detailed studies, which is continuously strengthened by symposiums conducted across the former Warsaw Pact borders. This present volume is committed to that objective. It is the product of a conference held in Mün-ster, Germany, in 2007, hosted jointly by the Netherlands Institute of Military History and the German Military History Research Institute.

According to chapter authors Kaplan, Diedrich, and Bruno Thoss, Cen-tral Europe, what NATO designated as its Central Sector, always remained the epicenter of the Cold War. Interest, therefore, focuses on the strategic ideas and operational plans of both alliances in Central Europe in general, and in northern Germany in particular. The plain reaching from Pomerania in the east to the Atlantic in the west was ideal terrain for tanks. Only the courses of the Oder, Elbe, Weser, Ems, and Rhine Rivers, and the densely populated area west of the Elbe, posed noteworthy terrain obstacles. Con-sequently, NATO expected the enemy to approach on this axis with a heavy, perhaps the heaviest, concentration of his ground and tactical air forces, pre-sumably in combination with a thrust by the Baltic Fleet against the Baltic exits and Jutland. The Soviet, Polish, and East German military units faced the mixed force of German, British, Netherlands, and Belgian divisions of the Northern Army Group (NORTHAG) of the Central Region.

Kaplan and Matthias Uhl emphasize that the West overestimated the threat posed by the Soviet Union in the 1940s and 1950s.[25] Even after having approved the attack on South Korea on 25 June 1950, Stalin adhered to his defensive course in his military and security policy. Evans quotes the Brit-ish commander-in-chief of NORTHAG, General Sir Richard Gale, who in September 1955 stressed that the Soviet armed forces had established a de-fensive posture. He thus came to the conclusion that the military deterrence measures of the West were obviously adequate. Viktor Gavrilov and, simi-larly, Diedrich write that in Moscow's eyes, the advanced conventional armed forces of the Soviet Union in Germany, Austria, and Hungary compensated for the nuclear threat posed to the Soviet economy by the United States. The Soviet Union would actually have pushed through to the Channel only in response to a nuclear attack. At the time, the Soviet Union had not yet been able to match the Americans in terms of nuclear assets. The Soviets therefore sought to deter the Anglo-Saxons with conventional weapons and with the threat of taking Western Europe as a hostage.[26]

As Diedrich notes, the Soviet military presence also facilitated the consol-idation of the cordon sanitaire in Eastern Europe. That was meant to protect the Soviet Union from another invasion if the "imperialist powers" went at each other's throats again, a development that was extremely probable from the Marxist-Leninist perspective. Moreover, Stalin had hoped to prevent the formation of a bloc in the west through diplomatic efforts and Russia's influence on the western Communist parties. Had Stalin succeeded, the Soviet Union would have had sufficient political influence over a conglomeration of bourgeois small and medium-sized powers, ideally with Communists in the government. When the Soviets later advocated a collective security system in Europe, ideally without North American participation, their objective was basically the same as it had been in the 1940s. During those years, however, the United States foiled Soviet intentions with the Marshall Plan and the reconstruction of West Germany. According to Gavrilov, the Soviet Union perceived both initiatives as a threat to its legitimate security interests.

The spiral of fear did indeed begin to revolve more quickly in 1948. The Stalinization of Eastern Europe in response to the American challenge boosted the foundation of the Atlantic alliance, which sooner or later would include West Germany. At the same time, the internal resistance against the Soviet consolidation of Eastern Europe hardly abated. On the contrary, the people there saw their chance after Stalin's death in 1953. From Moscow's perspective, real de-Stalinization and the reform of Communism posed the risk of the states of their European cordon sanitaire defecting to NATO with flying colors, as did indeed happen after the Cold War had ended.[27] American secretary of state John Foster Dulles proclaiming the aim to roll back the Soviet Union from Eastern Europe could hardly have been perceived by the Stalinists as anything but a confirmation of what they expected from a politician of a major capitalist power.

The states of Western Europe welcomed the decision made under the influence of the Korean War to transform the North Atlantic pact into an institutional military alliance as a guarantee of their sovereignty. The deployment of four American divisions to West Germany after 1951, described by Donald A. Carter in his chapter, had to be followed up with the armament of the Federal Republic of Germany. The American soldiers otherwise would have found themselves in a strategic vacuum, in which they would have been annihilated during an emergency. Without German support, it would have been almost impossible to hold even the line of the Rhine River. BAOR would have withdrawn immediately to that position, according to Evans. The working assumption was that one-third of the British forces would not have reached the Rhine in the event of a Soviet surprise attack, and those troops that did reach the river would not have been capable of defending it.

Even France had to yield to the logic that in an emergency it would not be possible to defend Western Europe without German troops. The leadership in Paris was no less afraid of the defeated Germans than of the Russians. More than anything, however, the French feared the Germans and Russians together. In the end, the integration of West Germany into the Atlantic and European alliances was the lesser evil, especially since a reasonably stable glacis was formed east of the French border. Similar, albeit less frightening, thoughts were entertained in London.

In his chapter Kaplan questions whether NATO did indeed establish more military security. We are inevitably reminded of the contemporary concerns of George F. Kennan about a militarization of America's policy of containment. According to Kaplan, the value of the American nuclear umbrella continually decreased following the detonation of the Soviet nuclear bomb in September 1949. The initial Western plan to assemble more than thirty divisions in Western Europe, which would have been able to put a halt to any rapid advance by Soviet ground forces, ultimately failed because of the subliminal belief that more butter might be a more reliable means to keep the Communists in check than more guns.

The Netherlands may be taken as an example for this deeply rooted attitude, as Jan Hoffenaar explains in his chapter. Consequently, according to Thoss, NATO forces based in northern Germany—BAOR and Belgian, Netherlands, and Canadian units—would until well into the 1950s have been able to defend no more than a few bridgeheads east of the Rhine against a Soviet attack. Carter shows in his chapter that after their deployment to Europe, the American divisions had to transfer almost all their well-trained personnel to Korea. Evans writes that BAOR faced similar problems. Hoffenaar notes that the Netherlands army was still being built up until well into the 1950s and hardly met the capability requirements of the alliance during this period.

Originally, the West German divisions were intended to reinforce the already existing allied forces. However, the buildup of the West German Bundeswehr, which had begun in 1956, proceeded much more slowly than planned. All the same, by 1963 the West Germans fielded forty-two tank and fifty-two mechanized battalions, including appropriate tube and rocket artillery support and a tactical air force. That force constituted what Hammerich describes as a "respectable army." Initially, the German units only filled the gaps left by the reductions in British, French, and later American forces. According to Thoss, the task of the NATO units was to force the adversary to concentrate his troops for attack, and by doing so to create high-payoff targets for nuclear strikes. The Western powers' aversion to the existence of too many West German armored divisions reflected the continuing mistrust they felt toward their German ally.

In contrast, the West German army was convinced that nothing other than major armored units could effectively delay a thrust against the Rhine.

As Carter writes, the former Wehrmacht generals were able to impart their philosophy to their American counterparts, who had no experience in fighting the Soviet army. Many protagonists of the former Wehrmacht were convinced that although Adolf Hitler had lost the eastern campaign on the strategic level, they themselves had successfully fought against an enemy who clearly outnumbered and outgunned them, and the key to that success had been the superior manner in which the Germans conducted operations. Consequently, the Americans later accepted the German preference for deploying major armored units in a battle of maneuver, especially since the U.S. Army had the strong and powerful field artillery forces to support such a strategy. Of course, the air superiority the Americans had been accustomed to from World War II was anything but assured. In hindsight, moreover, there is the question of whether the alleged or real lessons learned from World War II in the east campaign could be transferred to western Germany, which is comparatively densely populated and narrow, and where the terrain south of the Teutoburg Forest and the Harz Mountains regions is often rather mountainous.

The nuclearization of operational planning after around 1954 is explained by Evans, in his chapter, using BAOR as an example. BAOR's task was to hold up the Warsaw Pact's advance for two days to ensure the execution of the supreme allied commander, Europe's (SACEUR) atomic strike plans. Tactical nuclear air strikes were then planned to cover the British withdrawal to the Rhine. British army officers naturally questioned the alliance's capability to coordinate adequately the land and air battles. The British also feared that the American-influenced plans of the Central Army Group (CENTAG) to fight a battle of maneuver would allow the enemy to encircle BAOR units. Carter writes that since 1953 the U.S. Seventh Army had indeed practiced mobile tactical nuclear warfare on the ground and fielded the appropriate guns and missiles. The U.S. Army established Pentomic Division force structure between 1957 and 1959 to enhance its nuclear firepower, while simultaneously economizing on personnel and ensuring that the forces could disperse in a manner necessary to survive nuclear warfare. Above all, the U.S. Army did not want to be forced out of the nuclear war business in favor of the air forces.

Hoffenaar in his chapter writes that the Netherlands also carried out a similar force structure reform. He further notes that East German observers of the NORTHAG exercise BATTLE ROYAL had questioned as early as 1954 whether nuclear fires could compensate for a lack of troops. In their opinion, an attacker with a large number of forces and few nuclear weapons was superior to a defender with a small number of forces and many nuclear weapons. At that time the Soviet ground forces had hardly any tactical nuclear weapons at their disposal. In 1957, however, the Sputnik satellite indicated the significant progress of the policy of arming the Soviet forces with nuclear weapons, as discussed by Gavrilov in his chapter. It was only a matter of time before they would be able to launch a nuclear attack on American territory.

As the years went on, it became clearer that the United States was not willing to bear the same risk of nuclear extermination that their European allies faced. The intention to mount a flexible response to Soviet military attacks instead of opting for massive retaliation plunged NATO into a deep crisis. From 1960 the Anglo-American nuclear powers intended to defend Western Europe initially with conventional means in the event of a conflict. Consequently, the U.S. Army in Europe returned in 1961 to a more traditional and proven divisional structure, as Carter notes. It reduced its dependency on tactical nuclear weapons and again trained for conventional combined-arms combat operations. Hoffenaar notes that the Netherlands also made a similar adjustment. The Kennedy administration wanted to limit a possibly inevitable nuclear war in Europe in order to buy time for crisis management. The Federal Republic and all the other exposed NATO countries resented the corresponding loss of security and hoped—in vain, of course—for a little more co-determination in nuclear matters.

As Thoss and Hammerich stress, the Germans, too, considered the rapid transition to total nuclear warfare under the strategy of Massive Retaliation to be questionable. Such a strategy would mean that the territory of both German states would inevitably be devastated by nuclear weapons. In the 1960s five German divisions and two each from the United Kingdom, the Netherlands, and Belgium were ready—at least on paper—to halt a Soviet attack directly behind the Inner-German Border. On the one hand, the Germans had succeeded in convincing the alliance of the need for establishing a forward defense. But as Hammerich notes, the British and French were reluctant to redeploy their forces. According to Hoffenaar, the Netherlands I Corps was unable to make satisfactory arrangements to deploy to its staging areas in North Germany until 1967.

The West German army, in particular, hoped to have to resort to tactical nuclear weapons only as a last resort, even in a forward defense scenario. The German air force harbored as few illusions about this as the British military. Hammerich concludes that until the 1970s, nuclear weapons would have had to have been launched as soon as the enemy tried to do anything more than execute a border skirmish. Such a minor action was not very probable. Hoffenaar agrees with Hammerich's key argument by writing that it was the task of the Netherlands divisions even in the 1960s to defend the line of the Weser

River in coordination with the British for at least two days until SACEUR had executed his atomic strike plan. NORTHAG, the army group influenced primarily by the British, had the command over the NATO divisions deployed in North Germany to the Elbe River. According to Aldrich, the integrated NORTHAG staff devoted its peacetime attention to ensuring compliance with NATO training standards, joint exercises, and military reconnaissance. Nuclear target planning was another of its tasks. In addition, this staff was a means for the British to keep an eye on the armed forces of their German ally.

In contrast to the Anglo-Saxons and relying on its own future national nuclear potential, France stuck to the concept of massive retaliation. Its decision to take its military forces out of the NATO integrated command structure—and the consequent renunciation of the supreme command of NATO forces in Central Europe as a direct superior to NORTHAG command—might have increased the coherence of the alliance. The disputes over burden sharing were aggravated by the Americans' demand for conventional rearmament. Kaplan and Herman Roozenbeek write that the Central Sector had to reroute the vital supply lines from west-to-east to north-to-south, an undertaking that was completed before 1970. Consequently, the Central Sector suffered a further loss of operational depth.

While in the West the Berlin and Cuban missile crises (1958–1962) served as reasons for the alleged increase in the importance of conventional armed forces, the Soviets made a dramatic change in their strategy as a response to the nuclear stalemate, as Uhl, Gavrilov, and Diedrich explain.[28] Until then, the role of the Warsaw Pact had been more of a symbolic counterpart to NATO.[29] Following the Berlin crisis, the Pact was likewise transformed into a real military alliance, assigning an offensive role to the armed forces of the Eastern European allies in the so-called first strategic echelon of the joint armed forces. It was only from this time on that the East German National People's Army (NVA) gradually developed into a hard-hitting force. According to Diedrich, the three NVA divisions based in the north were put under Polish supreme command of the Coastal Front (army group). Together with the Baltic Sea forces, the Coastal Front was designated to advance to Schleswig-Holstein, Jutland, and on to the North Sea. The NVA Third Army would have supported the central army group under Soviet supreme command during its advance on the Ruhr area and Lorraine.

The Soviet armed forces were now systematically reequipped with tactical nuclear weapons, and even the Eastern allies received modern arms and nuclear means delivery systems. Moreover, the Soviets trained part of their strategic nuclear arsenal on Europe. Western military politicians saw limited advances as the most probable threat, since anything else would hardly be compatible with the strategy of Flexible Response. In contrast, their potential enemies planned a Blitzkrieg without or after only a very short period of mobilization. Such an offensive would open with massive deep nuclear strikes and subsequently be supported initially by forty-five and later one hundred divisions.

Diedrich emphasizes that the Soviet Union adhered to the principle that it is always better to have military superiority over the enemy and to fight that enemy in a military conflict on his territory from the onset. Correspondingly, the Soviets directed a large share of their resources into superior offensive capabilities. It is no wonder that the West perceived this as a threat. Nevertheless, the offensive strategy of the Soviet leadership was not necessarily an indication of their intent to conquer Western Europe by military force. Over the course of its history Russia had defeated in the depths of its own territory powerful invaders, from Charles XII and Napoleon to Hitler. The Soviet Communist leadership, however, could not be sure of the loyalty of the Eastern European populations outside the immediate sphere of Soviet rule. A purely defensive strategy, therefore, was out of the question. The Soviets' own sphere of rule could only be held together if the military conflict was shifted rapidly into the depth of the enemy's territory. The longer a war lasted, the greater the risk of internal erosion of Communist rule. Diedrich notes that the GDR consequently structured its territorial organization for not only fighting saboteurs and NATO commando units, but also combating "counterrevolutionary" actions committed by its own population.

As Dimitri Filippovych writes, the logistics units of the Soviet armed forces were therefore adjusted in size, equipment, and organization to support and sustain a possibly uninterrupted offensive into the depth of the enemy's territory. Diedrich explains that the NVA fielded a complete range of logistics units and facilities to support the Warsaw Pact armed forces on its territory. For example, the small NVA with a war-strength of 280,000 troops was organized to provide thirty transportation battalions for the Soviet armed forces alone. And as Filippovych notes, during the large-scale exercises staged by the Warsaw Pact in the 1960s, military transportation units always trained intensively in supporting the forces with bridging equipment and ferries across the Vistula, Oder, and Danube Rivers. The existing bridges across those rivers were indeed high priorities in the target list of SACEUR's atomic strike plan. In any case, these exercises do not support the conclusion that the Warsaw Pact was planning limited aggressions. Rather, the forces of the first strategic echelon were to be followed by a second strategic echelon that would carry the offensive to the Atlantic. The Soviet Union adhered to this strategy until 1987.

As a matter of fact, the Soviet logistics system in 1968 did not prove to be quite as good as intended. The invasion of Czechoslovakia was accompanied by considerable problems, although the Czechoslovakian army did not put up any resistance. Of course, the NATO apparatus did not look so good either. Its key leaders were not at their posts because of a lack of preparation and the inadequate functioning of the communications links. As is so often the case, the ideas of the strategic planners came up against the harsh reality of military facts.[30]

Hammerich concludes that even if the Soviet army had not resorted to nuclear strikes, German I Corps in the NORTHAG sector would hardly have been able to mount a mobile defense as intended against a massive advance in the 1960s. German I Corps had neither the required forces nor a sufficiently deep space of maneuver. Moreover, the adversary probably would have had air superiority. Consequently, German I Corps continued to consider resorting to the massive use of nuclear artillery and atomic demolition munitions (ADM), the latter producing a particularly high level of fall-out contamination. Note that the nuclear devices would have been detonated mostly on West German ground. It is hardly surprising, as Hoffenaar emphasizes, that the operations plan of Dutch I Corps, which was deployed forward toward the Elbe, also depended on the early use of tactical nuclear weapons against any enemy units that broke through.

According to Roozenbeek, materiel readiness remained the Achilles' heel of NATO's forces. In both war and peacetime, this was a national responsibility of the member states. Their respective armed forces consequently had different arms and equipment. Accordingly, the member states had to stock many different spare parts and types of ammunition. The NATO demand for standardization always failed to be met because of the self-interests of member states when it came to armament, although they did begin to pursue cost-saving joint developments in the 1960s. Logistics, then, became more important because of the sharp rise in the requirements for petroleum, oil, and lubricants (POL) and ammunition of the largely mechanized units whose advantage lay in their firepower. In his chapter, Filippovych also examines in detail a similar challenge on the Eastern side.

The supplying of forces with POL, ammunition, and spare parts during the period of thirty battlefield days, over long distances, and under conditions of nuclear warfare within a national framework and responsibility, was the crucial enabler of the integrated operations of NATO's integrated commands. There were no clear provisions governing the authority of the NATO commands to redirect the supplies from the forces of one member state to those of another. Understandably, the respective member countries were leery of indirectly subsidizing those allies that did not maintain their stocks at the required levels—and who relied on the adoption by NATO of a pragmatic solution in an emergency. The concern of the small Benelux states was whether they would get sufficient supplies at all in such an emergency. All in all, the war reserves in the NORTHAG sector generally remained below the established level of thirty battlefield days. Until the 1970s at least, Flexible Response remained a myth, simply because of the lack of military capabilities to mount a conventional defense.[31] Hoffenaar considers NORTHAG's operation plans to be similarly contradictory, even after NATO's official change of strategy in 1967–1968.

Marxist-Leninist thinking attributed NATO's logistics problems to the regressive character of capitalism, whose industries would inevitably compete for the largest defense profits. The Warsaw Pact, indeed, benefited from having mostly uniform Soviet equipment, especially since the concept of defense economics had little if any tradition in the Eastern European states—except for Czechoslovakia. According to Diedrich, the East German NVA was equipped with Soviet materiel based on Soviet planning norms.

NATO did achieve some success in establishing a logistical infrastructure. As Roozenbeek notes, the sky-rocketing demand for aircraft fuel—not least for the alliance's nuclear-armed fighter bombers—prompted NATO to build a jointly financed pipeline system as early as the 1950s. An early-warning system, air bases, and in the 1960s a control and reporting system were also financed within the framework of an infrastructure program. Nevertheless, the tensions between the member states' national interests and the common purpose of the alliance continued to reduce the military effectiveness of NATO, and do so to this day.

A mixture of dominance and partnership characterized both alliances. But in the Warsaw Pact the mutual dependence between the leading power and its allies was far more in the favor of the Soviet Union. The relationship between the latter and its Eastern European allies was by no means free of tensions either. After all, even Communist party leaders gave priority to national interests. Compared to the Western European allies, however, the competing national interests of the Warsaw Pact had much less effect because of two factors. The worldview of the Eastern European Communists was more or less identical to that of their Soviet comrades. Simultaneously, the leaders of the Eastern European countries depended on the Soviet Union's support, because the level of acceptance by their own people was often rather low. In contrast, the elites and the peoples in the Western European states expected their governments to bring national interests to bear within the alliance. Thus, armaments cooperation, even in a European context, remains rather complicated to this day.

Aldrich notes that the enemy's growing capability to launch surprise attacks with units that presumably had managed to become combat ready within a very short space of time increased NATO's military requirement for reliable early warning information. In fact, NATO staffs depended mainly on intelligence provided by the respective national services. Those services occasionally were infiltrated successfully by the enemy, the more notorious examples being the British "Cambridge Five" and the West German "Felfe Case." The Americans, British, and Canadians were hesitant to provide NATO with information from their Anglophone strategic signals intelligence network. The information collected by the British Military Mission to the Soviet Forces in Germany (BRIXMIS) was an important source for NORTHAG, as was the signals intelligence collected along the Inner-German Border. In the event of war, long-range reconnaissance units and observers scheduled to be left behind would have identified targets for NORTHAG's tactical nuclear weapons. Those assets, however, probably would have been neutralized rapidly by the adversary.

According to Uhl, the fact that the Soviet military in the 1960s did not neglect the expansion of its conventional armed forces did not indicate the intent of launching a purely conventional offensive. Such an option did not exist until the 1970s.[32] Rather, it reflected the respective Soviet military services' demands for a balanced share in future armaments programs. Khrushchev's objective had been to secure the Communist future with more butter, more missiles, fewer soldiers, and less unlimited despotism.[33] His successors, however, sponsored the growth of the military-industrial complex—which had helped them to reach power—with more missiles and many soldiers, but less and less butter. Under other auspices they did what Eisenhower had rejected when he worried about the civilian essence of society. According to Aldrich, the intelligence services of the Eastern bloc had infiltrated NATO to such a degree that Soviet strategists and military politicians could hardly escape the conclusion that the armed forces of the Western alliance in Europe were neither willing nor able to conduct an offensive deep into Warsaw Pact territory.

Citing East Germany as an example, Hoffenaar and Diedrich demonstrate that the obligatory Marxist-Leninist ideology had the effect of a magnifying lens. The major capitalist powers could do nothing but harbor aggressive intentions, as historical experience allegedly had taught. Consequently, NATO in general and the Federal Republic in particular became a military threat, even though the excellent results of NVA military intelligence from 1964 on suggested rather the opposite. By overestimating allied plans, the Eastern side could at least feel themselves justified. During Exercise LIVE OAK, the Americans, British, and French explored the possibility of clearing the land route to Berlin by military force. The NVA responded by concentrating a considerable number of forces around Berlin. This might explain what—from the Western viewpoint—was an implausible Eastern training scenario based on the initiation of hostilities by NATO advancing into the territory of the Eastern alliance.

The Eastern bloc interpreted the West German military's push for a relocation of the defensive lines to the Inner-German Border, their concern about a sufficiently early nuclear strike in case of emergency, and the Federal government's efforts to obtain a say in nuclear arms matters as preparations for war by those who had already participated in the National Socialist war of annihilation against the Soviet Union. Consequently, East German military intelligence searched for indicators of an imminent attack just as eagerly as did their NORTHAG counterparts. According to Hoffenaar, NVA officers interpreted NATO's transition to the strategy of Flexible Response quite correctly as a signal of weakness, but also as a sign of increasing aggressiveness. What from the American perspective was meant to facilitate crisis management, the East Germans understood as the imperialists' attempt to improve their position for the final exchange of blows.

This volume does not so much examine from different angles the military strategies of the Eastern and Western alliances during the phase of their paradigm shifts in the 1950s and 1960s; rather, it focuses on how these shifts were reflected in the operational ideas and plans. Flexible Response generally has been considered an appropriate strategy in the age of weapons of mass destruction. This notion was almost exclusively derived from documents reflecting the intentions and goals of high-level politicians and the ideas of the great strategists. But as soon as the allied forces' military prerequisites are examined in depth, this generally accepted notion begins to totter.

At least until the early 1970s, NATO's conventional capabilities were so inadequate that the adoption of a conventional strategy seemed nothing but absurd, for at the same time, the Warsaw Pact nuclearized its strategy. The nonchalance, noted by Diedrich, with which Eastern strategists regarded the impact of nuclear weapons on the terrain, as well as on the physical and psychological constitution of their forces, seemed hardly less absurd. The fact that ground troop commanders planned their operations as if the opponent did not have tactical nuclear weapons at his disposal was not, however, peculiar to the Eastern militaries. Many Bundeswehr army general officers would have preferred to do completely without nuclear weapons, considering the degree to which the operational commanders planned to use them as a matter of course on German territory. On the one hand, the use of such weapons would have lain waste what they were supposed to defend. On the other, the assumed or actual superiority of their own units in conventional combat would not be of much value if both sides used a vast number of nuclear weapons. Conventional warfare would, of course, be feasible only if the Eastern opponent obliged the NATO forces in Europe by aiming at a limited objective with limited forces. That, of course, was anything but probable.

The idea of connecting the acceptance of a limited war with as high a nuclear threshold as possible was, of course, only an unrealistic intellectual construct when seen from the Western European perspective.[34] Consequently, France stuck to its deterrence strategy of using a small but adequately effective strategic nuclear force to retaliate on a massive scale. It likewise dispensed with any costly and probably ineffective protection scheme for the civilian population. Similar to Anglo-Saxon thinking was the notion that France would probably participate in NATO's ground war as long as it was waged east of the Rhine. This is the purpose for which the French ground forces were equipped with tactical nuclear weapons. It provided Paris the option to defend its German glacis with conventional and nuclear means. France would have used its strategic potential only if its own territory had been attacked.

From America's perspective, it was plausible to gain time at first for crisis management by confining any conflict to the European side of the Atlantic, before committing collective suicide. NATO's new flexibility had the possible advantage of preventing a global nuclear war from breaking out accidentally. Its disadvantage, however, of which contemporaries were also aware, was the time required for the political decision-making process to agree on an appropriate response. That played into the hands of an opponent who was prepared to make surprise moves and commit massed forces. In case of doubt, the opponent could use this edge in time at the least to reduce considerably the capability of the European allied forces to fight a nuclear war.

Flexibility promised an illusory way out of the horrors of a global nuclear war. The more automatic response option was horrible but clear. The necessity for each side to demonstrate credibly to the opponent how ready it was to die for its own freedom was a key factor in both cases. In the end, it was probably more the risk of mutual nuclear extermination than it was NATO's doubtful conventional capabilities that caused the various national leaders to refrain from making adventurous decisions and to maintain the inclination toward détente.

NATO's official declaration of détente in 1967–1968 marked a more important paradigm shift than did Flexible Response. The latter aimed at the Warsaw Pact's military capabilities, while the focus of the Harmel Report aimed at its political intentions. The alliance took up the Warsaw Pact's proposals regarding the establishment of a European security system. Détente became an integral part of the alliance's strategy.[35] Agreement on a European system was reached with the signing of the Helsinki Final Act in 1975. Thus, the Soviet Union and its allies harvested the fruits of the military buildup they had consistently pursued for more than two decades, including outward equality, recognition of the borders established in 1945, and material relief through economic cooperation.

The price, however, soon came due. In compelling the Soviet Union and its allies to commit themselves to human rights and the exchange of information, the West facilitated its strategic objective of peacefully breaking up totalitarian Communism. This commitment offered a point of reference for the opposition movements in the Communist states, which could not be easily ignored by the state parties and their secret police forces in the attempts to suppress those movements. In the end, the aging Soviet elites and their Eastern European counterparts acted their age. The need for security in the present day was more important than the risks involved for the future. Nonetheless, they hoped that they themselves would not have to experience the effects of their actions. Soon after Erich Honecker celebrated the triumphs of the GDR's decadelong struggle for sovereignty and recognition during his state visits to Bonn in 1987 and to Paris in 1988, the GDR collapsed in 1989–1990. Although it had a large standing and well-armed military equipped with considerable stocks of ammunition—as had the Soviet Union, which imploded shortly after it—that force proved just as useless as the once-feared state security service.

D. K.

Notes

1. See, for example, Wilfried Loth, "Der 'Kalte Krieg' in der historischen Forschung," in *Der Westen und die Sowjetunion*, ed. Gottfried Niedhart (Pader-

born, 1983), 155–75, as well as the more recent article by Georges-Henri Soutou, "00L'historiographie actuelle de la Guerre froide entre révisionisme et nouvelles re- cherches," *Revue d'histoire diplomatique* 122 (2008): 187–92.

2. Such is the conclusion of Odd Arne Westad, introduction to *Reviewing the Cold War: Approaches, Interpretations, Theory,* ed. Odd Arne Westad (London, 2006), 1–23, here p. 1, and also Douglas J. Macdonald, "Formal Ideologies in the Cold War: Toward a Framework of Empirical Analysis," in *Reviewing the Cold War,* ed. Wes- tad, 180–204, as well as the overall view by Georges-Henri Soutou in *La Guerre des Cinquante Ans: Le conflit Est-Ouest 1943–1990* (Paris, 2001). John L. Gaddis, *We Now Know: Rethinking Cold War History* [Oxford, 1997]) had revaluated the importance of ideology already some years after the Cold War ended and emphasized this as- pect in his more recent diplomatic history *The Cold War: A New History* (New York, 2007). Bernd Stöver, in *Der Kalte Krieg 1947–1991: Geschichte eines radikalen Zeitalt- ers* (Munich, 2007), bases his system-theoretical interpretation in a similar way on the assumption of a dominating ideological and sociopolitical antagonism.

3. See Soutou, *La Guerre des Cinquante Ans,* 11–12, 17.

4. See Richard Saull, *Rethinking Theory and History in the Cold War: The State, Military Power and Social Revolution* (London, 2001), esp. 59–63.

5. See Vojtech Mastny, *Learning from the Enemy: NATO as a Model for the War- saw Pact* (Zurich, 2001), 20–31.

6. The stand-by organization based on NATO—a platform for exerting con- spiratorial influence. See Daniele Ganser, *NATO's Secret Armies: Operation Gladio and Terrorism in Western Europe* (London, 2005).

7. David S. Painter and Melvyn P. Leffler speak of "imbalance" in "The End of the Cold War," in *Origins of the Cold War: An International History,* ed. Melvyn P. Leffler and David S. Painter, 2nd ed. (New York, 2005), 333. See also Charles S. Meier, "The Cold War as an Era of Imperial Rivalry," in *Reinterpreting the End of the Cold War: Issues, Interpretations, Periodizations,* ed. Silvio Pons and Federico Romero (London, 2005), 17–19; Soutou, *La Guerre des Cinquante Ans,* 15; Westad, introduc- tion to *Reviewing the Cold War,* 19.

8. See the similar argument in Stöver, *Der Kalter Krieg,* 463–64.

9. See Gaddis, *We Now Know,* 284; and Vojtech Mastny, "Imagining War in Eu- rope: Soviet Strategic Planning," in *War Plans and Alliances in the Cold War: Threat Perceptions in the East and West,* ed. Vojtech Mastny, Sven G. Holtsmark, and An- dreas Wenger (Abingdon, 2006), 37–38.

10. See Marilena Gala, *Il Paradosso Nucleare: Il Limited Test Ban Treaty come primo passo verso la distensione* (Florence, 2002).

11. See Bernd Greiner (ed.), *Heiße Kriege im Kalten Krieg* (Hamburg, 2006).

12. On the complexly intertwined national and international approaches that ul- timately brought about the global phenomenon, see Leffler and Painter, *Origins of the Cold War.*

13. See http://www.php.isn.ethz.ch/ (accessed 27 January 2009) and http://www.

wilsoncenter.org/index.cfm?fuseaction=topics.home&topic_id=1409 (accessed 27 January 2009). On this topic see also the Internet edition of the Protocols of the National Defense Committee of the GDR, which also includes references to the politics of the Warsaw Pact: http://www.nationaler-verteidigungsrat.de/.

14. See Westad, introduction to *Reviewing the Cold War*, 1, 18; Soutou, *La Guerre des Cinquante Ans*, 10.

15. See Mastny, "Imagining War in Europe," 15.

16. See the conclusions drawn in the three-volume edition of *A History of NATO: The First Fifty Years*, ed. Gustav Schmidt (Houndmills, 2001), as well as the most recent overview by Lawrence S. Kaplan, *NATO Divided, NATO United: The Evolution of an Alliance* (Westport, Conn., 2004). Since 1998 the Military History Research Institute (MGFA) has published a series of studies titled "Entstehung und Probleme des Atlantischen Bündnisses."

17. See http://www.nato.int/archives/strategy.htm (accessed 20 January 2009).

18. See Dieter Krüger, *Brennender Enzian: Die Operationsplanung der NATO für Österreich und Norditalien 1951 bis 1960* (Freiburg, 2010), which drew on a study of the "emergency defense plans" of the Headquarters Allied Land Forces Southern Europe in Verona, analyzing microfilmed documents from the SHAPE archives in Mons, Belgium.

19. See Vojtech Mastny and Malcolm Byrne (eds.), *A Cardboard Castle? An Inside History of the Warsaw Pact, 1955–1991* (Budapest, 2005); Torsten Diedrich, Winfried Heinemann, and Christian F. Ostermann (eds.), *Der Warschauer Pakt: Von der Gründung bis zum Zusammenbruch 1955 bis 1991* (Berlin, 2009).

20. See Petr Luňák (ed.), *Plánování nemyslitelného: Československé válečné plány 1950–1990* (Prague, 2007).

21. See Gaddis, *We Now Know*, 282.

22. Even David Miller, in his thoroughly commendable book *The Cold War: A Military History* (London, 1998), studies the potentials, plans, and problems of the players in succession rather than really comparing them.

23. See Jan Hoffenaar and Christopher Findlay (eds.), *Military Planning for European Theatre Conflict during the Cold War: An Oral History Roundtable Stockholm 24–25 April 2006* (Zurich, 2007).

24. See as an assumedly first approach Mastny, *Learning from the Enemy*.

25. See also Petr Luňák, "War Plans from Stalin to Breshnev: The Czechoslovak Pivot," in *War Plans*, ed. Mastny, 71–75; Mastny, "Imagining War in Europe," 16–17.

26. See Aleksandr Fursenko and Timothy Naftali, *Khrushchev's Cold War: The Inside Story of an American Adversary* (New York, 2006), 39–40.

27. See ibid., 128–29, 140–41.

28. See also Matthias Uhl, "Storming on to Paris: The 1961 Burya Exercise and the Planned Solution of the Berlin Crisis," in *War Plans*, ed. Mastny, 46–71; Mastny, "Imagining War in Europe," 22–28.

29. See Mastny, *Learning from the Enemy*, 9–13.

30. See Mastny, "Imagining War in Europe," 30.

31. See Francis J. Gavin, "The Myth of Flexible Response: United States Strategy in Europe during the 1960s," *International History Review* 23 (2001): 847–75.

32. See also Mastny, "Imagining War in Europe," 28–29.

33. See William Taubman, *Khrushchev: The Man and His Era* (New York, 2003), esp. 507–28; Fursenko and Naftali, *Khrushchev*, 22–23, 242–48.

34. Luňák, "War Plans from Stalin to Breshnev," 83.

35. See Csaba Békés, "The Warsaw Pact and the CSCE Process from 1965 to 1970," in *The Making of Détente: Eastern and Western Europe in the Cold War, 1965–75*, ed. Wilfried Lothand and Georges-Henri Soutou (London, 2008), 201–20; Andreas Wenger, "NATO's Transformation in the 1960s," in *Transforming NATO in the Cold War: Challenges beyond Deterrence in the 1960s*, ed. Andreas Wenger, Christian Nuenlist, and Anna Locher (London: Routledge, 2007), 221–42, esp. pp. 235–37.

A Note on the English Edition

The German federal government's translation service, Bundessprachenamt, initially translated the preface, the introduction, and nine of the fourteen chapters of this book into English. Five of the chapters were originally written in English. I edited the entire work, ensuring that the English translations flowed smoothly and that specialized military terms and concepts were properly translated. Place names have been anglicized in the form most familiar to English-language readers; hence, Cologne and Munich are used, rather than Köln and München. Map symbols conform to standard NATO practice for military graphics. I have made every effort to ensure the citations are as full and accurate as possible; however, the contributions of the fifteen authors represent five different countries, with differing standards for references and citations.

D. T. Z.

Abbreviations and Common Terms

ACE	Allied Command Europe
ACE-LCC	Allied Command Europe Logistic Coordination Center
ADM	atomic demolition munitions
AFCENT	Allied Forces Central Europe
AFNORTH	Allied Forces Northern Europe
APC	armored personnel carrier
ATAF	Allied Tactical Air Force
ATGM	antitank guided missile
BAOR	British Army of the Rhine
BGS (Int & Sy)	brigadier, General Staff (Intelligence and Security)
BND	Bundesnachrichtendienst (German Federal Intelligence Service)
BRIXMIS	British Military Mission to the Soviet Forces in Germany
Bundeswehr	The joint military forces of the Federal Republic of Germany
CANUKUS	Canada–United Kingdom–United States
CENTAG	NATO Central Army Group, subordinate to Allied Forces Central Europe
CEPS	Central European Pipeline System
CIA	Central Intelligence Agency
CINCENT	commander-in-chief, Allied Forces Central Europe
CINCNORTH	commander-in-chief, Allied Forces Northern Europe
CINCSOUTH	commander-in-chief, Allied Forces Southern Europe
COMINT	communications intelligence
COMLANDCENT	commander, Land Forces Central Europe
COMNORTHAG	commander, Northern Army Group
DC	Defense Committee
EDC	European Defense Community
EDP	emergency defense plan

EGA	East German army
EUCOM	United States European Command
FALLEX	Fall Exercise
FEBA	forward edge of the battle area
FRG	Federal Republic of Germany
FROG	free rocket over ground
front	a Soviet army group
G-2	General Staff Section 2, Intelligence
G-3	General Staff Section 3, Operations
GDP	general deployment plan
GDR	German Democratic Republic
GOSPLAN	Gosudarstvennyi Komitet po Planirovaniyu (Soviet State Committee for Planning)
GRU	Glavnoy Razvedovatel'noy Upravlenie (Soviet Military Intelligence)
GSFG	Group of Soviet Forces in Germany
HQ	headquarters
HUMINT	human intelligence
ICBM	intercontinental ballistic missile
ICC	NATO Northern Army Group's Intercept Control Centre
IRBM	intermediate-range ballistic missile
KGB	Komityet Gosudarstvyennoy Bezopasnosti (Soviet Union's primary intelligence agency)
KT	kiloton, explosive power in thousands of tons of TNT
LANDCENT	Allied Land Forces, Central Europe
MC	Military Committee
MI6	Britain's Secret Intelligence Service, once known as Military Intelligence 6
MIRV	multiple individually targeted reentry vehicle
MLF	Multilateral Force
MRBM	medium-range ballistic missile
NATO	North Atlantic Treaty Organization
NBC	nuclear, biological, and chemical
NORTHAG	NATO's Northern Army Group, subordinate to Allied Forces Central Europe
NVA	Nationale Volksarmee (National People's Army, the military force of the German Democratic Republic)
Panzer division	Bundeswehr armored division

Panzer Grenadier division	Bundeswehr mechanized infantry division
POL	petroleum, oil, and lubricants
PTRB	mobile nuclear weapons unit
PVA	Polnischen Volksarmee (Polish People's Army)
RAF	Royal Air Force
REFORGER	Return of Forces to Germany, annual American exercise
ROAD	Reorganization Objectives Army Division
SACEUR	supreme allied commander, Europe
SAS	Special Air Service
SED	Sozialistische Einheitspartei Deutschlands (the Communist Party of the German Democratic Republic)
SHAPE	Supreme Headquarters Allied Powers Europe
SHD	special handling detachment
SIGINT	signals intelligence
SIS	Secret Intelligence Service, Britain's MI6
SITCEN	Situation Center
SLAR	side-looking airborne radar
SLBM	submarine-launched ballistic missile
SPD	Sozialdemokratische Partei Deutschlands (the Social Democratic Party of the Federal Republic of Germany)
SRBM	short-range ballistic missile
SRS	Special Reconnaissance Squadron, Royal Armoured Corps
Stasi	Ministerium für Staatssicherheit (Ministry for State Security of the German Democratic Republic)
TO&E	table of organization and equipment
USAREUR	United States Army, Europe
VHF	very high frequency
WINTEX	Winter Exercise
WUDO	Western Union Defense Organization

Introduction

The Plans of the Warsaw Pact and NATO

Jan Hoffenaar and Dieter Krüger

On 22 and 23 March 2007, military historians from Russia, the United States, and Eastern and Western Europe convened to discuss the military operational plans developed during the Cold War. With the opening of the archives, we are gaining ever greater knowledge of the conflict between East and West during that period. The conference was an initiative of the Netherlands Institute of Military History (NIMH) and was organized in cooperation with NIMH's German counterpart, the Militärgeschichtliches Forschungsamt (Military History Research Institute, MGFA) in Potsdam. It took place in Münster, Germany, and was sponsored by the Center for Netherlands Studies and the German/Netherlands I Corps headquarters, which is based there. The conference focused on the war plans for the European Central Sector during the 1950s and 1960s. The choice for the period was logical, as the archival records for that time are relatively accessible. That was also the period when both sides were armed to the hilt and facing each other across the Iron Curtain.

Professor Lawrence S. Kaplan, America's "Grand Old Man" of historical research into the Cold War, gave the inaugural lecture. In his presentation Professor Kaplan traced the overview of the most important international developments during the period, the dominating feature of which was the strong distrust from the start between the two major powers—the United States and the Soviet Union. Each action was seen as yet more evidence of the other power's bad intentions, contributing to the spiral of the costly conventional and nuclear arms race.

It does not appear now that the Soviet Union had aggressive intentions. It did, however, have plans to attack immediately (the strategic offensive) in the event of war breaking out. And from 1960 on, the Soviets had plans to use nuclear weapons within the framework of Warsaw Pact operations. Those conclusions emerged strongly in the presentations by Colonel Dr. Viktor A. Gavrilov, the chief of the Division of Foreign Military History, Institute of Military History, Ministry of Defense, Moscow, and Dr. Matthias Uhl of the German Historical Institute, Moscow. When it became clear that the Americans were not going to leave Europe after World War II, the Soviet Union concentrated on consolidating its spheres of influence in Eastern Europe. Past events, such as the German invasion of the Soviet Union in 1941, made the Soviet political leadership very distrustful of Western intentions. If, according to Moscow, a war in the near term became inevitable, then an offensive with all available resources would be the best form of defense.

The most important military archives in Moscow, incidentally, are still tightly sealed. What we do know of the operational plans stems from the analyses of the various military exercises of the period, the records of which have been dug out of the various archives of the former member states of the Warsaw Pact. A key example is the 1967 TROJKA war game conducted by the Nationale Volksarmee (National People's Army, NVA) of the German Democratic Republic, and which has been analyzed by Dr. Torsten Diedrich of the MGFA.

The NIMH historian Professor Jan Hoffenaar showed in his contribution on intelligence gathering in the Warsaw Pact that the leaders in the Kremlin and in East Berlin knew full well that NATO had no aggressive intentions. They did, however, maintain the image of an aggressive NATO, which supported the Marxist-Leninist worldview. And, as already noted, recent historical experience justified the maintenance of such an image of the enemy. In addition, the Federal Republic of Germany's accession to NATO in 1955 was less than reassuring to the Eastern bloc. Last but not least, the Kremlin needed to maintain this negative view of the enemy in order to keep the Warsaw Pact intact.

Various contributions from historians from different NATO countries focused on the preparations for a potential military confrontation. Dr. Bruno Thoss of MGFA provided a clear overview of the development of NATO's strategic and operational planning. Lieutenant Colonel Dr. Helmut Hammerich of MGFA; Dr. Robert Evans of the Army Historical Branch, Ministry of Defence, London; and Professor Hoffenaar discussed the operational preparations of the armed forces of the Federal Republic of Germany, the United Kingdom, and Belgium and the Netherlands, respectively. Each NATO member state had its own specific interests, problems, and solutions.

The well-known British intelligence specialist Professor Richard J. Aldrich of the University of Nottingham gave the conference participants important insights into NATO's operational intelligence work.

The contribution of Dr. Donald A. Carter of the U.S. Army Center of Military History in Washington, D.C., was especially noteworthy for his explanation of how differently the military commanders of the 1950s—the veterans of World War II—and those of the 1960s viewed nuclear weapons. The former found the use of these weapons, especially on the battlefield, to be self-explanatory, whereas the latter, the general officers of the 1960s, saw the weapons first and foremost as a political deterrent.

The enormous increase in the number of tactical nuclear weapons among the armed forces of both sides led to far-reaching reorganizations of those forces. Mobility, mechanization, nuclear hardening, and smaller independent units were key concepts. NIMH historian Herman Roozenbeek illustrated clearly in his presentation how NATO's logistics development along those lines lagged behind its armament developments. The phased advance of the allied line of defense—from the Rhine-IJssel River line to the Weser-Fulda line to the Elbe River—was in itself a major factor in the continual lag in logistics. Professor Dimitri Filippovych, head of the Department of Military History, Academy of Military Science, Ministry of Defense, Moscow, gave an interesting presentation on the question of how operational logistics adapted to nuclear warfare over the years.

In closing the conference, Dr. Gregory Pedlow, chief of the Historical Office, Supreme Headquarters Allied Powers Europe, Mons, Belgium, offered a well-balanced summary lecture. All in all, the conference contributed significantly to enhancing our knowledge of the military aspects of the Cold War. The contributions are now published in this volume for the benefit of a wider audience of historians, professional soldiers, and general readers. Our special thanks to the Association of the United States Army for its generous support, as well as to the University Press of Kentucky for publishing the book.

1

Strategic Problems and the Central Sector, 1948–1968

An Overview

Lawrence S. Kaplan

Western Europe's vulnerability to a Soviet thrust from East Germany was arguably the most pressing concern of the five powers that signed the Brussels Pact in March 1948. It was the most persuasive reason for the European allies to seek an American commitment to their defense. While the Soviet threat was not France's most visible worry in this period, the danger from a potential Soviet attack, coupled with a concomitant Communist internal uprising, was sufficient to convince the military and political elites of all but the Gaullist non-Communist parties to subsume their fears of a revived Germany under the greater fear of Soviet aggression. It was the nightmare of Communist hordes overwhelming a relatively defenseless West as they quickly marched across the North German plain to the English Channel or through the Fulda Gap in Hesse to split West Germany in half. British field marshal Sir Bernard Law Montgomery's often-quoted remark during his service as commander of the Western Union Defense Organization (WUDO) in 1948 that all the Soviets needed to reach the Channel was an adequate supply of shoe leather created an image that was difficult to eradicate.[1]

It did not matter that the Soviets in the Stalin era may have had no intention of invading the West; they still had expectations of the collapse of the capitalist societies through their internal weaknesses, abetted by active Communist parties in such countries as France and Italy. What did matter in 1948 was the perceived need by the British and French foreign ministers, Ernest Bevin and Georges Bidault, to lure the United States into the new Western Union. Only an assured American role in the defense of the West would calm European nerves and provide the psychological as well as military basis for the economic recovery promised under the Marshall Plan. The creation of WUDO under the leadership of Field Marshal Montgomery with French general Jean de Lattre de Tassigny as his subordinate commander of the land forces was consciously designed to show the Americans that Europe was doing its part by rearming and integrating its forces—but not much more. In 1948 WUDO was waiting for the completion of the North Atlantic Treaty that would incorporate its activities in an enlarged organization.[2]

While the Soviet Union's view of the West in the early Cold War years was not a mirror image, there were elements of the same suspicions that were found among the future Atlantic allies. Despite Communist expectation of the impending doom of all capitalist nations, the Soviets anticipated aggressive actions against them before their demise. Communist control of Eastern Europe, including Czechoslovakia after the coup of February 1948, was not sufficient to ensure security in the face of the West's hostility.

When the United States and the United Kingdom combined their occupation zones in 1948 to help restore the German economy, the Soviets were convinced that this was a prelude to the creation of a dangerous Germany intent on reclaiming its lost territories. To forestall such an eventuality they encouraged subversive activities among the Communist parties in Western Europe and instituted a blockade of the Western allies' access to the portions of Berlin assigned under the Yalta agreements of 1945. The Soviet Union failed to prevent either the formation of NATO or a unified West German state, but continued to present itself in the 1950s as the champion of a unified Germany freed from U.S. occupation.[3]

Whether NATO provided the security Europe demanded in 1948—and afterward—is a question not easily answered. Whether it was necessary in light of the continuing debate over Soviet capabilities as well as intentions is also a question for historians to answer. But in the matter of perceptions there was a transatlantic conviction in 1948 and 1949 that Europe was in peril and that only the United States could redress the imbalance by joining Europe not as an observer or as cheerleader, but as a participant in the process.

The immediate aftermath of the creation of NATO inspired some confidence on the erroneous assumption that U.S. B-29s based in Omaha, Nebraska, and armed with atomic weapons would provide a sufficient deterrent to Communist aggression as the Soviet armies hovered over Western Europe.

The Soviet explosion of an atomic device in August 1949 dissolved that illusion. But the American short-range defense plan in that year would have removed U.S. forces to Europe's periphery in the event of an attack, until the Anglo-American allies were prepared to liberate the Continent once again. Discontent with this plan led to NATO's acceptance of a medium-term defense plan that put the defense line at the Rhine and IJssel Rivers rather than at Gibraltar or Britain. This decision in March 1950 at least embraced France but left the Netherlands east of the Rhine and IJssel and West Germany and Denmark outside its scope. Nevertheless, it was a step in the right direction.[4]

The combination of the Soviet acquisition of an atomic bomb, the loss of China to Communism, and the Korean War in 1950 only intensified European insecurity. The possibility that the United States might abandon its new allies to meet its more traditional concerns with Asia and the Pacific was quickly resolved in favor of Europe in 1950 and 1951 in the aftermath of the Korean War. The reorganization of the alliance's organization from regional planning groups into a military machine prepared to respond to aggression with sufficient force either to inhibit such action or to repel it was evidence of this determination. The Brussels meeting of the North Atlantic Council in December 1950, six months after the North Korean invasion, established a Supreme Allied Command in Europe—under the leadership of General of the Army Dwight D. Eisenhower, the West's most trusted general—in which the central sector of defense, West Germany, was the major focus of NATO's concern. The commitment of four divisions to those already in place in Europe was an additional assurance of deepening U.S. involvement. The most dramatic illustration of the alliance's intentions came in February 1952 at the Lisbon meeting of the council when plans for fifty divisions were made.

Over the span of the next few years, allied confidence in the deterrent effect as well as the defense capabilities of the NATO build-up underwent considerable strain. The most immediate, and in some ways the most sensitive, issue was France's resistance to German rearmament, even when couched in a carefully framed context. This should not have been a surprise. Even before NATO came into being there was a bond between the Soviets and the French over limiting German sovereignty, whether the issue at hand was German control of the Ruhr or the ultimate creation of a West German government in Bonn. Nothing was more divisive in French relations with Anglo-Americans than the latter's pressure to reconstruct Germany. It took clear demonstrations of Communist malevolence to push France into acceptance of a limited German sovereignty in the form of the Basic Law creating the Federal Republic one month after the North Atlantic Treaty was signed.[5]

The Korean War made the use of German resources and manpower even more imperative. If the war in a divided Korea was a prelude to a war in a divided Germany, as many in the West feared, then there was no choice but to bring West Germany into the alliance in one way or another. To postpone facing this reality as long as possible, France agreed to a German role in Europe's defense, under special and stringent circumstances and then only after intense American pressure. The initial effort in the Pleven Plan in the fall of 1950 was to allow the creation of German military units in battalion strength in a European army that would be incorporated into an integrated NATO force. Authorship was attributed to Premier René Pleven in October, but like the Schuman Plan establishing a Franco-German coal and steel community, it was the brainchild of French economist Jean Monnet. Unlike the practical Schuman Plan, the Pleven idea was an act of desperation, designed to stave off U.S. efforts for immediate German rearmament. To soften the impact of such a German contribution, the United States would offer more troops itself and lead an integrated military command in Europe, as arranged in the Brussels meeting of the North Atlantic Council in December 1950.

In the short run France succeeded in winning for Europe American troops and American generals in a NATO command, while managing to hold off the German role through a European Defense Community (EDC) that would include twelve German divisions. NATO would be in control, and there would be thirty divisions drawn from the other members of the EDC.

France bought time to adjust to changes. While the United States fulfilled its end of the bargain immediately, French demands for additional guarantees from the Anglo-Americans who did not participate in the EDC led to seemingly unending delays in putting the EDC into action. The treaty establishing the community was signed in May 1952, but France's ratification was postponed until August 1954 after the allies rejected the latest protocols demanded by France. The French National Assembly nominally defeated the treaty on a procedural issue, but it was more likely because of concern about the loss of an independent army. French national pride was at stake. This was arguably more important at that moment than the long-standing reluctance to accept a German role in the defense of the West. The Federal Republic did join the alliance less than a year later with French approval under an arrangement wherein the Western Union was enlarged to include West Germany, and that country would agree to refrain from producing nuclear, biological, or chemical weapons.[6]

That the defense of German territory would be the most important NATO concern was implicit in Supreme Allied Commander Eisenhower's geographic division of forces in 1951 into northern, central, and southern sectors. The southern flank created the most difficulties because of British expectations of holding that command. The British did have an admiral as commander-in-chief, Allied Forces Northern Europe (CINCNORTH), but this did not compensate for their failure to win command of the Mediterranean area, which had always been regarded as a British lake, their link to their empire beyond Suez. An American admiral was appointed commander-in-chief, Allied Forces Southern Europe (CINCSOUTH), largely because the U.S. Sixth Fleet was the most significant entity in that area. But it was more significant if less controversial that Eisenhower himself initially retained overall control of the Central Sector. Soviet forces were massed along the Inner-German Border. This was where deterrence was vital.

But in the period between 1950 and 1954 the anticipated German contributions to NATO were in abeyance even as "the year of maximum danger" was moved from 1954 to 1952. Opposition to German participation in the alliance was not confined to France. From Germany itself there were protests from Left and Right. The Social Democrats may not have been in power, but they were articulate in expressing their concern that joining NATO would put Germany back on the path of militarism and a revival of Nazism. From the Far Right came the conviction that a NATO connection would foreclose opportunity for reclaiming territories lost in World War II. Their spokesmen lacked faith in the West's interest in reunification. Chancellor Konrad Adenauer himself, an ardent believer in incorporating West Germany into the West, appeared on occasion to play the East against the West in advancing Germany's progress toward full sovereignty.[7]

Further undermining the promise of the Lisbon decisions of 1952 was an early recognition on the part of the transatlantic allies that the build-up of fifty divisions in Europe was impossible to achieve. When Eisenhower took office as U.S. president in 1953 he acted on an assumption that he must have recognized earlier as NATO's supreme allied commander in Europe, that the fifty divisions envisioned in 1952 would not materialize. Eisenhower's exhortations to Europeans notwithstanding, the allies would not risk the fragile economic recovery achieved through the Marshall Plan being undercut by a military build-up. Nor would the United States be willing to do more than had already been pledged. Given the stalemate in 1953 with respect to a German contribution, the Eisenhower administration initiated a "New Look" defense policy that would see tactical nuclear weapons as a substitute for troops on the ground. Should the Soviets fail to be impressed, there was also the deterrent pressure of massive retaliation against any Soviet act of aggression.[8]

The nuclear strategy did not fully substitute for troops on the ground to face the formidable 175 divisions that the adversary presumably could bring to bear. NATO's intention in the event deterrence failed was to keep the enemy as far east as possible in a defense along the Inner-German Border. West Germany's entry into the alliance made a stand at the East German border vital if only for domestic reasons. The function of ground forces then was to hold on just long enough for America's nuclear power to be deployed. Such was the thinking of the NATO Military Committee's force-planning document MC-70. By the mid-1950s thirty divisions were as much as the alliance could put together and were considered an adequate minimum at the time.[9]

How credible was this strategy in the eyes of the allies as they contemplated its effect on the Warsaw Pact adversaries? True, West Germany was now part of the alliance and its manpower presumably would make a difference. Yet there were too many factors subverting the defense plans in the Central Sector. The principal partners—Britain, France, and Germany—each raised unsettling issues. Britain in financial distress proposed in 1956 to withdraw one-third of the British Army of the Rhine, which if implemented would be a psychological as well as military blow to defense planners. A compromise was devised whereby some forces in Britain would, if necessary, be earmarked for NATO, which postponed further withdrawals. France's reasons for failing to meet troop commitments were more pressing and more rigid. This time it was not fighting in Indochina but insurrection in Algeria that diverted French resources; five divisions were reassigned from Europe to North Africa. And the twelve German divisions whose addition to NATO forces had been long promised were delayed when domestic opposition forced Adenauer's government to postpone the introduction of conscription. Adenauer's problems were not helped by the impact of the NATO air exercise CARTE BLANCHE in June 1955, which estimated that 1.3 million Germans would be killed in a surprise Soviet air attack.

The inability of the allies to meet their force goals in the mid-1950s was complicated by the continuing Communist campaign to paint NATO as a disrupter of European peace. The Soviet Union's acceptance of the Federal Republic's membership in NATO, the arrangement for Austrian neutrality in the Cold War, and the creation of the Warsaw Pact in 1955 all seemed to indicate a softer policy toward the West. In fact, the model of the Warsaw Pact presumably was NATO itself. The purpose in promoting a conference in Geneva was to set in motion an all-European security treaty that would drive American troops from Europe. The Soviet view seemed to have won support from such prominent figures as George Kennan, who had deplored the militarization of NATO in a widely publicized radio speech in 1957. The allies were encouraged by Soviet premier Nikita Khrushchev's unilateral troop cuts of one million men in 1956.

In these circumstances it was unlikely that NATO could achieve even the modest build-up of conventional forces that had been the goal of the Eisenhower administration. The nuclearization of NATO as the organization's main deterrent seemed inevitable. Still, the addition of German troops, the deployment of tactical nuclear weapons, and the assumption that sufficient conventional forces were available to provide a credible shield gave some sense of confidence about confronting the Soviets on relatively equal terms by 1957.

But by the end of that year the Soviet launching of Sputnik, an earth satellite, shattered this fragile sense of security as it implied Soviet superiority in the mastery of intercontinental ballistic missiles (ICBMs). Sputnik raised fears in Europe and the United States that the Soviet Union would dominate the world from outer space. Instantly, America's invulnerability was challenged, with serious implications for the security of its European allies. Would the United States maintain its commitment to Europe if its own territory was subject to attack? This was the kind of question that General Charles de Gaulle, president of France in the Fifth Republic, asked the NATO allies as well as his countrymen. The United States did its best to calm its allies by accelerating its own ICBM program, by establishing nuclear weapon stockpiles in Europe, and by planning deployment of intermediate-range nuclear missiles in countries that would accept them—Turkey, Italy, and Britain. The supreme allied commander, Europe (SACEUR), General Lauris Norstad, made a point of emphasizing the sword as well as the shield that NATO possessed in its armory.[10]

These initiatives were not successful of themselves in coping with European doubts about the solidity of the American commitment to Europe. They spawned, however, two major approaches to European security that might not have been adopted had Sputnik not changed the transatlantic dialogue. One of them unsurprisingly was a demand by European allies for their own nuclear weapons, something France had done independently with its *force de frappe*. It was West Germany that still felt itself a junior partner in the NATO enterprise based on the terms of its admission to the alliance in 1954. Acquiring its own nuclear capability would give it a feeling of equality that its leadership had found lacking. Defense Minister Franz Josef Strauss personified this aspiration as he appeared to embrace a Gaullist position. The American response may have been discomfited by Strauss's rhetoric but still had to deal with Europe's perceived need for a more satisfactory role in nuclear affairs. Sputnik reminded its allies that if the United States should reduce or abandon its commitment to their defense, a nuclear weapon of their own could be a necessity.

The new wave of uncertainty unleashed by Sputnik produced the second approach in the form of a U.S. proposal from two quite different sources to dismantle the nuclear monopoly—or at least oligopoly, inasmuch as Britain and France possessed their own nuclear weapons. SACEUR General Lauris Norstad proposed making NATO the fourth allied nuclear power by having its own nuclear component. The virtue of this proposal was its potential to defuse tensions, particularly in Germany, over a feeling of inferiority to the nuclear states and to remove fear of American abandonment in the face of its own vulnerability to Soviet nuclear power. His plan was intended not only to appease German restiveness but also to arrest France's movement toward disengagement from NATO's military responsibilities. West Germany and other members of the alliance would then have a role in the defense of Europe they had not played before.

The Norstad Plan, however, was quickly enveloped into a U.S. State Department program with somewhat different purposes. Instead of a conventional army equipped with nuclear weapons, as Norstad intended, the State Department envisioned a naval force under European control armed with Polaris missiles, which eventually would lead to an independent European nuclear force. Norstad's idea was always to have the nuclear armies under the supreme commander's authority. The resulting Multilateral Force (MLF, as it was called) was pursued for a time by the United States, but hesitantly and for good reason. There was an element of fraud in the arrangement. Europeans would buy the weapon but the nuclear warhead would remain in American hands. The French regarded the program with contempt. Only Germany retained an interest because of the loosening of restraints it promised. The MLF quietly disappeared in 1965 under the weight of other challenges to allied unity. But before it left the NATO stage, the MLF at least was a testament to America's continuing commitment to Europe's security.[11]

A more serious reconsideration of NATO's military role surfaced at the end of the Eisenhower administration when skepticism over the utility of massive retaliation penetrated the consciousness of leading members of the administration. Before his death in 1959, Secretary of State John Foster Dulles expressed his doubts about its credibility should an accidental or a minor outbreak of violence at the Inner-German Border automatically let loose ICBMs. The specter of retaliation loomed large after Sputnik. In this context former army chief of staff General Maxwell D. Taylor spoke for the new Kennedy administration in formulating a doctrine of Flexible Response. This doctrine took a long time to win NATO acceptance. Not until 1967 did it become NATO policy. Until then the United States was almost alone in deprecating nuclear weaponry. In fact, Robert S. McNamara, U.S. secretary of defense from 1961 to 1968, became convinced that nuclear warfare was an impossibility, a mutual suicide pact if it were ever to be employed. He believed that any nuclear weapon, even a tactical weapon, would result in a conflict that inevitably would escalate to the stage of ICBMs.

While McNamara was undoubtedly the most influential American politician in security and military matters in that decade, he encountered formidable opposition in winning the European allies to Flexible Response. None of them, however, would equate this doctrine with American abandonment of Europe, as de Gaulle implicitly but repeatedly suggested. For him it was only natural for a country to consider its own defense above that of any ally. The other allies did not share this existential distrust of the American pledge. After all, U.S. troops were well established in the territories of most of the members. Yet the implications of Flexible Response troubled them all. Notwithstanding the doomsday consequences of implementing the doctrine of Massive Retaliation, the allies worried about the process of Flexible Response. It involved graduated escalation, avoiding a massive strike in response to a minor incident. Nuclear weapons would be employed only at the last stage of conflict when lesser reactions had been exhausted. The trouble with this approach to aggression was the suspicion that the nuclear option would never be exercised, and that Western Europe would be devastated by a Warsaw Pact ground offensive before the United States would bring its nuclear power into action.

In May 1962 McNamara unveiled his conceptions of the defense of the West before his allies at the Athens meeting of the North Atlantic Council. His speech at that session received attention primarily for his disparagement of nuclear weapons in the hands of the European allies. But the major thrust of his lecture to the allies was the continuing—indeed, increased—importance of conventional, nonnuclear forces to cope with Soviet aggression.[12]

The Berlin crises in 1958 and again in 1961 were case studies of the most serious problems that NATO faced. They were provocative acts that might have led to nuclear war that neither side wanted. And this arena was in the Central Sector, even though a divided Berlin was not part of West Germany, and hence not part of NATO's formal responsibility. Yet the challenge that Nikita Khrushchev, energized by Sputnik, raised inevitably touched NATO, threatening its integrity. By demanding that the Western allies negotiate with the German Democratic Republic to make West Berlin a "free city," he in effect asserted East Germany's sovereignty over Berlin. If a treaty were not concluded within a six-month period, Khrushchev would turn over the Soviet Union's functions to the East German government. Although Khrushchev backed off from his ultimatum in 1959, the threat remained in effect and was renewed in 1961 during the Kennedy administration.

The three major allies did not respond to this challenge through North Atlantic Council action, since Berlin officially remained outside NATO's responsibility. Instead, they organized a tripartite command structure, known as LIVE OAK, under General Norstad. This in essence was his third hat, in addition to his NATO and U.S. military responsibilities, and required approval of the French and British, and subsequently German authorities, before any action could be taken. Inevitably, the LIVE OAK structure involved NATO as supply convoys going into Berlin were periodically harassed in these years. NATO's secretary-general complained of being uninformed of plans made in LIVE OAK. And inside the tripartite command there were differences. The United States pressed for conventional forces to restore access rather than rely on an airlift, as in 1948, while the British would prefer trying an airlift again rather than resorting to ground action. De Gaulle was convinced that Khrushchev was bluffing, and determined to do nothing rather than negotiate under pressure.

De Gaulle was right. The notorious Berlin Wall built in the summer of 1961 reflected the desperate efforts of the Walter Ulbricht regime to arrest the exodus of East Germans fleeing to the more prosperous West. Khrushchev deferred to East German pressure, and the three NATO powers accepted the result. Nevertheless, the crisis over Berlin led to a dangerous confrontation in October when a U.S. diplomat refused to deal with East German police upon entering the Soviet zone of East Berlin. Soviet and U.S. tanks then faced each other at Checkpoint Charlie. President Kennedy had already authorized the deployment of thirty-seven thousand troops to the Central Region as an earnest of the U.S. commitment to the defense of West Berlin. Both sides retreated, although Soviet harassment on the ground and in the air continued sporadically over the next few years. Ultimately, Khrushchev failed to intimidate the West; the Soviet Union signed its own peace treaty with East Germany without reference to the West's status in West Berlin.[13]

The increasing tensions generated in the Berlin crisis did affect Soviet strategy. The crisis marked a shift from a defensive strategy in place since Stalin's time to an offensive strategy anticipating conquest of all Western Europe that involved training Warsaw Pact armies for an invasion of NATO Europe. It would include full use of nuclear weaponry, including a preemptive nuclear strike. But the rising influence of the Soviet military in the early 1960s was counteracted by deepening divisions within the Warsaw Pact countries—subversion from Romania and conflicting priorities of Poland and East Germany—as well as worry over the split with China.

At the same time that the Warsaw Pact was expanding its interest in nuclear warfare, the United States was backing McNamara's strong stand in favor of raising more conventional forces. In 1962 NATO had only twenty-four of the thirty divisions promised by 1966 for the land central command. The U.S. and Canadian forces were in place, but the others were considerably understrength. The Europeans resisted. Aside from the increasing German contribution in the Bundeswehr there was no increase in conventional strength in the Central Sector. Only two of France's six divisions in Germany were committed to NATO. Canada reduced a third of its aircraft squadrons in Europe, while the Dutch, like the French, reduced the overall size of their armies. Part of Europe's resistance to American pressure may well have been resentment against the undiplomatic approach of the secretary of defense. More significant was a sense that increasing NATO's ground forces would lessen not increase security, unless the United States showed more determination to use nuclear weapons. An absence of the nuclear option would only embolden the Soviets to initiate incidents, considering the advantage they enjoyed through their massive conventional forces in Germany and in the Warsaw Pact countries.

From a West German perspective, the subject of ground troops was itself almost a taboo. Since a ground war would take place on German soil, its aim was always deterrence, to show the adversary that the West would make aggression too painful to initiate. Should deterrence fail, the most forward deployment possible was the alternative, even if unsatisfactory. That attitude put a premium on nuclear weapons of all kinds. In brief, Germans believed that NATO could never withstand a Soviet attack by conventional forces without resorting to nuclear weaponry.

Americans persisted in their campaign to induce Europeans to increase their ground forces. McNamara felt he had two strong arguments to support his case. One of them was a Pentagon study that claimed that NATO had exaggerated the size and strength of Soviet divisions, which were considerably smaller than those of the Western allies, and more important, were not as well equipped. Consequently, the McNamara Pentagon judged that by recognizing the shrunken size of Soviet divisions and enhancing the capabilities of the West's, there would be rough equality on the ground should the Soviets venture an attack.[14]

To further bolster the morale of the NATO allies, McNamara experimented with the concept of the BIG LIFT in 1963—namely, the rapid deployment of U.S. divisions from their base in Texas to assigned positions in Germany. An entire division would be flown to Europe, draw its equipment there, and be ready without delay to participate in NATO maneuvers—or, in a worst-case scenario, be thrust immediately into combat.

The virtue of McNamara's interpretations of the relative strength of the competing forces in Germany and his confidence in a rapid transportation of U.S. troops across the Atlantic were drawbacks in European, particularly German, minds. For one thing, they rested on the assumption that the European allies would fulfill their obligations to increase their own forces. Second, Europeans were skeptical that the relative troop strength of the opposing forces was calibrated as accurately as the Pentagon claimed. Third, and perhaps the most damaging, was the concern that deterrence would be affected negatively by keeping American troops in America rather than having boots on the ground in Europe. McNamara missed the psychological element in boasting of the greater efficiency of his program. He concentrated on the cost element, how much money would be saved by his emphasis on the airlift.

Europe's residual fears that America would abandon its allies were nourished in the mid-1960s by the increasing American involvement in Southeast Asia. The Vietnam War resulted in a steady drain of U.S. troops from the European theater. At the same time that the United States was urging Europeans to increase their contributions to the alliance, it was withdrawing its own forces from Europe to build up its armies in Southeast Asia. Not that there was a mass evacuation of U.S. troops. But thousands in the most skilled positions in all three services moved from Europe to Asia. That movement was bound to increase allied nervousness about where the United States would place its priorities; memories of America's long-standing concerns with Asia and the Pacific were once again alive in Europe.

Almost at the same time that the Vietnam War was absorbing American energies, de Gaulle made his decision to remove France from NATO's military structure and to require the dismantling of all NATO installations in his country. Although his actions seemed abrupt, his policies prior to 1966 should have made them predictable. The effect of France's action on the Central Sector was immediate and potentially fatal. The infrastructure that contained the supply lines from the Atlantic to Germany had to be rerouted to the North Sea. The expulsion of NATO headquarters from France had an impact on the defensibility of the Central Sector. Supreme Headquarters Allied Powers Europe (SHAPE) was removed from Paris, to Casteau in Belgium, while the headquarters of the Allied Forces Central Europe (AFCENT) was moved to Brunssum in the Netherlands. But the north-south axis of communications and troop replacements was the more significant problem as supplies from the United States were transferred to German in place of French ports. Even if the dislocations were only temporary, the men in the field felt they had a major challenge ahead in redeploying garrisons without damaging their effectiveness.

Khrushchev welcomed de Gaulle's challenge to NATO, but only up to a point. He was pleased with the French president's objective to push the United States out of Europe and with his willingness to recognize the boundaries set at Yalta. Still, he considered the implications of France's relations with NATO. The French challenge offered a dangerous example for Romania and other members of the Warsaw bloc to follow. De Gaulle's visit to Moscow failed to revive the old Franco-Russian connection.

France's decisions could have been more disruptive than they were. NATO may have been expelled from France, but France did not surrender its commitments in Germany. A de Gaulle–Adenauer entente permitted French troops to remain in place in Germany. A more serious issue was the fraying of German-American relations over American demands for burden sharing. Unhappiness in Washington over the cost of maintaining forces in Europe had been building up since the Kennedy administration when discontent in the U.S. Senate threatened the removal of American troops unless Europeans, particularly Germans, helped solve the imbalance of payments. Trilateral negotiations that involved Britain as well ended with German help with British foreign exchange problems and with a specific pledge to purchase U.S. securities. This was in addition to previous bilateral agreements that mandated the Federal Republic to buy American military equipment to offset the costs of the American military presence in Germany.

None of the parties was fully appeased by the foregoing arrangements. U.S. senators continued to win resolutions asking the Johnson administration to reduce the size of U.S. forces in Europe unless Europeans took up more of the defense burden. Nonetheless, the solidity of the Central Sector was relatively unshaken despite the turmoil in the mid-1960s. A compromise was reached on the matter of dual basing of U.S. forces that allowed for only modest reduction of forces by 1968. The four hundred thousand American troops in 1962 declined to a little under three hundred thousand in 1968, but that reduction did not signal their eventual removal from Europe to serve in Southeast Asia. McNamara had won his argument that NATO had sufficient conventional force to cope with Soviet aggression. That the United States was moving toward de-escalation in Vietnam was a further indication that Asia was not to replace Europe in America's scheme of things. And the Czechoslovak crisis in 1968 proved to be a sober reminder to all NATO parties of the importance of maintaining vigilance in Germany.

Yet by the end of the 1960s NATO and the Warsaw Pact were in fact approaching a détente that was to flower for a time in the next decade. The Soviets had made a point of assuring NATO that the forcible removal of the liberal Czech government was not intended to alarm the Western allies, even as SACEUR General Lyman L. Lemnitzer was understandably nervous about the Warsaw Pact's military movements in Czechoslovakia. Although NATO's conciliatory activities were hardly symmetrical, the alliance was affected by two parallel influences at this time. One was the rising authority of the smaller allies, empowered by the departure of France from military decisions. They reluctantly had accepted the doctrine of Flexible Response in 1967. But they were wholeheartedly behind the drive toward détente reflected in the Harmel Report in that year. The United States accepted the new initiatives of the smaller nations, perhaps in part because of McNamara's conviction that nuclear war was mutually suicidal, and more likely because the Vietnam War had become such a drain on the energies and morale of America.

Despite the increasing military capabilities of the Warsaw Pact, incentives for détente were as strong in Moscow as they were in the NATO capitals. Unlike many of the NATO allies, the Soviets regarded the strategy of Flexible Response, hesitantly accepted by the North Atlantic Council in 1967, as more threatening than Massive Retaliation had been. The potential of a successful outcome of the Helsinki Process in 1969 trumped the benefits of a Warsaw Pact as a military instrument. The prospect of a détente that could legitimize territories acquired in World War II prevailed over objections from Warsaw Pact allies.

The issues that had divided the NATO allies in the past were not resolved by 1968: unequal military and financial burdens that so disturbed Americans and the continuing suspicions of Europeans that America was not fully committed to the defense of Europe survived at the end of the decade. Neither perspective was fair or accurate, but NATO could live with them both.

What is evident throughout the twenty-year period under review was that at all times the Central Sector, the German front, dominated NATO councils, as it did for the Warsaw Pact, to the relative neglect of the northern and southern fronts. Norway and Turkey bordered the Soviet Union, but despite the proximity of the Soviet base in the Kola Peninsula and despite the increasing power of the Soviet navy in the Mediterranean, they produced nothing comparable to the tremors that the Soviet presence in East Germany created among the NATO allies or that NATO forces in West Germany created in the Warsaw Pact. Repeatedly over the years, Italian generals raised alarms over the possibility of Soviet armies marching across Yugoslavia and pouring into the Po Valley through the gap at Nuova Gorizia. They felt that the leaders in Paris and Brussels, Washington and Bonn, were not listening. Although they may not have been correct, they had to recognize that NATO's primary concerns centered on the dangers from the east, not from the north or south. In retrospect, the alliance's priorities were justified.[15]

Notes

1. Many of my judgments about NATO's early years have been drawn from two studies in particular: *NATO 1948: The Birth of the Transatlantic Alliance* (Lanham, Md.: Rowman & Littlefield, 2007) and *The United States and NATO: The Formative Years* (Lexington: University Press of Kentucky, 1984).

2. Lawrence S. Kaplan, "An Unequal Triad: The United States, Western Union, and NATO," in *Western Security: The Formative Years, European and Atlantic Defence, 1947–1953,* ed. Olav Riste (Oslo: Norwegian University Press, 1985), 107–27.

3. Vojtech Mastny, *The Cold War and Soviet Insecurity: The Stalin Years* (New York: Oxford University Press, 1998).

4. Lawrence S. Kaplan, *NATO before the Korean War, April 1949–June 1950* (Kent, Ohio: Kent State University Press, in press), chapters 5 and 6.

5. Lawrence S. Kaplan, "Franco-American Relations in NATO," in *Les relations franco-américaines au XXe siècle,* ed. Pierre Mélandri and Serge Ricard (Paris: L'Harmattan, 2003), 245–62.

6. Kevin Ruane, *Rise and Fall of the European Defence Community: Anglo-American Relations and the Crisis in European Defence, 1950–1955* (Basingstoke, UK: Palgrave Macmillan, 2000).

7. Frank Ninkovich, *Germany and the United States: The Transformation of the German Question since 1945* (New York: Twayne, 1995).

8. Saki Dockrill, *Eisenhower's New-Look National Security Policy, 1953–1961* (Basingstoke, UK: Palgrave Macmillan, 1996).

9. Robert S. Jordan, "Norstad: Can the SACEUR Be Both European and American?," in *Generals in International Politics,* ed. Robert S. Jordan (Lexington: University Press of Kentucky, 1987), 73–92.

10. Erin Mahan, *Kennedy, de Gaulle, and Western Europe* (Basingstoke, UK: Palgrave Macmillan, 2002).

11. Lawrence S. Kaplan, "The MLF Debate," in *John F. Kennedy and Europe,* ed. Douglas Brinkley and Richard Griffiths (Baton Rouge: Louisiana State University Press, 1999), 51–65.

12. Lawrence S. Kaplan, Ronald D. Landa, and Edward J. Drea, *The McNamara Ascendancy, 1961–1965,* History of the Office of Secretary of Defense, vol. 5 (Washington, D.C.: Historical Office, Office of the Secretary of Defense, 2006), chapter 12.

13. Lawrence S. Kaplan, "The Berlin Crisis: Views from the Pentagon, 1958–1962," in *International Cold War Military Records and History: Proceedings of the Conference,* ed. William W. Epley (Washington, D.C.: U.S. Army Center of Military History, 1996), 65–86.

14. Alain Enthoven and K. Wayne Smith, *How Much Is Enough? Shaping the Defense Program, 1961–1968* (New York: Harper & Row, 1971).

15. Lawrence S. Kaplan, "Reflections on Reactions to European Integration," in *Von Truman bis Harmel: Die Bundesrepublik Deutschland im Spannungsfeld von NATO und Europäischer Integration,* ed. Hans-Joachim Harder (Munich: R. Oldenbourg, 2000), 1–18.

2

Aims and Realities

NATO's Forward Defense and the Operational Planning Level at NORTHAG

Bruno Thoss

At its formation, NATO basically represented a regional alliance with its leading powers as global actors. The classical strategic thinking of the Anglo-Saxon sea powers had to be coordinated with the demands of their continental partners for an effective defense of Western Europe. In all its strategy papers during the Cold War, NATO concentrated defense planning on three major principles: an overall defensive concept; maximum efficiency by minimal expenditure; and burden sharing.[1]

The United States, too, gave geostrategic priority to the Atlantic over the Pacific regions.[2] But the sea powers regarded the Western European continent as only one of several pivotal points of Western security. A possible war over Europe would have been decided in the North Atlantic as the central region of transatlantic security. The peripheral seas, like the Baltic and the Mediterranean, also were considered to be nearly as important geostrategically as the European continent. Furthermore, the Soviet Union could focus on the Middle East to attack Western security through its dependence on oil.[3] As a consequence, a lengthy process of mutual persuasion was necessary until the area between the North Sea and the Alps was accepted as the most vulnerable sector of NATO's eastern front. Document DC (Defense Committee) 13 of March 1950 read: "Because of its material resources, dense population, high industrial potential, and the strategic values of its central geographical position, the conquest of the Western European Region would represent a major and perhaps decisive victory." For the Soviet Union, the centers of heavy industry along the Rhine and Ruhr, in southern Belgium, and in northern France, as well as the ports of Hamburg, Bremen, Rotterdam, and Antwerp, would be "their primary objective in war."[4] An invasion, therefore, "would in all probability develop through the North German Plain." Because of its topography, which was the most suitable vicinity for the eastern tank armies, the area's seizure would also with one stroke break up the NATO defense into two spaces linked only by the sea.[5]

Initial Response

Because of a lack of sufficient armed forces, however, the initial NATO response would have been one of delaying, and even an evacuation of the continent at a very early stage. Confronted with this gloomy perspective, the members of the Brussels Pact tried from spring 1948 to make the Rhine front "impenetrable" from the onset. But that goal was far from achievable because many of the Western powers had strong military forces deployed outside of Europe.[6] The United States expected the Europeans to prove themselves prepared and to strengthen their self-defense.

NATO's strategy paper MC (Military Committee) 3 of October 1949 postulated the mission to "arrest and counter as soon as practicable the enemy offensives against the North Atlantic Treaty powers by all means available." The whole concept, however, was questionable because "initially, the hard core of ground forces will come from the European nations."[7] Western European responsibility for initial self-defense was combined with a conditional early reinforcement from overseas, depending on the situation at other key points of the conflict. Defense starting at the Rhine was in military terms nothing but a declaration of intent. At the Rhine and the IJssel the British, Dutch, and Belgian forces were to hold the Northern Sector from the North Sea to Remagen. Adjacent to them, French and American troops would defend the upper Rhine to Basel. Eventually, French forces, possibly including the Swiss army, were to secure the Alps to the Mediterranean.[8] But since the Europeans did not have sufficient troops, they could defend only temporarily until powerful assistance was provided from overseas. In the event that it did not arrive in time, the Europeans had to resign themselves to the American plan to withdraw to the Atlantic or over the Pyrenees, and maybe even to North Africa.[9]

For the years to come NATO planned to extend its defenses eastward of the Rhine. Such a plan depended heavily on the Federal Republic of Germany (FRG), not only its territory but also its manpower and material resources. As early as 1948 the future German defense planner, General Adolf Heusinger, prepared a study for United States European Command that considered the battlefield between the North Sea and the Alps as the focus of the fight for Europe. The Rhine River line would serve as a fixed base.[10] The territory east of the river would be defended not by lines based on the terrain, but rather through a mobile defense. The superior Soviet forces advancing from the German Democratic Republic would have to be channelized into northern Germany, with Schleswig-Holstein being the northern and the Hessian mountains the southern anchors of the defense. Those were to be held at all costs in order to threaten the attacker's deep flanks. If the "puny ground forces" of NATO could not be reinforced, the enemy "would not need to fight but simply to drive" on the tank trails of northern Germany.[11]

Heusinger had support within NATO. The alliance planners, too, pretended that "defense should be conducted in an active manner making full use of mobility and offensive action whenever opportunity offers."[12] But in fact the lack of combat-ready divisions would have limited any possibilities to exploit such opportunities. The main burden would have to be borne by the British Army of the Rhine (BAOR), whereas the Dutch and Belgian forces were at best suited for conducting a defense at the Rhine, but not beyond. All the plans after 1951 had arriving American reinforcements committed initially in southern Germany and in the Fulda Gap.[13]

Joint operational planning could finally start after the establishment in 1951 of the unified command structures.[14] Based on the lower Rhine, the Northern Army Group (NORTHAG) consisted of four British, two Dutch, and two Belgian divisions plus one Canadian brigade.[15] The basic concept was to initiate defensive action beginning at the Elbe, followed by a fighting withdrawal across the Weser to the Rhine. At first, however, NATO was not capable of conducting defensive action beyond the Rhine and the IJssel. Possibly some fixed positions could be held east of the Rhine, which would threaten the advancing enemy's flanks. But the actual backbone of the defense was not the ground troops; it was rather the British air forces, which were based primarily in East Anglia. Their mission was to provide close air support to the ground forces and interdict the battlefield in order to block reinforcements in depth from the Soviet Union.[16]

During and after its conference in Lisbon in 1952 NATO intended as soon as possible to build up a strong shield of forces and to integrate the future German divisions as part of a European Defense Community.[17] But those hopes were dashed before that year ended. Because of the delays until 1955 in its admission to the alliance, the FRG could not start building its force of twelve divisions, half of which were planned for NORTHAG.[18] Furthermore, the Benelux countries were for economic reasons unable to reorganize their armed forces as rapidly and efficiently as required.[19] For the present, then, operations east of the Rhine remained wishful thinking. The so-called Rhine barrier would be the largest natural obstacle, extensively re-inforced by artificial measures, including widespread flooding in the north-east of the Netherlands and an entire system of prepared barriers in northern Germany—demolished bridges and intersections and temporarily flooded river valleys.[20]

But such measures would not slow down effectively the enemy's rapid breakthrough to the Atlantic. As early as 1952, therefore, the British and Americans made the strategic decision to substitute the unavailable required ground forces with increased nuclear firepower—the concept of Massive Re-taliation.[21] In December 1954 the European allies accepted the introduction of tactical nuclear weapons into the force structure of NATO.[22] According to MC 48, for the alliance to effect an efficient forward defense it needed both "highly trained and mobile forces with an integrated atomic capability . . . to prevent a rapid overrunning of Europe."[23]

Tactical Nuclear Weapons

From mid-1955, Germany as a new NATO partner tried to bring its own defense thinking to bear on the alliance. German military leadership hoped that the fielding of the German divisions would provide an operation-capable mass in the midterm, which would enable the alliance to conduct a mobile ground-air battle on the North German plain, with or even without the resort to the controlled use of nuclear weapons.[24] The German insis-tence on a Bundeswehr solidly based on tank divisions met with predictable skepticism. NATO planners, however, did agree to a gradual shifting of the defensive lines from the Rhine to the German eastern frontier as soon as the build-up of the German divisions would permit. But in NATO terms, op-erational "mass was henceforth to be measured in kilotons, not force levels, the tactic called for destruction instead of mobility and capture."[25] NATO expected the Bundeswehr to provide a screen of light troops rather than tank divisions operating over large areas. Thus a "gap theory" emerged for the management of combat operations east of the Rhine. The objective was to induce the enemy to concentrate his forces for attack, thus offering lucra-tive targets for nuclear strikes. The mobile defensive forces—more infantry than tank heavy—were to act only as a conventional trip wire to trigger the decisive nuclear hammer.[26]

The situation deteriorated further when the British began to thin out BAOR, even before the Germans could complete the establishment of their I Corps in northern Germany.[27] Forward defense east of the Rhine was not possible under such conditions, except with the extensive use of atomic weapons. The NATO exercise LION NOIR in March 1957 made this conclusion more than obvious to all the participants. As the exercise demonstrated, the enemy would have penetrated the North German plain within a few days and could have been prevented from crossing the Rhine only by the use of one hundred tactical nuclear weapons. This was—as the supreme allied commander, Europe (SACEUR), admitted in 1959—only "a more forward strategy in certain areas."[28]

In 1957–1958 the first five German divisions were assigned to NATO, three to NORTHAG.[29] The summer 1958 European Defense Plan for Central Europe now accepted a forward defensive line at the Weser River. The Germans, however, remained aware that "within the scope of NATO there will be no more than delaying actions forward of the Rhine."[30] Formally, NORTHAG now could count on a Dutch, a German, a British, and a Belgian corps. But the British army had already evacuated its forward-based stations in lower Saxony. The British redeployed their units farther to the west while reducing their personnel strength, from seventy-seven thousand men in 1957 to forty-five thousand in 1963.[31] In response, NORTHAG asked for two Dutch divisions to deploy to the Weser region, in addition to the two Belgian divisions that had been advanced across the Rhine. But it was only after the erection of the Berlin Wall in 1961 that the Netherlands met NATO's request to station Dutch military units in Germany. Initially, the Dutch based a light brigade east of the Weser, and then after 1963, an armored brigade.[32]

Gradually, then, the defensive lines advanced toward the east. But even at the end of the 1950s, NATO forces were short on numbers and effectiveness, while the German rearmament program proceeded very slowly. By that point it would take the attacker only five days to push NORTHAG's defensive line back to the Ems River in the west. During the 1959 NATO exercises a stronger position on the Weser was considered too optimistic. Still, the opinion continued to prevail that only the Rhine could be defended effectively and successfully.[33] Even in 1960 and 1962 NORTHAG did not plan to assemble combat-capable forces beyond the Weser. The area to the east would be kept under observation and possibly turned into a nuclear target area.[34]

Such a situation was completely unacceptable for the Germans. In the late 1950s, therefore, General Heusinger considered the idea of fortifying greater sectors of Germany's eastern border.[35] But the blocking of the routes of advance into the FRG for only a few days would have required NATO to use atomic demolition munitions (ADM).[36] NORTHAG exercise MAKE FAST VIII in the summer of 1960 exposed the differing approaches very clearly. To the surprise of his British, Dutch, and Belgian allies, all of whom adhered to the NATO concept of a primarily nuclear defense, the commanding general of German I Corps instructed his subordinate commanders to use tactical nuclear weapons only in an extreme emergency. In fact, NATO's fragile scheme of defense depended on the use of tactical nuclear weapons "from the outset." In NATO terms, "any delay in their use—even measured in hours—could be fatal."[37] On the other hand, American analysts cautioned early on that the free use of nuclear weapons would threaten "the destruction of Europe." Washington harbored no illusions that nuclear deterrence had already produced psychological self-deterrence among the European allies.[38]

Forward Defense

By 1963 the Bundeswehr had grown to ten of its planned twelve divisions— five assigned directly to NORTHAG. In response, NATO moved its defensive line forward to the Iron Curtain. The Dutch units in the north were assigned to cover the sector south of Hamburg. The defense line of this Netherlands I Corps was extended incrementally forty kilometers to the south in order to link to the reserves of the adjacent German and British corps. On the Dutch southern flank German I Corps was tasked with preventing a penetration into the Lüneburger Heath north of Hanover. Next to the Germans, BAOR deployed from Hanover to the Harz Mountains. Its southern flank was secured by Belgian I Corps. The British and German tank divisions were held together in Westphalia as an operational reserve. In the air, NORTHAG was supported by the British, German, Dutch, and Belgian air forces under the command of the Second Allied Tactical Air Force.

On paper, the defense of the North German plain was based on a rather impressive force—five German, four British, two Dutch, and two Belgian divisions. But BAOR continued to thin out its conventional units and compensated for the reductions by increasing the number of short-range missiles. German I Corps still had serious shortcomings in its logistics support system. All the NORTHAG divisions were in the process of mechanization and motorization to achieve the required armored mobility on the battlefield, largely in response to the continuing and ultimately successful German pressure for the concept of mobile defense. That concept had become a common feature of the defensive plans of Allied Forces Central Europe (AFCENT),[39] which in turn meshed with the demands of the Kennedy administration to reduce the overall dependence on nuclear weapons in favor of increased conventional options.[40] At first the Europeans feared such a change would result in the separation of their own security from the transatlantic security. The Germans in particular wondered whether nuclear deterrence would actually work to prevent the outbreak of a European war. Would the Americans really risk a worldwide nuclear war merely to defend a politically important but nonetheless local outpost like West Berlin? Thus, it was not before 1967–1968 that the Flexible Response doctrine, which combined nuclear and conventional defense options, was finally issued.

In order for NORTHAG forces to operate flexibly, as was now required, they needed extensive modernization, which had to be achieved in the environment of an oil crisis and an economic recession. The necessary extension of the logistical communications lines across the Rhine caused additional strain because the available areas were already overcrowded with military infrastructure. Finally, alternate airfields had to be established throughout the area to facilitate the dispersal of the air forces to prevent them from being neutralized by an enemy first strike. Force ratio comparisons with the ever far-superior enemy and the still-limited operational capability of the NATO forces, however, did not allow for a purely conventional defense, even though the defensive lines had been moved forward. Thus, the extensive use of nuclear weapons on the battlefield remained an essential prerequisite for any successful defense.[41]

The British in particular thought that a nonnuclear defense within their zone of operations was not feasible for longer than three or four days. Once the enemy crossed the Weser, he had to be attacked with nuclear weapons, otherwise the battle would be lost. Once again, this focused NATO's attention on a special type of weapons, ADM. The military advantages of ADM were twofold: they could delay an enemy attack close to the border, and at the same time they could minimize the risk of nuclear escalation because they would be detonated on NATO territory. But that was exactly their greatest psychological disadvantage. The ADM would destroy what the NATO forces were supposed to defend, the FRG's territory, its infrastructure, and—if not evacuated in time—its population. Initially the German defense planners had agreed with NATO commanders that ADM had to be used to secure the so-called vital areas. But the weapon lost its military value because its employment remained fully in U.S. hands, thus preventing detonation in time.[42]

Skepticism

What had changed since 1963 were the now commonly accepted guidelines of new operational flexibility. But the military means had not increased to the same extent. Thus, the effectiveness of forward defense would inevitably continue to be linked to a controlled early use of tactical nuclear weapons. Nonetheless, two NORTHAG senior officers, Belgian general Robert Close and British general Sir John Hackett, retained their skepticism even through the mid-1970s.[43] In their respective best-selling books they warned that given its insufficient defensive capabilities, NATO in the course of a European war ran the risk that the enemy would advance up to the Rhine and eventually to the Atlantic coast within just a few days—particularly on the main front of the North German plain. But by that time NATO was no longer relying exclusively on a military defense. The Harmel Report of December 1967 posited an effective stabilization of the security situation in Europe, and in particular at the key point in northern Germany.[44] The basic concept had become one of combining continued military efforts with a policy of détente.

Notes

1. See *NATO Strategy Documents 1949–1969*, ed. Gregory W. Pedlow (Brussels, 1997).

2. Regarding the theories of Sir Halford Makinder's geopolitical main topics of the Eurasian "heartland" and its "rimlands" Western Europe and East Asia into U.S. strategic thinking, see John Lewis Gaddis, *Strategies of Containment: A Critical Appraisal of Postwar American National Security Policy* (New York, 1982), 57–65; see also Stefan Fröhlich, *Zwischen selektiver Verteidigung und globaler Eindämmung: Geostrategisches Denken in der amerikanischen Außen- und Sicherheitspolitik während des Kalten Krieges* (Baden-Baden, 1998), 125–50.

3. JIC 435/12, "Soviet Intentions and Capabilities," 30 Nov. 1948, quoted by Christian Greiner, "Die alliierten militärstrategischen Planungen zur Verteidigung Westeuropas 1947–1950," in *Von der Kapitulation bis zum Pleven-Plan*, Roland G. Foerster et al., Anfänge westdeutscher Sicherheitspolitik, 1945–1956, vol. 1 (Munich, 1982), 197–201. See also Norbert Wiggershaus, "Nordatlantische Bedrohungsperzeptionen im 'Kalten Krieg' 1948–1956," in *Das Nordatlantische Bündnis 1949–1956*, ed. Klaus A. Maier and Norbert Wiggershaus (Im Auftrag des Militärgeschichtlichen Forschungsamtes), Beiträge zur Militärgeschichte, vol. 37 (Munich, 1993), 18–21; and Christian Greiner, "Die Entwicklung der Bündnisstrategie 1949 bis 1958," in *Die NATO als Militärallianz: Strategie, Organisation und nukleare Kontrolle im Bündnis 1949 bis 1959*, ed. Christian Greiner, Klaus A. Maier, and Heinz Rebhan, Entstehung und Probleme des Atlantischen Bündnisses bis 1956, vol. 4 (Munich, 2003), 39–41.

4. DC 13, "North Atlantic Treaty Organization Medium Defense Plan," 28 Mar. 1950, *NATO Strategy Documents,* 153.

5. Ibid., 146.

6. See Nigel Hamilton, *Monty: The Field Marshal, 1944–1976* (London, 1986), 753–58.

7. MC 3, "The Strategic Concept for the Defense of the North Atlantic Area," 19 Oct. 1949, *NATO Strategy Documents,* 6.

8. Greiner, "Die alliierten militärstrategischen Planungen," 301–3 and 311–15; regarding early hopes for a military cooperation of the Swiss army, see Bruno Thoss, "Geostrategie und Neutralität: Die deutsch-schweizerischen Sicherheitsbeziehungen im Spannungsfeld von Neutralitätswahrung und NATO-Verteidigung," in *Die Schweiz und Deutschland 1945–1961,* ed. Antoine Fleury, Horst Möller, and Hans-Peter Schwarz (Munich, 2004), 183–86.

9. Robert A. Wampler, *Ambiguous Legacy: The United States, Great Britain, and the Foundation of NATO Strategy, 1948–1957,* 2 vols. (Ann Arbor, 1996), 4–12; Greiner, "Entwicklung der Bündnisstrategie," 49–63; Bruno Thoss, *NATO-Strategie und nationale Verteidigungsplanung: Planung und Aufbau der Bundeswehr unter den Bedingungen einer massiven atomaren Vergeltungsstrategie 1952 bis 1960,* Sicherheitspolitik und Streitkräfte der Bundesrepublik Deutschland, vol. 1 (Munich, 2006), 17–38.

10. Georg Meyer, *Adolf Heusinger: Dienst eines deutschen Soldaten 1915 bis 1964* (Hamburg, 2001), 359–70.

11. See Heusinger's appreciation of the military situation, summer 1950, in ibid., 375.

12. See Heusinger's "Die Verteidigung Westeuropas," 1949/50, in ibid., 372–75.

13. Bruno Thoss, "The Presence of American Troops in Germany and German-American Relations, 1949–1956," in *American Policy and the Reconstruction of West Germany 1945–1955,* ed. Jeffry M. Diefendorf, Axel Frohn, and Hermann-Josef Rupieper (Cambridge, 1993), 413–15.

14. Greiner, "Entwicklung der Bündnisstrategie," 74–82.

15. Heinz Rebhan, "Der Aufbau des militärischen Instruments der NATO," in *Die NATO als Militärallianz,* ed. Greiner, Maier, and Rebhan, 210–17.

16. Robert S. Jordan, *Norstad: Cold War NATO Supreme Commander: Airman, Strategist, Diplomat* (London, 2000), 84–96.

17. Rebhan, "Aufbau des militärischen Instruments," 220–26.

18. Thoss, *NATO-Strategie und nationale Verteidigungsplanung,* 127–29.

19. Helmut R. Hammerich, "Invasion oder Inflation: Die Aufrüstung Westeuropas und ihre wirtschaftlichen Auswirkungen auf die NATO-Mitgliedstaaten 1949–1954," *Militärgeschichte* N.F. 8 (1998): 30–35.

20. Thoss, *NATO-Strategie und nationale Verteidigungsplanung,* 613–20.

21. Ibid., 39–63.

22. Greiner, "Entwicklung der Bündnisstrategie," 117–28.

23. MC 48 (Final), "The Most Effective Pattern of NATO Military Strength for the Next Few Years," 22 Nov. 1954, *NATO Strategy Documents,* 241.

24. Thoss, *NATO-Strategie und nationale Verteidigungsplanung,* 88–96.

25. Robert C. Richardson III, "NATO's Nuclear Strategy: A Look Back," *Strategic Review,* no. 9 (Spring 1981): part 2: 41.

26. Axel F. Gablik, *Strategische Planungen in der Bundesrepublik Deutschland 1955–1967: Politische Kontrolle oder militärische Notwendigkeit?,* Internationale Politik und Sicherheit, vol. 30/5 (Baden-Baden, 1996), 71–73.

27. Saki Dockrill, "Retreat from the Continent? Britain's Motives for Troop Reductions in West Germany, 1955–1958," *Journal of Strategic Studies* 20 (1997): 45–70.

28. Meeting of the British Chiefs of Staff with SACEUR General Norstad, 1 Oct. 1959, Public Record Office, London, DEFE 3276, COS (59) 61.

29. Helmut R. Hammerich, Dieter H. Kollmer, Martin Rink, and Rudolf J. Schlaffer, *Das Heer 1950 bis 1970: Konzeption, Organisation, Aufstellung,* Sicherheitspolitik und Streitkräfte der Bundesrepublik Deutschland, vol. 3 (Munich, 2006), 135–41.

30. Paper Führungsstab der Bundeswehr (Fü B) regarding SACEUR's EDP 2-58, 19 Nov. 1957, Bundesarchiv-Militärarchiv, Freiburg, BW 2/2668.

31. Dockrill, "Retreat from the Continent?," 59.

32. Jan Hoffenaar and Ben Schoenmaker, *Met het blik naar het Oosten: De Koninklijke Landmacht 1945–1990* (The Hague, 1994), 166–74. See also Hoffenaar's chapter "The Dutch Contribution to the Defense of the Central Sector" in this volume.

33. For the Statement of the Supreme Commander, Seventh (U.S.) Army, in May 1959 and the heavy controversy in the German public, see Thoss, *NATO-Strategie und nationale Verteidigungsplanung,* 577–78.

34. Briefing for the meeting of the British Chiefs of Defense Staff with the U.S. Chiefs of Staff, 18 Sept. 1963, Public Record Office, London, DEFE 4/157, IP Note 28/63, Appendix E.

35. Thoss, *NATO-Strategie und nationale Verteidigungsplanung,* 597–99.

36. For analysis and documents about the NATO exercise MAKE FAST VIII, see Reiner Pommerin, "General Trettner und die Atom-Minen," *Vierteljahrshefte für Zeitgeschichte* 39 (1991): 637–54; see also Thoss, *NATO-Strategie und nationale Verteidigungsplanung,* 540–41.

37. MC 48, "The Most Effective Pattern of NATO Military Strength for the Next Few Years," 22 Nov. 1954, *NATO Strategy Documents,* 242.

38. Bernard Brodie, "Strategy Hits a Dead End," in *The Development of American Strategic Thought, 1945–1969,* ed. Marc Trachtenberg, 6 vols. (New York, 1988), vol. 3, part 2, 91–95.

39. Hoffenaar and Schoenmaker, *Met het blik,* 170.

40. Jane E. Stromseth, *The Origins of Flexible Response: NATO's Debate over Strategy in the 1960s* (Oxford, 1988), 26–35. The West European and German reactions are discussed in Bruno Thoss, "Bündnisintegration und nationale Verteidigungsinteressen: Der Aufbau der Bundeswehr im Spannungsfeld zwischen nuklearer

Abschreckung und konventioneller Verteidigung (1955–1968)," in *Die Bundeswehr 1955 bis 2005: Rückblenden-Einsichten-Perspektiven,* ed. Frank Nägler (Im Auftrag des Militärgeschichtlichen Forschungsamtes), Sicherheitspolitik und Streitkräfte der Bundesrepublik Deutschland, vol. 7 (Munich, 2007), 33–35.

41. For NATO's defense planning under the conditions of Flexible Response, see Hammerich et al., *Das Heer,* 110–21.

42. Interview with General Johann Adolf Graf von Kielmansegg, 24 June 1997, Militärgeschichtliches Forschungsamt, Zeitzeugen-Schrifttum.

43. Robert Close, *L'Europe sans défense? 48 heures qui pourraient changer la face du monde* (Brussels, 1976); and Sir John Hackett, *Der Dritte Weltkrieg: Hauptschauplatz Deutschland* (Munich, 1978).

44. Helga Haftendorn, "Entstehung und Bedeutung des Harmel-Berichts der NATO von 1967," *Vierteljahrshefte für Zeitgeschichte* 40 (1992): 169–221.

3

Soviet and Warsaw Pact Military Strategy from Stalin to Brezhnev

The Transformation from "Strategic Defense"
to "Unlimited Nuclear War," 1945–1968

Matthias Uhl

Drawing in part on recently acquired sources from Russian archives, this chapter presents an overview of the changes in Soviet military strategy from 1945 through the end of the 1960s. It examines how nuclear weapons transformed the strategic thinking of the Soviet armed forces during the Stalin, Khrushchev, and Brezhnev eras, and concludes that Soviet military plans for war in Europe—which in the eyes of Soviet military planners was the decisive theater—became increasingly more offensive because of the assumption that nuclear weapons would be used. Such thinking ultimately was based on the premise that Western Europe could be overrun in a very short time, thereby forcing by means of military operations a decision favorable to the Soviet side in the struggle between the opposed social and political systems.

The chapter starts by briefly examining Stalin's strategy of "strategic defense," the aim of which was to secure the areas of Soviet influence won after World War II. It then outlines, using the example of the 1961 BURYA command and staff exercise, the concept of "unlimited nuclear war" in Western Europe, as conceived by Nikita Khrushchev and his military commanders. This rash strategy met with some resistance in the ranks of the Soviet military leadership. Finally, it sheds some light on how the military-industrial-academic complex in the Soviet Union armed the Soviet forces with the weapons necessary for offensive warfare, how the Warsaw Pact countries were increasingly involved in the armaments effort, and how their forces were to support the Soviets more effectively in the potential struggle for Western Europe.

From Stalin to the Warsaw Pact

Following the end of World War II, Soviet premier Joseph Stalin initially was concerned with holding and consolidating the positions won by the Red Army in Europe. He thought it was necessary to defend the areas of Soviet influence in east-central and Eastern Europe against feared Western attacks. Considering the strategic weakness of his own armed forces, the dictator precluded any offensive measures for the time being. The operational plans developed for Poland and Czechoslovakia under Soviet direction in 1951, for example, required those countries to limit themselves exclusively to the defense of their own territories.[1] The *Plan for the Active Defense of the Territory of the Soviet Union,* submitted by the Soviet General Staff in 1947, specified the mission for defensive armies to smash the enemy in the border-defensive zone at the outset of hostilities. A counterattack would then be launched that included the reserves of the Soviet Supreme Command, which would have the mission of inflicting a crushing defeat on the aggressor and "securing the invulnerability of the boundaries established by international agreement after World War II."[2]

During the end of the 1940s and the beginning of the 1950s, Soviet military strategy refocused toward its new enemies, the United States and its European NATO allies. Initially, the Soviet Union could counterpose a superiority in conventional armaments to the nuclear superiority of the Americans. Although the first Soviet atomic bomb had already been tested in 1949, nuclear weapons would not be available to Soviet forces in any significant numbers until later. Soviet air forces did not receive their first operational atomic bombs until 1954. The following year, the Soviets initiated the storage of nuclear weapons in the central and military depots of the Ministry for Mid-Level Mechanical Engineering. Soviet land forces and the navy had to wait until the end of the 1950s for nuclear warheads, and the air-defense units had to wait even longer.[3]

Thus, Soviet military strategy still depended on strong conventional power during the second half of the 1950s, as nuclear weapons were available only to a very limited degree. Nevertheless, operations were planned with the objective that "Soviet Forces will reach the English Channel on the second day of war."[4] How this ambitious goal was to be achieved was not clear, since the average attack tempo at that time amounted to not more than thirty to thirty-five kilometers per day and the Group of Soviet Forces in Germany (GSFG) had not yet been restructured as an offensive force. The Soviet military leadership saw its mission as one of holding the NATO forces for forty-six hours in case of an attack, after which the second strategic echelon would arrive and shift to an offensive toward the Channel coast.[5]

After the foundation of the Warsaw Pact in May 1955, which included the establishment of the Supreme Command of the Unified Warsaw Pact Forces, the military and political antagonism between the Soviet Union and the United States developed into a confrontation between the NATO and Warsaw Pact military blocs. By the end of the 1950s that confrontation was shaped essentially by the rapid development of military technology. Development and deployment of strategic nuclear forces were the most important tasks. For the Soviet Union that meant a primary reliance on their Strategic Missile Forces. At the same time, a new military strategy developed during this period—the strategy of general nuclear-missile warfare, which in turn sparked a radical transformation in Soviet thinking on the conditions, character, course, and outcome of armed confrontation.[6]

During the Fourth Session of the Supreme Soviet of the Soviet Union in January 1960, Nikita Khrushchev publicly proclaimed the strategy of comprehensive nuclear-missile warfare as the new military doctrine of the USSR, which indicated clearly that the Soviet political and military leadership by the early 1960s no longer considered the use of exclusively conventional forces as a viable strategic option. Missiles and nuclear weapons had too drastically transformed the combat capabilities of the armed forces. Nuclear firepower opened a new dimension that made it possible to deliver a crushing blow against any aggressor on his own territory.[7]

Under such conditions, the need for a structure that separated strategic attack and strategic defense became obsolete. Soviet military theoreticians stated unequivocally that in nuclear war there was only one choice—either attack or defeat.[8] According to a Soviet doctrinal handbook of the early 1960s: "Soviet military doctrine sees concerted offensive operations as the only acceptable form of strategic actions in nuclear warfare, and stresses that strategic defense contradicts our view of the character of a future nuclear war and of the present state of the Soviet armed forces. . . . Under modern conditions, passivity at the outset of a war is out of the question, for that would be synonymous with annihilation."[9]

In the context of the second Berlin crisis of 1961 it became apparent that the Soviet military was dependent on combat-capable allies for the accomplishment of its war objectives. According to a Central Intelligence Agency (CIA) assessment, the Warsaw Pact consequently changed from being an "alliance on hold" to an "important element of Soviet security and military policy."[10] The BURYA command and staff exercise was an element of this new strategic alliance framework, one that was oriented toward delivering a crushing defeat to a presumed enemy by means of the massive use of nuclear weapons and the occupation of his territory by the forces of the Unified Supreme Command.

BURYA and Warsaw Pact War Planning for Central Europe

The planning scenario for the BURYA exercise was based on the actual conditions of the armed forces of the two military blocs in the Western Theater of War. It involved Eastern bloc officers simulating combat actions conducted on the territory of West Germany, Denmark, Belgium, Holland, and France.[11]

The point of departure for the exercise assumed that the Soviet Union on 4 October 1961 signed a unilateral peace treaty with East Germany. Attempts by the Western powers on the afternoon of 5 October 1961 to restore by military means the lines of communications to West Berlin would, according to the scenario of the Supreme Command of the Unified Warsaw Pact Forces and the Soviet General Staff, result in a nuclear-missile strike at 1200 hours on October 6, triggering a war that would end with conquest of Paris and the breakthrough of Warsaw Pact forces to the Channel coast on 16 October 1961.[12]

Since the exercise area included the entire West European theater of war, the staffs of all the Warsaw Pact fronts planned for that theater took part in the maneuver.[13] At the start of the exercise the Central Front, consisting of the GSFG and the East German army (Nationale Volksarmee, NVA), and the Southwestern Front, consisting of the Czechoslovak army and the Soviet Southern Group of Forces, were at full combat readiness. The Warsaw Pact forces thus had a total of forty-two divisions ready to go into action as of the first day of hostilities. In the course of the notionally planned operations, three additional fronts of the second echelon were then committed to the battle within three to five days. These units were the Coastal Front, consisting of the Polish army, and the 2nd Central Front and the Western Front, which were to operate from the territories of East Germany and Czechoslovakia, respectively, and which were composed of Soviet units. With the commitment of those three additional fronts, the Supreme

Command of the Unified Warsaw Pact Forces would have more than one hundred divisions available for its attack on Western Europe by the fifth day of operations.[14]

Those one hundred divisions were to be grouped into five tank armies and twenty combined-arms armies. The tank armies were the most important offensive element of the fronts. According to the thinking of the Soviet military leadership, they had great offensive power, high mobility, and low vulnerability to the nuclear weapons of the enemy. As armored wedges they were to penetrate deeply into the operational depth of the enemy after the first nuclear strike, rip open his strategic front, and deprive NATO of the capability of further organized resistance. With an average attack speed of one hundred kilometers per day, the Warsaw Pact tank armies were to reach the Atlantic coast as fast as possible.[15]

While the tank armies could be committed along the entire depth of the front of operations, the military leadership of the Warsaw Pact planned an attack depth of up to four hundred kilometers for the combined-arms armies. Here too, the daily attack speed was to be not less than one hundred kilometers per day. With the support of the nuclear weapons at their disposal, they were to destroy major enemy troop concentrations independently and "sweep aside anything in their way that might resist their advance or hinder them."[16]

During the BURYA command and staff exercise, the Supreme Command of the Unified Warsaw Pact Forces thus tried for the first time to simulate through large-scale war games a military confrontation between NATO and Warsaw Pact forces. In their planning studies for the BURYA exercise, the military planners of the Unified Supreme Command assumed strikes in the Western theater of war with a total of more than 2,200 nuclear weapons. In that operational sector the "Westerners" had 1,200 nuclear weapons, of which 30 percent were missiles and 70 percent aircraft-delivered weapons, while the "Easterners" had 1,003 warheads, of which 85 percent were mounted on missiles and 15 percent on aircraft. The Warsaw Pact weapons were in the hands of the Strategic Missile Forces, the fronts, and the armies. The total explosive force of the nuclear weapons potentially used by NATO and the Warsaw Pact would have been approximately equal.[17]

The results of the war games coincided with the calculations of the Soviet General Staff. In late 1959 and early 1960 the Soviet planners estimated that the destruction of 1,200 targets would be necessary "to eliminate our potential enemies," as Khrushchev had put it in an internal speech to the Soviet military leadership. It was unmistakably clear that this meant not merely the destruction of the adversaries' immediate military potential, but first and foremost the destruction of their economic war-making capacity and their general foundations of life. "This means the destruction of the administrative and industrial centers in Europe as well as in Asia and America, but mainly in America," Khrushchev said.[18] Some seven hundred nuclear weapons strikes would be necessary to "smash our enemies" in Europe, according to the Soviet president and Communist Party chairman.[19]

From the available information, the West German Bundeswehr assumed the Warsaw Pact forces intended to launch their first strategic nuclear strike within thirty minutes of the initiation of hostilities, attacking a total of 1,200 stationary NATO targets in the European theater of war, 422 of which were in West Germany. Bundeswehr planners assumed that there would be some 400 additional nuclear attacks on such mobile targets as troop concentrations and nuclear weapons. This large number of nuclear strikes would completely paralyze the West German political and military leadership for eight to ten days. NATO forces would, it was thought, suffer extremely heavy losses in this first nuclear strike, with 75 percent of the nuclear weapons based in West Germany being destroyed immediately, along with 90 percent of the radar installations and airfields. Forty percent of the troops in the strike zones were expected to fall victim to nuclear attack. The losses in weapons, equipment, and technological infrastructure would be as high as 60 percent. The combat power of the active NATO divisions in West Germany would be reduced to the point of combat ineffectiveness.[20]

By the third day of hostilities, when the "Easterners" were to commit the Western Front and the 2nd Central Front as the second strategic echelon, the troops of the Warsaw Pact were supposed to have reached the Danish border, the Weser River, and the Ruhr valley, and would then establish their first bridgeheads on the west bank of the Rhine between Mainz and Worms. At the same time, other Eastern forces would occupy Nuremberg and Munich. On the fifth day of hostilities the tank elements of the 1st Central Front, supported by nuclear strikes in the area between Bonn and Mannheim, would cross the Rhine with two tank armies and advance 140 kilometers farther westward. Simultaneously, the forces of the Coastal and Western Fronts would occupy the northern part of the Jutland peninsula and reach the borders of the Netherlands and Belgium. By the end of that fifth day, the Unified Supreme Command would order the Warsaw Pact fronts to continue the advance, reaching a line running along the Burgundy Canal to Châlons-sur-Saône and Morez by the tenth day of the fighting. The BURYA exercise ended with the establishment of the follow-on mission to continue to destroy NATO forces on the territory of the Benelux countries and France.[21]

The BURYA exercise demonstrated that the military leadership of the Warsaw Pact at the beginning of the 1960s believed that it was possible to defeat in a very short time the NATO forces based in Western Europe. BURYA seemed to confirm the opinion of the Soviet General Staff at that time that all of continental Europe could be brought under the control of the Warsaw Pact within ten to fifteen days by means of massive nuclear strikes. For the military and political leadership of the Soviet Union, and hence of the Warsaw Pact, defense was an obsolete strategic option. It was replaced by attack and offensive action, for "under the condition of nuclear war, only '*Blitz*' operations can ensure victory."[22]

Nuclear Romanticism or Radioactive Chaos?

Recent Russian publications show clearly that the strategic-missile forces of the Soviet Union were integrated into the military operations in Central Europe. Their commitment to combat was designed to ensure that the initial hostilities between NATO and Warsaw Pact forces would be decided quickly in favor of the Eastern bloc.[23] The strategic missile units had practiced nuclear first-strike procedures in the context of earlier war games conducted between 20 and 25 May 1961. The commitment of the Twenty-Third Rocket Army and the XLI Rocket Corps was designed to smash an enemy's surprise attack "on one of the continental theaters of war within two days, using massive nuclear-missile strikes with 460 medium-range and 108 intercontinental missiles against his targets."[24] An anticipated attack was to be preempted a few hours prior to its launch by a nuclear strike. The fact that 70 percent of the targets were military-industrial centers, strategic airfields, and missile-launching facilities, of which 60 percent were to be destroyed with medium-range missiles, suggests the rehearsal of a preemptive nuclear war in Europe. Moreover, the missile exercise was directly associated with another maneuver held between 24 May and 2 June 1961 in East Germany west of Berlin, with the participation of the GSFG and the NVA. The objective of that exercise was to conduct an "offensive in depth and [force] a crossing of the Rhine."[25] In the context of that exercise, too, the Warsaw Pact forces managed to prosecute the war in their favor through the commitment of numerous nuclear weapons. The outcome of the operation was "decided by the crossing of the Rhine. The enemy had no realistic possibility of preventing [the Soviets from] reaching the Channel and Atlantic coasts."[26]

The concrete civilian and military effects that the massive use of nuclear weapons in Europe would have on the operations of the armed forces was of no particular interest in the context of Soviet planning. Rather, they assumed the socialist camp would be able to survive the enemy's first nuclear strike, thanks to the socialist structure of the economic system and the political unity of the people. The "imperialist bloc," of course, had neither of those advantages.[27] There were, however, some Soviet generals and admirals who did indeed acknowledge the problems of unlimited nuclear warfare. In a letter to Khrushchev, for example, Rear Admiral Konstantin I. Derevyanko questioned the "nuclear romanticism" of his General Staff colleagues:

> Only one small item would be interesting: Which planet do these people intend to live on in the future, and to which earth do they plan to send their troops to conquer territories? What use would it be to us in this condition? Can they even imagine the chaos into which they are throwing our troops? . . . I don't know, but I assume that the next strategic goal of our forces in the initial period of the war will be the occupation of the territories of the aggressor countries in the West European central sector by means of a rapid thrust and attack by our forces—especially airborne and motorized units—in order to reach swiftly the Atlantic coast. How narrow minded can the person be who created radioactive barriers with contaminated soil, water and air in the path of our troops along the entire breadth of the front? Never will we achieve an attack speed of 100 kilometers a day. On the contrary, the attack would grind itself to a halt. By this indiscriminately massive use of nuclear weapons on a small and narrow area like Western Europe, we would not only be accepting millions of radioactively contaminated civilians, but, because of the prevailing westerly [winds], would also be radioactively contaminating millions our own people for decades—our armed forces and the population of the socialist countries, including our own country as far as the Urals. . . . We must put an end to the triumphant thinking associated with the power of our nuclear missiles. They have their strategic possibilities, but they cannot decide the many different facets and processes of modern combat.[28]

The Soviet head of state, however, did not acknowledge these weighty objections. Instead, he passed along the letter unread to the secretaries of the Central Committee of the Communist Party of the Soviet Union (CPSU) and to Minister of Defense Rodion Malinovski.

The command and staff exercises carried out by the Warsaw Pact during this period were designed largely to test the feasibility of the operational plans for Central Europe developed by the Soviet General Staff. Thus, for example, the strategic objectives of the Polish army as defined in the 1961 Operational Plan (OP-61) coincided entirely with the maneuver objectives of the Polish Coastal Front during the BURYA command and staff exercise.[29] Evidently the Soviet General Staff also considered the operational plans developed for the East German NVA. Those plans, however, were not turned over to the East Germans until the summer of 1962.

The extent to which the Czechoslovak maneuver objectives in the summer of 1961 also coincided with the operational plan developed by the Soviet Supreme Command requires closer examination in the Czech files. Initial research indicates that during an exercise conducted in September 1961, Czechoslovak forces together with those of the NVA and the GSFG were to reach the Bonn-Metz-Strasbourg line within seven days. During another war game conducted in December 1961, the front formed by the Czechoslovak People's Army had the mission of advancing to the Besançon-Belfort area in the "shortest possible time," using 130 nuclear weapons.[30] The operational plan drafted by the General Staff of the People's Army of Czechoslovakia in 1964, which remained in effect until at least 1968, was also based on executing deep thrusts using at least 131 nuclear weapons on German and French territory. Together with the troops of the GSFG, now designated the 1st Western Front, the forces were to cross the Neckar and Rhine in coordination with airborne landings, and occupy the Langres, Besançon, and Epinal areas within seven days. The main effort was to be directed along the Nuremberg-Stuttgart-Strasbourg axis, while Munich was to be taken by a supporting attack.[31]

Records released in 2006 by the Polish General Staff on the operational planning of the Warsaw Pact also prove that an exclusively conventional option for a war in Central Europe was not seriously considered until after 1968. In the thinking of the military leaders, the intended operational attack tempo of up to ninety kilometers per day could be maintained only through the use of nuclear weapons.[32]

The Material Underpinnings of the Strategy of Unlimited Nuclear War in Europe

The fact that Warsaw Pact and Soviet forces further reinforced their conventional capabilities after the removal of Khrushchev in 1964 resulted apparently not so much from any fundamental change of strategy, but rather from

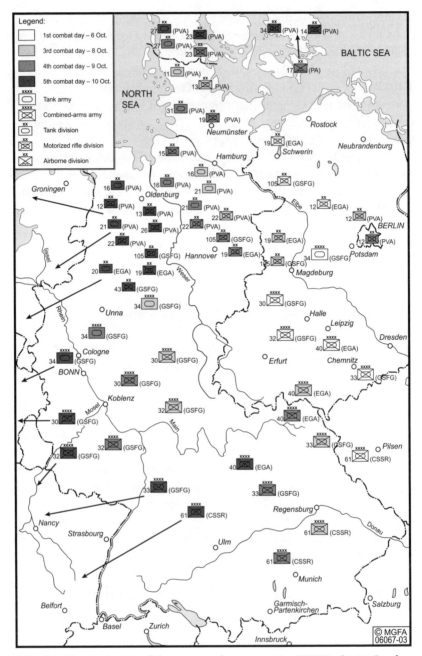

Map 3.1. Situation map of the command post exercise BURYA (6–10 October 1961). BA-MA, DVW-1/6289-2, fol. 304.

the Soviet military's intent to restore the balance between the branches of the armed forces, which to their thinking had been distorted by the deposed Soviet party boss. An examination of recently accessible Soviet records, however, shows that the neglect of the conventional element was probably more perceived than real. While the total budget of the Soviet Ministry of Defense had climbed by about 50 percent between 1957 and 1963, procurement expenses doubled during the same period, from 2.91 billion rubles in 1957 to 6.17 billion rubles in 1963.[33] The most important cause of this drastic increase in procurement expenditures was the Soviet military's effort to equip

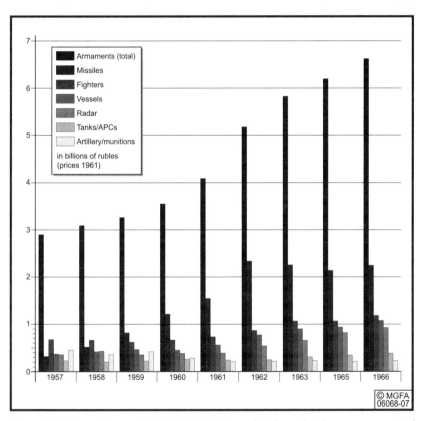

Figure 3.1. Expenditures of the Soviet Ministry of Defense for the procurement of armaments, 1957–1966. RGAE, 4372/76/320, fol. 7, Spravka, On expenditures of the Ministry of Defense for the procurement of armaments, 28 Nov. 1957; RGAE, 4372/79/59, fols. 85–86, Spravka, On the shipment of armament supplies to the Ministry of Defense, 16 Nov. 1960; RGAE, 4372/80/185, fol. 274, Spravka, On armaments shipments to the Ministry of Defense, 1961–1963, 24 Nov. 1962; RGAE, 4372/81/1222, Draft for the procurement of armaments for 1966, 27 Oct. 1965.

its units with strategic, operational, and tactical nuclear weapons, because "the most important strategic missions should be carried out with ballistic missiles."[34] Expenditures in this area rose from 320 million rubles in 1957 to 2.515 billion rubles in 1963, an increase of more than 780 percent. Moreover, the Soviet air force and navy also profited to a considerable degree from the increased procurement budget, with both forces able to carry out considerable modernization with new armaments programs.

There is no actual conformation, however, of the previous assumption that the conventional forces had to be prepared to accept cuts as the support of the nuclear forces increased. The expenditures for armored vehicles, for example, rose slightly, while only the corresponding expenditures for artillery, ammunition, and individual weapons dropped. The overall combat strength of the Soviet forces did not necessarily decrease as a result of the nuclear build-up, because the army had received considerable quantities of new artillery during the previous years.

A comparison of the armament expenditures with actual production figures between 1957 and 1963 does show some peculiarities. First, it is apparent that the disproportionate expenditures for missiles caused only a relatively slight increase in strategic capabilities in this area. At the same time, however, there was a considerable increase in the military capabilities deployable against Europe. More than seven thousand medium- and short-range missiles alone were produced for the Soviet forces between 1957 and 1963—evidence that the Soviet military leadership saw the European continent as the "decisive battleground" in any armed conflict between the two systems. This is confirmed as well by the continued high production levels for tanks, armored personnel carriers, cannon, and combat aircraft.

Nonetheless, the Soviet armed forces evidently were not equipped for a nuclear conflict until 1961. Up to that point the Soviet army had only a very limited nuclear capability. Moreover, the high production output of such defensive weapons as air defense and antitank guided missiles may appear surprising, but it fitted neatly into the Soviet offensive strategy. The former had the mission of protecting the overextended and vulnerable infrastructure against NATO's "interdiction tactics," designed to disrupt the movement of reinforcements from the Soviet Union to Central Europe during any armed conflict. The antitank missiles were designed to defeat any flanking attacks by Western armored units.[35]

In order to keep pace with the Soviet units in support of this military strategy, the forces of the other Warsaw Pact countries had to be equipped with the most modern technology and armaments. The Soviet General Staff

	1957	1958	1959	1960	1961	1962	1963	1966
Ballistic missiles	264	477	829	1,409	1,811	1,620	2,010	1,115
ICBMs	0	3	20	40	92	195	200	340
R-7 A (SS-6)	–	3	20	40	35	12	–	–
Launchers R-7 A (total)	–	–	3	2	–	–	–	–
R-9 A (SS-8)	–	–	–	–	10	35	40	10
Launchers R-9 A (total)	–	–	–	–	–	16	16	–
hard sites	–	–	–	–	–	6	6	–
R-16 (SS-7)	–	–	–	–	47	148	160	50
Launchers R-16 (total)	–	–	–	–	49	45	81	–
hard sites	–	–	–	–	15	12	21	–
R-36 (SS-9)	–	–	–	–	–	–	–	70
Launchers R-36	–	–	–	–	–	–	–	63
UR-100 (SS-11)	–	–	–	–	–	–	–	210
Launchers UR-100	–	–	–	–	–	–	–	220
IRBMs/MRBMs	130	225	365	550	507	540	320	–
R-5 M (SS-3)	80 (+50 R-2)	200	25	–	–	–	–	–
Launchers R-5 M	12	36	36	–	–	–	–	–
R-12 (SS-4)	–	25	340	550	452	420	200	–
Launchers R-12	–	6	54	160	236	151	12	–
R-14 (SS-5)	–	–	–	–	55	120	120	–
Launchers R-14	–	–	–	–	10	37	27	38
SRBMs	134	190	390	679	1,092	725	1,380	740
R-11/R-11 M (SCUD)	134	190	390	314	234	–	150	–
Launchers R-11	4	45	56	34	42	–	–	–
R-17 (SCUD-B)	–	–	–	–	68	225	300	400
Launchers R-17	–	–	–	–	13	70	70	50
Luna/Luna-M (FROG)	–	–	–	365	790	500	900	340
Launchers Luna	–	–	–	80	100	100	92	n/a
Temp (SS-12)	–	–	–	–	–	–	30	60
Launchers Temp	–	–	–	–	–	–	–	20
SLBMs	–	59	54	140	120	160	110	35
R-11FM (SS-N-1B)	–	59	54	50	–	–	–	–
R-13 (SS-N-4)	–	–	–	90	120	150	80	–
R-21 (SS-N-5)	–	–	–	–	–	10	30	25
R-27 (SS-N-6)	–	–	–	–	–	–	–	10
PTRBs (mobile nuclear weapon units)	n/a	10	55	96	119	34	83	33
SA-missiles	1,796	2,699	5,884	8,218	8,894	9,000	10,320	2,750
S-25 (SA-1)	1,218	1,400	1,130	600	65	900	800	850
S-75 (SA-2)	578	1,299	4,754	7,581	8,404	6,900	7,990	1,000
S-125 (SA-3)	–	–	–	100	425	1,200	1,500	500
S-200 (SA-6)	–	–	–	–	–	–	30	400
SAM-batteries	30	130	182	205	250	255	235	70
AA-missiles	4,000	7,300	11,192	12,308	17,724	8,480	13,265	10,150
Cruise missiles	371	642	668	1,113	1,054	1,380	1,035	370
Fighters	1,031	692	525	883	722	513	712	599
Interceptors	613	546	348	689	496	297	418	493
Fighter bombers	–	–	102	118	177	104	199	64
Bombers (TU-16/22)	382	125	37	50	39	102	85	30
Bombers, strategic:	36	25	38	26	10	10	10	12
T-95	14	10	18	17	10	10	10	12
3M	26	15	20	9	–	–	–	–
Transporters	5	53	150	110	58	100	140	110
Helicopters	239	273	n/a	240	148	245	150	95
Tanks	2,436	2,380	2,281	2,599	2,723	2,270	2,588	1,762
APCs	2,366	2,202	2,255	2,065	2,046	2,520	2,154	2,122
ATGMs	–	–	–	–	2,000	5,200	5,000	12,600
Launch complexes	–	–	–	–	80	220	120	891
Artillery	4,885	2,897	1,634	1,287	720	580	895	970
Submarines – Atom	–	1	1	4	6	12	9	11
Submarines – Diesel	27	13	19	18	19	11	7	7
Cruisers	–	1	–	–	–	1	–	2
Destroyers	9	4	–	5	4	2	1	3
Frigates	8	8	2	6	5	7	11	9
Submarine chasers	9	50	60	2	–	13	20	21
Missile boats	–	7	n/a	22	12	14	13	26

© MGFA
06069-07

Table 3.1. Armaments shipments to the Soviet Ministry of Defense, 1957–1966. RGAE, 4372–GOSPLAN files, 1957–1966.

thought such modernization necessary to prevent the "imperialist enemy" from achieving any crucial initial success by launching a sudden strike with missiles and nuclear weapons. Instead, the forces of the Soviet Union's allies would destroy the enemy's nuclear-weapons capacity with *"Blitzkrieg*-like speed," and move immediately to the nuclear counterattack.[36] The non-Soviet allied armies of the Warsaw Pact, therefore, had to adopt not only the new Soviet combat doctrine, as outlined, for example, in *Soviet Field Manual 62,* but they also had to modernize considerably and be equipped with the newest weapons developments from the Soviet Union.[37]

Between 1962 and 1965 the armed forces of East Germany, Czechoslovakia, Bulgaria, Romania, Poland, and Hungary were programmed to receive more than 880 new fighter aircraft, 555 helicopters, 6,075 tanks, 17,312 armored vehicles, and extensive supplementary equipment. Simultaneously, the Soviets ordered that the armies of all these countries be equipped with the most modern missile capabilities. By the end of 1965 the European armies of the Soviet Union's allies were to be supplied with 104 antiaircraft missile detachments, 84 antitank guided missile batteries, and 5 land-to-sea missile defense batteries. The navies of Poland, Bulgaria, Romania, and East Germany were also to receive a total of 28 missile-armed high-speed boats under a project designated 205/OSA. The total value of these Soviet arms deliveries to the Warsaw Pact countries between 1962 and 1965 was an estimated 2.8 billion rubles.[38] By comparison, the State Planning Commission of the Soviet Union estimated the total Soviet arms production for 1961 at 4.1 billion rubles.[39]

Nonetheless, the Soviet General Staff and the Supreme Command of the Unified Warsaw Pact Forces increasingly wanted to reinforce more than just the conventional capabilities of the Eastern European armies. Beginning in 1961, the forces of the Soviets' allies were for the first time armed with operational and tactical nuclear-weapon delivery systems.[40] Through 1963 the Soviets equipped fourteen rocket brigades of the non-Soviet Warsaw Pact armies with the R-11M/SCUD-A-type missile, and another forty rocket detachments with the Luna/FROG-5-type missile.[41]

The build-up of Warsaw Pact conventional forces continued throughout the mid-1960s. The peacetime strength of the NVA, for example, rose from 90,000 to 120,000 troops between 1962 and 1970, while the planned wartime mobilization strength was boosted from 200,000 to 280,000 troops. The rationale, according to the Supreme Command of the Unified Warsaw Pact Forces, "lies in the requirements *engendered by the occupation of the territory of the enemy"*(original emphasis).[42] Later, in 1969, the Central

Committee of the CPSU decided to increase the table of organization and equipment (TO&E) strength of the Soviet divisions from 8,000 to 12,000 troops, especially increasing once again the power of the divisional artillery.[43] That did not mean, however, that Soviet thinking had abandoned the dominant importance of nuclear capability. The doctrine still defined an attack characterized by "high speed, fast and deep penetration, and sudden initiation, coupled with mobility and the use of nuclear, chemical, biological, and conventional firepower, and the use of airborne and seaborne landings, as well as the strong use of air power."[44]

That doctrine formed the basis of the 1969 command and staff exercise Zapad-69. The objectives of the exercise were the strategic marshaling of allied forces in the theater of war and the "conduct of offensive operations at the outset of the war." The mission of the Eastern European forces was to repel a potential enemy attack and defeat NATO forces in the Central European theater of war. To accomplish that mission, the Warsaw Pact was organized into five fronts formed from the Soviet army's Belorussian and Transcarpathian Military Districts; the Polish, Czechoslovak, and East German armies; and the GSFG.

According to the exercise scenario, the notional attack by the "Westerners" was conducted initially with conventional weapons. The Warsaw Pact also initially responded conventionally. The NATO offensive toward Berlin was to be crushed by the fire of 1,400 artillery pieces and twelve waves of fighter-bomber strikes at regimental strength. At the same time, the Warsaw Pact forces were to counterattack and penetrate toward the Rhine in the direction of the Ruhr and Frankfurt. They were to be reinforced continually by the units of the second strategic echelon. Within two days, the front line stood two hundred kilometers east of the Rhine River. The Warsaw Pact attack also developed momentum in the direction of Kiel. The follow-on planning postulated the occupation of Denmark the next day, which would include air and sea landings on the island of Zeeland. Within five days of the start of the war, the forces of the Northern Front were to occupy the northern parts of West Germany and the Netherlands and seize the Jutland peninsula. The Central Front of the Combined Forces was to concentrate its attack in the direction of Frankfurt, cross the Rhine, and reach the German-French border within three to five days. The plan for that attack included the insertion of two airborne divisions between Koblenz and Wesel. The Southern Front was to occupy southern West Germany, seize the key Danube and Rhine crossings, and within two days further develop the attack in the direction of Ettingen, near Basle, Switzerland. On the fourth day of the war the exercise scenario assumed that NATO, unable to withstand the offensive with conventional forces, would shift to the use of nuclear weapons. The Warsaw Pact would then respond with a counterstrike. The short conventional phase of the notional war in Europe thus ended, and the strategy of general nuclear warfare and of a far-reaching offensive was once again initiated, at least on the side of the Warsaw Pact.[45]

The Zapad-69 exercise once again demonstrated the great significance the Soviet High Command assigned to the Rhine River as the main defensive line of the Western European alliance. In his evaluation of the exercise, Soviet minister of defense Marshal Andrei Grechko noted that the loss of the Rhine River line would "bring the entire European group of NATO forces to a critical situation and would for all practical purposes mean the loss of Europe for the enemy."[46] Even as late as 1982, Soviet General Staff chief Marshal Nikolai Ogarkov emphasized that the control of the Rhine "would decide the outcome of the war."[47]

By the end of the 1960s an assessment issued by the West German Federal Intelligence Service (Bundesnachrichtendienst, BND) projected that the Warsaw Pact forces were capable without mobilization preparations of going into action immediately with a single echelon, executing combat operations in the form of a strategic attack operation into the Western theater of war beyond West Germany, reaching the French, Spanish, and Portuguese Atlantic coasts and the Spanish and French Mediterranean coasts within twenty days.[48] Because of the Warsaw Pact's increasingly strong conventional equipment at the unit level, the BND reached the conclusion that under such conditions, "the early recognition of attack preparations has become much more difficult."[49] In 1968 the Czechoslovak crisis effectively demonstrated that the military situation in Central Europe had approached a dangerous climax, which caused both alliances to pursue policies of détente and nonnuclear warfare options during the ensuing period.

In conclusion, the military doctrine, strategy, and operational warfare principles of the Warsaw Pact during the 1960s were fully oriented toward smashing the European NATO forces with rapid, deep penetration operations at an attack tempo of between eighty and one hundred kilometers per day in order to overrun the territory up to the Atlantic coast within twelve to sixteen days. The political, economic, and military-technological developments of the 1970s and 1980s did not result in a more realistic assessment of the Warsaw Pact's operational options. But according to former East German army officer Harald Kiesslich-Köcher, the strategic planning for the European theater of war was indeed aimed only at forcing the frontline NATO countries out of the war.[50]

Nonetheless, the fact that the Soviet General Staff continued to plan for airborne landings of Warsaw Pact forces in Denmark and in the Wesel area on the Rhine, and "for the capture of Paris,"[51] as well as massive nuclear strikes against NATO forces,[52] at least raises the question as to whether the changes in Warsaw Pact military strategy were of a thoroughgoing nature, or whether they must be seen as merely cosmetic corrections that constituted no real abandonment of the concept of the offensive and the associated massive use of nuclear weapons. Only in 1987, under the new Soviet secretary general Mikhail Gorbachev, did the Warsaw Pact receive a military doctrine that definitively excluded any option of attack or first use of nuclear weapons, and provided only for the defense of its own territory. But that change met with initial resistance by the armed forces, because the Soviet General Staff at the time still assumed "the aggressor could only be definitively crushed by determined offensive operations." Only gradually did the topmost leadership of the Soviet armed forces, and subsequently the Warsaw Pact, come to accept the concept that the defensive "in the strategic framework is no longer a forced type of warfare, but an intentional one."[53]

Notes

1. See Vojtech Mastny, "Imagining War in Europe: Soviet Strategic Planning," in *War Plans and Alliances in the Cold War: Threat Perceptions in the East and West,* ed. Vojtech Mastny, Sven G. Holtsmark, and Andreas Wenger (London, 2006), 16; Peter Luňák, "War Plans from Stalin to Brezhnev: The Czechoslovak Pivot," in *War Plans and Alliances in the Cold War,* ed. Mastny, Holtsmark, and Wenger, 73–76.

2. See M. A. Garelov, "Otkuda ugroza," *Voenno-istoricheskii zhurnal* 2 (1989): 24–25; David M. Glantz, *The Military Strategy of the Soviet Union: A History* (London, 1992), 180–88.

3. See *Strategicheskoe yadernoe vooruzhenie Rossii,* ed. P. L. Podvig (Moscow, 1998), 3–6; Mikhail P. Pervov, *Zenitnoe raketnoe protivovozdushnoi oborony strany* (Moscow, 2001), 104–6; *Rozhdennye atomnoy eroy. 12 Glavnoe upravlenie Ministerstva oborony Rossiiskoi Federacii: Opyt i razvitiya,* ed. N. S. Birjukov (Moscow, 2002), 64–68.

4. CIA Information Report, 29 Mar. 1957: Marshall Zhukov's speech to senior commanders of the GSFG, Parallel History Project on Cooperative Security (PHP), http://www.php.isn.ethz.ch/collections/colltopic.cfm?lng=en&id=16599&navinfo=14861 (accessed September 2007).

5. See ibid.; Russian State Archive of Sociopolitical History (hereinafter RGASPI), 17/165/154, fol. 108, Speech by Malinovski at the Central Committee meeting

with the chiefs of the military districts, 18 Dec. 1959; Federal Archive Koblenz (hereafter BA-Koblenz), B-206/126, fols. 86–90, BND: Military Situation Report. East. Annual report 1966, 30 Dec. 1966.

6. See *Istoriya voennoi strategii Rossii,* ed. V. A. Zolotarev (Moscow, 2000), 383; Andrej A. Gretschko, *Die Streitkräfte des Sowjetstaates* (Berlin, 1975), 98–101; Anatolij Gribkow, *Der Warschauer Pakt: Geschichte und Hintergründe des östlichen Militärbündnisses* (Berlin, 1995), 34–36.

7. See Speech by Khrushchev at the Fourth Session of the Supreme Soviet, *Pravda,* 14 Jan. 1960; Bernhard Bechler, "Der Raketenkernwaffenkrieg eine neue Qualität des bewaffneten Kampfes," *Militärwesen* 5 (1962): 658–60.

8. See Thomas W. Wolfe, *Soviet Power and Europe 1945–1970* (Baltimore, 1970), 199–201; Michail G. Ljoschin, "Die Streitkräfte der UdSSR zwischen Berlin- und Kubakrise: Wandlungen strategischer Prinzipien und Einsatzmuster?," in *Vor dem Abgrund: Die Streitkräfte der USA und der UdSSR sowie ihrer deutschen Bündnispartner in der Kubakrise,* ed. Dimitri N. Filippovych and Matthias Uhl (Munich, 2006), 36.

9. See German Federal Military Archive (hereinafter BA-MA), DVL-3/29942, fol. 38; 238, "Die Strategie des Kernwaffenkrieges," 1964 (unauthorized German translation of a Soviet top-secret handbook on nuclear warfare for the chiefs of the military districts of the Soviet Union).

10. *A Cardboard Castle? An Inside History of the Warsaw Pact, 1955–1991,* ed. Vojtech Mastny and Malcolme Byrne (Budapest, 2005), 7; CIA-NIE 12–65: Capabilities of Soviet General Purpose Forces, CIA-FOIA Reading Room, http://www.foia.cia.gov/docs/DOC_0000278467/0000278467_0001.gif (accessed September 2007), 12–65.

11. See *Zeittafel zur Militärgeschichte der Deutschen Demokratischen Republik 1949–1968,* ed. Karl Greese (Berlin, 1969), 147; Thomas M. Forster, *NVA—Die Armee der Sowjetzone* (Cologne, 1967), 224.

12. See BA-MA, DVW-1/6103, fols. 138–41, Presentation by Army General Heinz Hoffmann, evaluating the BURYA command and staff exercise, undated.

13. In Soviet military terminology, a "front" is a military strategic unit consisting of subunits and groups of various combat arms. It is roughly comparable to a Western army group, but unlike the latter, consists of organically structured forces.

14. See BA-MA, DVW-1/6289-2, fol. 305, Situation Map of the BURYA command and staff exercise between 1000 hrs. October 1 and 2200 hrs. October 5, 1962, undated; BA-MA, DVW-1/6103, fol. 137, Presentation by Army General Heinz Hoffmann, evaluating the BURYA command and staff exercise, undated; BA-Koblenz, B 206/181, Up. fol., BND Monthly Report, October, undated, 5–7.

15. See BA-MA, DVW-1/5203, fols. 56–58, Excerpt from the speech by Malinovski evaluating the BURYA command and staff exercise, undated; Igor' G. Drogovoz, *Tankovy mech SSSR* (Moscow, 1999), 10–16.

16. See BA-MA, DVW-1/5203, fol. 57.

17. See BA-MA, DVW-1/6103, fols. 153–54, Paper by Hoffmann on the evaluation of the BURYA command and staff exercise, 11 Nov. 1961; *Raketnye voiska strategicheskogo naznacheniya: Istoki i razvitie,* ed. Nikolai E. Solovtsov (Moscow, 2004), 244–45.

18. RGASPI, 17/165/153, fol. 15, Speech by Khrushchev at the meeting of the CPSU Central Committee with commanders, chiefs of staff, and members of the military councils of the military districts, 18 Dec. 1959.

19. RGASPI, 17/165/153, fol. 17.

20. See BA-MA, BW-2/2228, fols. 4–15, Study by the Command Staff of the Bundeswehr III 6: Combat Situation—Case A, 15 Dec. 1961.

21. See BA-MA, DVW-1/6103, fols. 139–40, Presentation by Army General Hoffmann, evaluating the BURYA command and staff exercise, undated; BA-MA, DVW-1/6103, fols. 153–55, Paper by Hoffmann on the evaluation of the BURYA command and staff exercise, 11 Nov. 1961; BA-MA, DVW-1/6303, fol. 25, Map of action by the Fortieth Army and the XLI Army Corps of the NVA, undated; Situation Report of the Commander of the Polish Coastal Front, 10 Oct. 1961, PHP, http://www.php .isn.ethz.ch/collections/colltopic.cfm?lng=en&id=20317&navinfo=16446 (accessed September 2007).

22. Anton M. Gastilovich, "The Theory of Military Art Needs Review," *Voennaya mysl' (Spetsvypusk)* 1 (1960): 6, CIA-FOIA Reading Room, http://www.foia.cia.gov/ docs/DOC_0000012299/0000012299_0001.gif (accessed September 2007). This article is an English translation of a top-secret special edition of the Soviet military journal *Voennaya mysl',* authorized only for army commanders and higher. From 1960 to 1962, Colonel Penkovski of the GRU gave the CIA three complete years of this journal, which are now accessible on the CIA website.

23. See *Raketnye voiska strategicheskogo naznacheniya,* ed. Solovtsov, 245–49; *Glavny shtab Raketnykh voisk strategisheskogo naznasheniya: Istorisheskii osherk,* ed. S. V. Khutorcev (Moscow, 2005), 143; Vladimir E. Aleksandrov, "Operatsiya 'Tuman,'" in *50 Raketnaya armiia. Kniga 2. Gody i sud'by. Chast' 2. Sbornik vospominanii veteranov-raketchikov,* ed. G. I. Smirnov (Smolensk, 1998), 53–58.

24. See *Raketnye voiska strategicheskogo naznacheniya,* ed. Solovtsov, 242–44.

25. See ibid., 243–44; Dieter Kürschner, "Zur Geschichte des Militärbezirkes III von 1956 bis 1961" (diss., Potsdam, 1987), 157–58.

26. BA-MA, DVW-1/8754, fols. 223–33, Speech by East German Defense Minister Hoffmann to the National Defense Council, 28 June 1961.

27. See Gastilovich, "The Theory of Military Art Needs Review," 4.

28. Russian State Archive of Contemporary History (RGANI), 5/30/372, fols. 7–9, Letter from Rear Admiral Derevyanko to Khrushchev of 1 Aug. 1961.

29. See Pawel Piotrowski, "A Landing Operation in Denmark," PHP, http://www .php.isn.ethz.ch/collections/coll_polex/piotrowski.cfm?navinfo=16446 (accessed September 2007); BA-MA, DVW-1/6289-2, fol. 304, Situation Map of the BURYA command and staff exercise, undated.

30. See *A Cardboard Castle,* ed. Mastny and Byrne, 20–23; Mastny, "Imagining War in Europe," 22–28; Petr Luňák, "Planning for Nuclear War: The Czechoslovak War Plan of 1964," *Cold War International History Project Bulletin,* no. 5. 12/13 (2001): 289–97.

31. Luňák, *Planning for Nuclear War,* 291–97.

32. See Gerhard Gnauck, "In sieben Tagen am Rhein," *Die Welt,* 9 May 2006.

33. See Russian State Archive of Economics (hereinafter RGAE), 4372/76/320, fol. 7, Spravka, On expenditures of the Ministry of Defense for the procurement of armaments, 28 Nov. 1957; RGAE, 4372/79/59, fols. 85–86, Spravka, On the shipment of armament supplies to the Ministry of Defense, 16 Nov. 1960; RGAE, 4372/80/185, fol. 274, Spravka, On armaments shipments to the Ministry of Defense, 1961–1963, 24 Nov. 1962.

34. RGAE, 29/1/600, fol. 134, Letter to the CPSU Central Committee on the development perspectives for long-distance and strategic bombers, 13 Mar. 1959.

35. See Bernd Lemke, Dieter Krüger, Heinz Rebhan, and Wolfgang Schmidt, *Die Luftwaffe 1950 bis 1970: Konzeption, Aufbau, Integration* (Munich, 2006), 199–248; Helmut R. Hammerich, Dieter H. Kollmer, Martin Rink, and Rudolf J. Schlaffer, *Das Heer 1950 bis 1970: Konzeption, Organisation, Aufstellung* (Munich, 2006), 107–17.

36. See Material on the Development of the Military Art in Conditions of Nuclear War, letter from Glavnoy Razvedovatel'noy Upravlenie (GRU) director General Petr I. Ivashutin to Marshal Matvey V. Zakharov, director of the academy of the General Staff, 28 Aug. 1964, PHP, http://www.php.isn.ethz.ch/collections/colltopic.cfm?lng=en&id=16248&navinfo=15365 (accessed September 2007); S. N. Kozlov, *O sovetskoy voennoy nauke* (Moscow, 1964), 65–66; V. A. Zolotarev, O. V. Saksonov, and S. A. Tiushkevich, *Voennaya istoriya Rossii* (Moscow, 2000), 619.

37. See BA-Koblenz, B 206/126, fols. 111–13, Military Situation Report. East. Annual Report 1966, 30 Dec. 1966.

38. See RGAE, 4372/79/792, fol. 106f., Spravka, On meeting the demand of the armies of the Warsaw Pact countries for military technology, 1961 to 1965, March 1961; BA-MA, DVW-1/53111, fols. 1–10, Agreement between East Germany and the USSR on the delivery of special equipment, 1961–1965, 6 June 1961. I thank Mr. Fritz Minow for his kind provision of this document. See also Anna Locher, Christian Nünlist, and Matthias Uhl, "The 1961 Berlin Crisis and Soviet Preparations for War in Europe," PHP, http://www.php.isn.ethz.ch/collections/colltopic.cfm?lng=en&id=16161 (accessed September 2007).

39. See RGAE, 4372/79/759, fol. 36, GOSPLAN Report to the CPSU Central Committee on the expected fulfillment of production targets for arms deliveries, 20 Dec. 1961.

40. See RGAE, 4372/79/792, fol. 106f., Spravka, On meeting the demand of the armies of Warsaw Pact countries for military technology, 1961 to 1965, March 1961; *Zur geschichtlichen Entwicklung und Rolle der NVA der Deutschen Demokratischen Republik* (Berlin, 1974), 200.

41. See RGAE, 298/1/77, fols. 118–22, Order of the State Commission for the Arms Industry of the USSR, No. KS-150/58 for the adoption of the R-11M missile into the arsenal of the Soviet army, 23 Apr. 1958; RGAE, 4372/79/792, fols. 24–65, appendix on the draft decision for the Political Advisory Commission of the Warsaw Pact; lists of arms deliveries to the respective participating countries, from 1962 to 1965, March 1961.

42. See BA-MA, DVW-1/18762, fol. 94, Draft Protocol on questions of the further development of the NVA, 1967–1970, 1967; DVW-1/18761, fol. 138, Draft Protocol, 1964.

43. See BA-MA, AZN 32885, fol. 14f., Memorandum by Grechko, 22 Dec. 1969.

44. BA-Koblenz, B 206/130, fol. 30, BND: Military Situation Report. East. Annual Report, 1968.

45. See Statements of Soviet General Staff Chief Marshal Matvei Zakharov on the evaluation of the "Zapad-69" war games, PHP, http://www.php.isn.ethz.ch/collections/colltopic.cfm?lng=en&id=21216&navinfo=15697 (accessed September 2007), 3–19.

46. Statements of the Soviet defense minister on the evaluation of the "Zapad-69" war games, ibid.

47. BA-MA, DVW-1/32643, fol. 125, Report on statements by Marshal Ogarkov, 14 Sept. 1982.

48. See BA-Koblenz, B 206/128, fols. 21–27, BND: Military Situation Report. East. Annual Report, 1967.

49. BA-Koblenz, B 206/130, fols. 36–37, BND: Military Situation Report. East. Annual Report, 1968.

50. See Harald Kiesslich-Köcher, "Kriegsbild und Militärstrategie der UdSSR," in *Rührt euch! Zur Geschichte der NVA*, ed. Wolfgang Wünsche (East Berlin, 1998), 581–87.

51. BA-MA, DVW-1/32643, fol. 76, Report on discussion between GDR Defense Minister Hoffmann, Soviet Defense Minister Ustinov, and Marshal Kulikov, Commander-in-Chief of the Unified Forces, 14 Sept. 1982.

52. See Statements of Soviet General Staff Chief Ogarkov on the evaluation of the "Zapad-77" war games, PHP, http://www.php.isn.ethz.ch/collections/colltopic.cfm?lng=en&id=21200&navinfo=15697 (accessed September 2007), 32.

53. See BA-MA, DVW-1/32659, fol. 67.

4

Waiting to Be Kissed?

NATO, NORTHAG, and Intelligence

Richard J. Aldrich

An intelligence chief once remarked, "Intelligence is regarded as a Cinderella service," and war is what changes Cinderella into the princess.[1] This analogy sought to capture the way intelligence had been badly neglected before 1939 and suddenly became critical to operations thereafter. These remarks, however, apply less well to the Cold War, a curious and prolonged period of peace, albeit of a precarious kind, during which intelligence agencies grew at an unprecedented rate. In contrast to the interwar period, intelligence during the Cold War was always big business, and by 1957 the United States was already spending close to $1 billion per year in this area.[2] Accordingly, one might look elsewhere for an analogy that will illustrate the relationship of intelligence to NATO's Northern Army Group (NORTHAG) during the Cold War. This chapter suggests that we might consider that of Sleeping Beauty— or Dornröschen, as she is known in German.

NORTHAG was established in 1952 as a NATO wartime multinational "command in waiting" that would assume its full functions with the onset of hostilities. We therefore might liken NORTHAG to the Slumbering Princess, waiting for many years for the magic kiss that would bring her to life. It seems to follow from this analogy that war might be the Handsome Prince that would awaken her. Ideally, however, the Slumbering Princess would be woken not by war, but by *timely warning that war was imminent*. In other words, in the context of NORTHAG, alerts and warning intelligence took on an important, even heroic role. As we shall see, intelligence, perhaps in the guise of the Handsome Prince, was central to the NORTHAG story and issues of its deployment.

Throughout the Cold War, NORTHAG headquarters (HQ) was the main wartime operational command for the NATO forces defending northern Germany. NORTHAG consisted of four national army corps from Belgium, Germany, the Netherlands, and the United Kingdom. Because the commander of the British Army of the Rhine (BAOR) also served as commander, NORTHAG (COMNORTHAG), the key headquarters functions of NORTHAG and BAOR overlapped and many officers were "double hatted." BAOR had its peacetime headquarters at Rheindahlen near Mönchengladbach, and on the eve of war it quickly would have reconstituted itself as the core component of a multinational NORTHAG headquarters. The duality between headquarters elements in BAOR and NORTHAG extended to intelligence. For example, the UK staff officer who served as brigadier, General Staff, Intelligence and Security (BGS [Int & Sy]), at BAOR also served as assistant chief of staff G-2 for NORTHAG.[3]

Although NORTHAG was primarily a wartime entity, limited elements were permitted to exist even in peacetime, providing transport, security, and communications. Typically, five different NATO signal units formed the NORTHAG Signal Group and were permanently assigned. The deputy commander of NORTHAG, often from the Dutch army, had special responsibility for encouraging joint NATO training and exercises. In order to encourage integration further, a single building was constructed at Rheindahlen that housed not only the headquarters of BAOR and NORTHAG but also those of Royal Air Force (RAF) Germany and of the Second Allied Tactical Air Force (2 ATAF).[4] This building was conceived in 1952 when the decision was made to situate NORTHAG headquarters to the west of the Rhine. The Rheindahlen HQ project was completed in 1954 and was accelerated by the impending Bonn Convention that brought the Federal Republic fully into being, because that event increased the cost of preexisting headquarters buildings that the United Kingdom previously had freely requisitioned in some of the most pleasant German spa towns.[5] For some unknown reason the new headquarters building was soon nicknamed "the Kremlin." NORTHAG also had an additional rear headquarters in some crumbling underground caves at Maastricht, together with a wartime mobile element at Rheindahlen that would "crash out" on the eve of war to a secret survival location, rumored to be in the vast forests near Aachen.

The presumption was that in wartime, HQ BAOR would become HQ NORTHAG by means of adding numerous non-British officers and an influx of reserve personnel. On 17 January 1952, General Sir John Harding, commander-in-chief of BAOR, explained that his headquarters had received some training for its new wartime role. It was being reorganized and by October 1952 would be "fully fit for its task as HQ Northern Group in war."[6] Dominating the command structure of NORTHAG had been a UK political objective throughout the 1950s. By 1952 the UK maintained four armored divisions in Germany. In 1956, when London began to contemplate some troop withdrawals, UK diplomats in Bonn advised that such reductions should be disguised by keeping four understrength divisions in Germany rather than two full-strength divisions. With four "light" divisions in being, and therefore four major generals, they asserted, "our case for retaining a British general in command of Northern Army Group will be strengthened." In 1956, with the creation of the new Bundeswehr, UK diplomats also emphasized the importance of being able "to keep a close eye on what the German forces are up to."[7]

NORTHAG's Priorities and Structures

NATO undertook little intelligence collection of its own during the Cold War.[8] In reality, NATO was largely fed with intelligence by its various national components, some of which preferred to keep the alliance on a rather meager diet. In wartime these restrictions would have been removed and NATO organizations at every level would have been deluged by the national agencies. The plan to send a wave of unfamiliar intelligence material to NATO amid the panic caused by an impending Warsaw Pact attack was never a very good one. As we shall see, during the 1960s that was a continual source of anxiety for NATO planners because nuclear decision making was growing in importance.[9] This chapter argues then that references to "NATO intelligence" are more plausible when we talk about its military centers, which included Supreme Headquarters Allied Powers Europe (SHAPE) at Mons and also at the operational-level army group headquarters, such as Rheindahlen.[10] Unlike the main NATO political headquarters, the various national corps focused on Rheindahlen had considerable intelligence-gathering assets of their own.

　　Cold War intelligence priorities diverged at different levels. In national capitals, a great deal of attention was focused on strategic nuclear forces. Within NATO, there was perhaps more interest in the dangers of a surprise conventional attack that many believed would be accompanied initially by the use of chemical but not nuclear weapons.[11] Beyond the initial war warning phase, NORTHAG required operational intelligence. This was essentially deep battlefield intelligence and included surveillance of enemy movements together with meteorologic and topographic information. In practice the requirement translated into a need for intelligence over the NORTHAG front and extending beyond the forward edge of the battle area (FEBA) to a distance of at least three hundred kilometers, and ideally to five hundred kilometers. The top priority was near real-time intelligence on enemy movements in this zone, which was essential to allow NORTHAG to concentrate resources against enemy thrusts, rather than dispersing its defensive forces thinly. It also would permit the tasking of artillery and air operations to slow the enemy down during the crucial early stages of an attack.[12]

NORTHAG's staff officers also worried about the structural changes to the command that would be made even as the headquarters rushed to its wartime survival location. Poor communications infrastructure together with an influx of reserve staff meant that the intelligence mechanisms were unlikely to function smoothly in the vital first few days of war. Perennial concerns about slow target acquisition times became worse during the 1960s. This was because NORTHAG intelligence was increasingly conscious of the ability of Warsaw Pact forces to operate equally well by night as by day, and perhaps under a blanket of near radio silence. Commanders wanted efficient reconnaissance at night and in bad visibility, but these capabilities were not available until the late 1970s.

Alert procedures were controversial within all NATO commands. This period witnessed an animated debate over supreme allied commander, Europe (SACEUR), "Counter-Surprise Military Systems," which connected warning and alert systems to states of readiness, mobilization of reserves, and practical measures such as aircraft dispersal. This in turn raised complicated matters of access to national intelligence on the brink of war. In the early 1960s there was confusion over exactly how SACEUR's Counter-Surprise Military Systems should work, given that much of NATO would receive only high-grade signals intelligence (SIGINT) once war had broken out. These problems reverberated at the operational level—in other words, at the level of NORTHAG.[13]

Many planners considered the warning times to be unrealistic and pressed for changes to the mobilization arrangements. On 14 March 1960, for example, General Alfred Ward, who was then COMNORTHAG, wrote to the four ministries of defense of his component national corps asking agreement to minimum deployments within the framework of SACEUR's Counter-Surprise Military Systems. His units were very dispersed in peacetime. COMNORTHAG requested that should intelligence trigger either State

Orange (warning of an attack within thirty-six hours) or State Scarlett (attack within one hour), he could "assume his full powers as a NATO commander" and at that point the full wartime chain of command would come into effect. Without this, he argued, much of the Dutch and Belgian corps would struggle to arrive at their deployment areas in time. In all four countries there was an initial reluctance to delegate full operational command authority before war started, since that implied the authority to open fire. They eventually agreed, however, to the wartime chain of command coming into effect with the counter-surprise procedures.[14]

During the approach of war, and probably during the vital first few days of combat, most of NORTHAG HQ's intelligence would have been provided by BAOR. Within BAOR the BGS (Int & Sy) oversaw intelligence operations at Rheindahlen. Accordingly, the origins of BAOR's intelligence system lie with the gradual shift of UK armed forces in Germany from an occupation role to a NATO defensive role. Immediately after World War II the UK's main intelligence element in the region was the Intelligence Division of the Control Commission Germany, one of largest intelligence organizations ever fielded by the UK.[15] As early as 1950, however, the Intelligence Division was winding down and more attention was being given to the activities of the intelligence elements of BAOR.[16] The intelligence and security branch of BAOR was an oddity among UK military commands because Germany was ideal for observing the Warsaw Pact. Therefore, unlike the intelligence branches of most regional commands, which merely fed assessments to senior staff officers, BAOR was a major collector of intelligence. BGS (Int & Sy) BAOR had also built up a "very close liaison" with the intelligence element of the American HQ U.S. European Command (EUCOM) farther south at Heidelberg.[17] For this reason BGS (Int & Sy) BAOR was given special protected status from any economies that were imposed by Whitehall in the 1950s.[18]

Over the next twenty years BAOR gradually expanded its collection capabilities with specialized collection elements. By the 1960s BAOR even had its own small security service and human intelligence (HUMINT) collection service, known respectively as the British Services Security Organization and the British Services Intelligence Organization.[19] There also were a number of dissemination units producing recognition material and handbooks on Soviet tactics for distribution to frontline units and junior commanders.[20] However, while these specialist collection units were valuable and provided NORTHAG with a reservoir of excellent information about their Warsaw Pact adversary, they were not the core of NORTHAG's wartime intelligence machine. In wartime the most important element would have been a series of intelligence cells that worked closely with operations and planning sections at every echelon. During the late 1960s and early 1970s there were severe worries about poor communications and data overload in this area. In common with much of NATO, NORTHAG intelligence elements lacked access to a secure voice system. NORTHAG intelligence officers who ran these cells also complained that they were prisoners of outmoded procedures. During exercises they spent much of their time compiling detailed intelligence summaries that were thought to be of doubtful value to commanders, and that might not even be read during the turbulent first few days of a conflict.[21]

Intelligence before the Outbreak of War

In the early years NORTHAG commanders complained of weak information on their adversary. Initially this complaint was justified. In January 1952 General John Harding, who presided over the establishment of NORTHAG, observed that our "intelligence cover of eastern Germany and Poland, on which we must depend for warning of attack, and information on Russian and Satellite forces, is poor and deteriorating," and he urged that "no effort be spared" to improve it. The Directorate of Military Intelligence in London agreed, commenting that this problem was "realized only too well" and adding that the remedial work would "take some time."[22] Although commanders in Germany wanted better intelligence on Warsaw Pact capabilities, what they wanted above all was reliable war warning. Forty-eight hours' warning meant a reasonable chance of survival, while only a few hours' warning spelled almost certain disaster. Throughout this period there was a prevailing paranoia that the Soviets would somehow manage a sneak attack. Events in Hungary in 1956 and Czechoslovakia in 1968 only increased their worries.

NORTHAG received some intelligence from UK national sources, including HUMINT and SIGINT. The UK's much-vaunted Secret Intelligence Service (SIS), also known as MI6, had several large stations across Germany and a large establishment in Berlin based at the former Olympic stadium.[23] SIS, however, had been a somewhat moribund organization during the war and failed to modernize itself sufficiently after 1945. Only with the advent of Dick White as MI6 chief in 1956 did serious reform begin. More important, all Western clandestine human operations into the Communist bloc proved difficult with a high rate of agent loss.[24] The Communist countries invested vast sums in internal security procedures of labyrinthine complexity, such as internal passports for moving from one locality to another. Although operations into East Germany—mostly from Berlin using former Wehrmacht personnel as agents—achieved some success, they became progressively more difficult after the erection of the Berlin Wall in 1961.[25]

SIS also suffered serious penetration. The case of Kim Philby is too well known to repeat here.[26] Rather more important with regard to Germany was another penetration agent, George Blake. Unbeknownst to his superiors, Blake had been influenced in his youth by members of his family, who were committed Communists. Stationed in Seoul, he was taken prisoner by the North Koreans in 1950, and during his confinement he volunteered to work for the KGB (Komityet Gosudarstvyennoy Bezopasnosti, the most important intelligence service of the Soviet Union). After his release, he was dispatched as a senior SIS officer in the Berlin station, where he compromised perhaps four hundred Western agents to the Soviets. Blake remained active until he was exposed by Michael Goleniewksi, a defecting Polish security service officer who came over to the Central Intelligence Agency (CIA) in 1959.[27] The equivalent German service, the BND (Bundesnachrichtendienst), seems to have fared little better. In November 1961, Heinz Felfe, a senior BND official, was arrested after it was discovered that he had been a double agent for the Soviets for many years. Through him, the Communists acquired detailed knowledge of German intelligence structures, and many agents were arrested and some executed.[28]

What then of SIGINT? Although this is a complex subject and hard to generalize, Soviet communications security improved markedly after 1948, and thereafter Soviet high-grade communications proved difficult to read until further breakthroughs in the 1970s. The majority of Western SIGINT conducted against the East during this period came either from relatively low-grade systems or from the monitoring of voice traffic. Nevertheless, sophisticated traffic analysis and direction finding, developed in the 1940s, ensured good product. In theory at least, this could have provided NORTHAG with war warning, since any deviation in normal patterns of signals traffic would have alerted the West to the possibility of attack. Although units might adopt radio silence, war preparations required many mundane activities, such as unusual movements of railway stock, which could be tracked through the interception of open communications. SIGINT also contributed heavily to Western knowledge about the Soviet order of battle. Innumerable "special operators" spent years along the Inner-German Border listening in to the operating habits of Soviet fighter defense forces.[29]

Ironically, the most daring of these SIGINT operations, the Berlin and Vienna tunnels, were compromised in 1955 by George Blake but remained effective for some time since the KGB feared compromising their agent.[30]

Moreover, the British, Americans, and Germans all operated large SIGINT installations along the Inner-German Border and in Berlin. After 1961 they used Teufelsberg, the highest point in Berlin, which gave better line-of-sight access to very high frequency (VHF) communications. The best technical intelligence systems, however, were national assets, so tasking was at best indirect and distribution to NORTHAG was limited to what London thought advisable. Thus, while the order of battle material provided to NORTHAG (constructed largely from low-grade SIGINT) was excellent, access to higher-grade material was limited. It was partly for this reason that NORTHAG commanders in Germany were anxious to expand their own peacetime col-lection capabilities.

NORTHAG's best asset was the British Military Mission to the Soviet Forces in Germany (BRIXMIS), which was established on 16 September 1946 under the Robertson-Malinin Agreement. It initiated an exchange of liaison missions, effectively teams of roving military attachés, whose task was to encourage good relations between the two occupation zones. They were joined later by parallel French and American missions and remained in being until October 1990.[31] The BRIXMIS teams were able to drive rela-tively freely within the German Democratic Republic (GDR), and soon conducted intelligence gathering on Warsaw Pact forces. BRIXMIS teams were given several intelligence tasks. They became the premiere source of technical intelligence on new Soviet equipment, examples of which were often "liberated." They provided invaluable information on order of battle and troop movements that could be cross-checked with SIGINT. Finally, and perhaps most important, the teams provided the most reliable source of war warning—since BRIXMIS were "eyes on the ground"—and could not be spoofed by techniques such as radio silence. Their missions were subjected to continual hostility, which even extended to the ramming of mission cars by military trucks.[32]

The activities of BRIXMIS had additional value for NORTHAG HQ. Their existence owed everything to direct agreements between the commander-in-chief of BAOR and his opposite number in the Soviet zone, and therefore Rheindahlen "owned" BRIXMIS completely. Accordingly, while BRIXMIS often worked in cooperation with London and the national agencies, it was a creature of and tasked by BAOR. Relations between the BRIXMIS chief of mission and the BGS (Int & Sy) at Rheindahlen were exceptionally close. That connection was reinforced by the fact that the mission officers, includ-ing its chief, were regular army officers and not Intelligence Corps specialist personnel. They related immediately to the operational needs of NORTHAG.

These missions also served as genuine crisis prevention systems.[33] More remarkable was that BRIXMIS managed to escape the financial constraints imposed on other intelligence agencies by end-of-occupation rules in 1955, since BRIXMIS was paid for by the Berlin Senate and effectively enjoyed an unlimited budget that allowed it to purchase the latest equipment.

Indeed, because of the serious depletion of the clandestine networks run by the BND and SIS during the late 1950s, and then the problems of the Berlin Wall in the early 1960s, BRIXMIS became increasingly important. BRIXMIS paid particular attention to Warsaw Pact deployment patterns, and the mission was pessimistic about the chances of detecting a surprise attack using SIGINT. Their roving patrols were conscious of break-out drills conducted successfully by entire divisions under radio silence. The GDR also had installed an elaborate network of landlines that provided for communications to remote locations and were immune to interception. Exactly how much war warning NORTHAG would receive was a matter of constant debate among the various intelligence elements in Germany.[34]

Intelligence Collection in War

The vital long-range intelligence required by NORTHAG HQ during the crucial first forty-eight hours of war was expected to come from a mixture of aerial reconnaissance, stay-behind patrols, and SIGINT. At army group level the primary operational need would have been to track the movement of reinforcements some three hundred kilometers beyond the FEBA in order to discern the Warsaw Pact's emerging battle plan and to counter its thrusts in a timely way. Self-evidently, nothing would come from the Western military missions inside East Germany, since these were peacetime activities functioning in the realm of defense diplomacy. In common with diplomats and military attachés in the East, BRIXMIS expected to be rounded up before any military action took place.

Remarkably, during the 1950s and the 1960s NORTHAG seems to have placed the greatest emphasis on the least technical of these options, human reconnaissance, often referred to in local parlance as "the Mk1 eyeball." From the onset of war the best intelligence from the Soviet rear areas would probably have been provided by stay-behind parties fielded by NATO special forces. These special forces had several roles in wartime, including the collection of intelligence, coup de main operations by small parties, coordination with partisans, and assistance to downed pilots. In the context of global war, however, collection of intelligence was the overwhelming priority for Special

Air Service (SAS)–type units. They had orders to give "particular reference to enemy atomic systems." Meanwhile, the only coup de main–type activities that were considered important were efforts to "destroy enemy nuclear weapons or missile sites."[35] NORTHAG's emphasis on special forces reflected a growing recognition that Warsaw Pact units might move too fast to allow aerial reconnaissance to provide effective targeting intelligence for artillery.[36]

By 1962 NORTHAG was busy developing a new force for this important role by adding a Special Reconnaissance Squadron (SRS) from the Royal Armoured Corps to 23 Special Air Service Regiment (23 SAS). During the initial alert, SRS was to hold the fort until the arrival of 23 SAS from the UK. Thereafter 23 SAS and SRS were to operate as a single unit, giving priority to observation of "nuclear units, formation HQs, amour, and bridging and ferrying equipment." Their main task was to focus the targeting for the Honest John and Corporal missile systems.[37] These special units were based at Paderborn and were equipped with high-frequency Morse to provide long-range and hopefully continued communications, even in an electromagnetic pulse environment. Considering the expected rapid rate of enemy advance, there was no need for these units to practice exotic skills to penetrate the enemy front line. Instead, the drill was to move forward quickly, usually by any available soft-skinned transport, and "stay behind." Preparations had become quite elaborate by the late 1960s, with pre-identified hides and stocks.[38]

All the component national corps of NORTHAG recognized the value of stay-behind operations. The Germans created the Fallschirmjäger Fernspähkompanie (Airborne Long-Range Reconnaissance Company), while the Belgians fielded two companies of para-commandos in this role. To the south, each American corps developed its own ranger-type companies dedicated to Long-Range Reconnaissance Patrols. Eventually NATO set up its own International Long Range Reconnaissance Patrol School run by Germany at Weingarten in Bavaria. Some of the American special forces units would have been equipped with atomic demolition munitions (ADM) in an attempt to slow the advance of Soviet armor.[39] NORTHAG was wholly dependent on American ADM teams attached by USAREUR at Heidelberg.[40] In September 1965 it was reported, "All ADM's in Germany are American devices which are allocated by SACEUR to Northern Army Group and are emplaced and fired by U.S. personnel."[41] By 1965, however, there was clearly a growing UK interest in developing national devices.[42] This interest reflected anxiety in NORTHAG about delays in deployment resulting from the possibility of complex political restrictions and custodial arrangements.[43]

During the late 1960s and early 1970s NORTHAG became increasingly concerned about the potential vulnerability of stay-behind parties and began to carry out research on their survivability. The largest program of research was carried out during 23 SAS's annual training exercise held in Germany during October 1973, code-named BADGER'S LAIR. Numerous SAS teams were deployed in the Soltau training area. Signals security teams conducted elaborate tests to investigate their vulnerability to interception. RAF units examined concealment procedures by overflying the SAS hide locations with thermal cameras, infrared systems, and monochrome photography. Vulnerability to dog patrols was also examined. To the dismay of the SAS, twenty-seven of the thirty-nine hides established during these tests were found within the first six hours by the patrols. Alsatian dogs were "highly successful" throughout the trials. Even more remarkable was success with electronic warfare sensor vehicles, which located not only hand-speed Morse code transmitters but also, to the surprise of the research team, burst-encrypted message traffic.[44] Partly because of the problem of moving special forces elements forward on short notice, NORTHAG also encouraged the establishment of an additional secret force of civilians who would conduct a mixture of intelligence reporting, sabotage, and demolition work. As early as 1952 General John Harding urged that war preparations must include a "German-manned stay behind sabotage organization."[45] By the end of the 1950s a shadowy civilian organization had come into being, code-named GLADIO.[46]

Alongside this human effort, NORTHAG also had its own SIGINT and electronic warfare capability, presided over by the NORTHAG Intercept Control Centre (ICC). The ICC exercised control over electronic warfare units like the UK's Number 225 Signals Squadron, based at Scharfoldendorf and later at Langeleben, close to the Inner-German Border. At corps level there were also Electronic Warfare Control Centres that worked as subordinate elements to the ICC. Their tasks included direction finding or position fixing against enemy HQs. These units provided an invaluable peacetime contribution through their work on the Soviet order of battle. They feared, however, that commanders overestimated their likely contribution in wartime. Some predicted that for the first twenty-four hours, the Warsaw Pact might advance on predesignated lines and maintain near radio silence. A further limitation was range of intercept. The primary mode of Warsaw Pact command and control was VHF radio, and the range over which it could be intercepted was about forty-five kilometers. Collectors had to be positioned as far forward as possible, exposing them to risk and forcing them to move frequently, which was not "conducive to the best COMINT [communications intelligence] collection." Moreover, Warsaw Pact communications security was improving. In 1969 British officials conceded that the result would be "lean intelligence collected by the SIGINT organization."[47]

During the late 1960s American and French units in the southern part of the Central Sector acquired effective ground surveillance radar systems; however, BAOR did not have such radar equipment until the 1970s. NORTHAG was greatly impressed by the U.S. Army's OV-1 Mohawk aircraft equipped with side-looking airborne radar (SLAR), which provided night-and-day and near all-weather capability. Operating in a stand-off mode, the SLAR Mohawk could detect large vehicles at ranges of up to seventy kilometers. NORTHAG hoped that the Luftwaffe units in 2 ATAF might decide to acquire the system. Although test systems flew in both German and French colors, this useful aircraft was never acquired by European forces.[48] Only during the mid-1970s did technology begin to provide alternative sources for NORTHAG. Unattended ground sensors, initially tested in Vietnam under the IGLOO WHITE program, began to become available in Europe. By the early 1980s these sensors had become a formidable intelligence instrument for NORTHAG and resolved many of its reconnaissance problems.[49]

NORTHAG also would have depended for longer-range intelligence on traditional aerial reconnaissance with cameras, conducted by 2 ATAF.[50] Second ATAF, however, had limited reconnaissance resources in Germany. Moreover, that source of intelligence would have diminished quickly because an aircraft attrition rate of some 60 percent was expected in the first week of war. Once battle commenced, aircraft vulnerability would have required low-altitude flying, which in turn would have limited the area that could be surveyed by airborne sensors. Effectiveness also was hampered by retaining aircraft under centralized control, requiring the requests for reconnaissance to travel through several command levels before being approved. By 1969 some reconnaissance aircraft worked with the individual corps within NORTHAG, and plans were developed to assign helicopters to armored reconnaissance units.[51]

Eastern Bloc Espionage and NATO Security

Improving the flow of strategic intelligence from national sources to NATO was much debated in Western capitals throughout the late 1950s and 1960s. The driver was the increased pressure on NATO's decision-making process, caused by a growing addiction to nuclear weapons. This in turn reflected the conventional military weakness of NORTHAG. The impediments to releasing better information were the obsessive secrecy that the CANUKUS countries (Canada, the United Kingdom, and the United States) attached to SIGINT, together with several high-level security scares in NATO in the late 1960s. The pressure to improve intelligence flow, however, was hard to resist. Accordingly, in late 1965 NATO's Special Committee set up a Working Group on Intelligence and Other Data Exchange, tasked with identifying "the kind of information which heads of government should have in order to take part in timely and meaningful consultations about the possible use of nuclear weapons."[52]

The British, Americans, and Canadians did not wish to reveal too much about their own Anglo-Saxon "closed shop" on strategic SIGINT, often referred to as CANUKUS arrangements.[53] The larger NATO commands had COMINT-handling cells known as special handling detachments (SHDs), which were effectively classified reading rooms where senior officers could consult intercept material. While many NATO countries participated in the SHD system, in practice this material was relatively low grade (up to the classification level of Secret). A separate system supplied medium-grade COMINT to "double-hatted" officers from the United Kingdom, the United States, and Canada. However, in peacetime no one in Europe seems to have received high-grade SIGINT. The presumption was that at the outbreak of war, the choice material would have been released widely.[54] NATO's political headquarters was the most problematic area, and thus the material passed to Brussels was "severely restricted" during peacetime. Although there was general agreement that in war "all intelligence is passed to NATO," there was no agreed timetable for changing to a war footing.[55]

Discussions about upgrading intelligence support for the political headquarters were also prompted by NATO's move from Paris to Brussels in 1968. NATO already had an analysis shop called the Intelligence Division, which produced assessments for the Military Committee. NATO now decided to create an additional Situation Center, or SITCEN, which was more warning-focused, with hopes for watch officers on a twenty-four-hour basis. The emphasis was on better support for crisis decision making.[56] Again, a key issue was the supply of COMINT from national sources. Previously, attached intelligence staffs from Canada, the United Kingdom, and the United States had seen the national material themselves, adding their background knowledge to the general discussions. But in May 1968 London and Washington were considering upgrading the direct flow of COMINT to NATO. Bill Millward, the director of requirements at Government Communications headquarters (GCHQ), traveled to Brussels to talk to military representatives. The result was joint UK/U.S. action to establish a NATO COMINT detachment within the Intelligence Division to serve both the Military Committee and the planned NATO SITCEN located at Evere. This process, however, was overshadowed by two security scares at Brussels during late 1968 and 1969.[57]

In retrospect, we now know that the penetration of NATO by Warsaw Pact intelligence was remarkably good and the East German foreign intelligence service achieved some notable successes.[58] At the time, the West was unaware of most of these penetrations. It was aware, however, of serious penetrations by the Romanian intelligence service. On 10 September 1968 a Turkish colonel named Nahit Imre, a member of NATO's international staff, was arrested by the Belgian security authorities while in possession of microfilm copies of some 1,500 NATO documents. As NATO's financial controller he held an A7 grade, which was the highest possible classification for a member of the international staff. He had been caught in a joint operation between the Belgian Security Service and the NATO Security Directorate, assisted by the CIA. The operation had been complex, "involving several double agents."[59] Imre's espionage covered the majority of papers submitted to NATO's Defense Planning Committee and the force goal proposals during the period 1969–1973. The main damage done by Imre was to underline to the Soviets the scale of NATO's weakness, notably in the NORTHAG area.[60] The Imre case caused real consternation in London. Ronnie Burroughs in the Foreign Office immediately saw the connection with plans to improve COMINT provisions for NATO. He wrote to the senior UK representative on the North Atlantic Council (NAC): "Another matter . . . is whether we are right to proceed with our plans to set up an all-NATO GCHQ cell at Evere. We have discussed this inter-departmentally, and have come to the conclusion that we should go ahead, but we would nevertheless be grateful if you would reconsider the matter and let us have your views."[61]

The UK delegation replied that London should still go ahead with the plan for a NATO GCHQ cell at Evere.[62] Within three months, however, NATO was shaken further by the unraveling of the "Roussilhe case." Francis Roussilhe was a French employee of the international staff who had worked for NATO since 1952 and had gradually risen to be chief clerk of the Document Translation Center. Since 1963 he had provided the Romanian intelligence service with at least five thousand NATO documents, including material classified as Cosmic Top Secret. As with Imre, Roussilhe was caught as the result of information from a high-level Romanian defector secured by the Americans.[63] The UK chiefs of staff took a "very grave view" of this, and many in London argued that the UK was putting its own forces at risk "by passing too much information to NATO."[64]

Two security problems confronted NATO security in Brussels. First, the presence of what were referred to as "floaters"—in other words, people from NATO countries who worked for international organizations who had therefore long ago lost contact with their own country and were unknown to their home security service. Roussilhe was one such person. Second, the move from Paris to Brussels meant that NATO now relied on the Belgian Security Service, which, while energetic, was smaller than its French counterpart and had less capacity to keep known Communist agents under surveillance.[65]

Why did the development of a SIGINT distribution center at NATO still go ahead? The answer probably lies with the constrained nature of the initial proposal by NATO's Special Committee. The proposed improvement was about intelligence that might influence "a timely decision to release nuclear weapons." It specifically was about material to be made available during the critical period between consultation on a developing security situation and "request for the release or use of nuclear weapons." In other words, there was never any intention to supply NATO with significant COMINT during "normal" times. During the 1967 Middle East War, the United Kingdom and the United States provided NATO with most of its intelligence, requiring the laborious production of "specially tailored" documents that hid sources and methods.[66] Perhaps more important was the widespread recognition in 1968 of the need for higher-grade command and control links between NATO and its subordinate commands.[67] In 1970 NATO began a serious effort to address its communication problems. Member states signed up to a large-scale program designated the NATO Integrated Communications System. The long-term objective was to afford rapid, secure, and survivable communications to NATO's senior political and military echelons.[68]

In retrospect, northern Europe seems like the Cold War's frozen front—a place where little happened. However, repeated crises, beginning with Hungary in 1956, had in fact placed growing emphasis on warning and intelligence. In the 1960s further crises over Berlin, Cuba, Vietnam, and then Czechoslovakia in 1968 proved deeply unsettling. Moreover, throughout the 1960s there was growing awareness that NATO's conventional inferiority, especially in the NORTHAG sector, might prompt calls for the early use of nuclear weapons. All this generated considerable strain on intelligence, command, and communications. Anxiety was only increased by the Yom Kippur War of October 1973. That episode demonstrated excellent Arab deception and poor Israeli intelligence analysis, combined with indecisiveness about whether or not to mobilize. In Europe, senior policy makers saw that the same underlying problems would be faced by NATO compounded by the need for inter-allied consultation. Some thought that the Warsaw Pact's large standing forces made "surprise attack an attractive option," and that NATO had done relatively little work on how to respond to a surprise attack.[69]

Equally, this sense of vulnerability contributed to developing détente in the 1970s. An agreement that defused tensions over Berlin was signed in March 1970. More important was the treaty signed between the two Germanys in December 1972, which allowed both to be members of the United Nations.[70] All this was accompanied by arms control agreements, verified by intelligence. Arguably, the intelligence effort by both NATO and the Warsaw Pact countries had contributed to this improvement in relations. Complex warning indicators gave NATO commanders at least the hope of forty-eight hours' war warning and rendered surprise attack a less tempting option. In the 1960s at least, espionage seems to have persuaded some Warsaw Pact leaders that NATO intentions were benign.[71] Yet the onset of détente and *Ostpolitik* also provided opportunities to accelerate the intelligence war. Accordingly, collection agencies in Germany remained active until the end of the Cold War.

Notes

I am most indebted to Tessa Stirling of the UK Cabinet Office for access to documentation that has contributed to this essay. I would also like to record my thanks to those who have shared their memories.

1. These comments were made by UK director of Naval Intelligence (DNI) Edmund Rushbrooke, see ADM 223/297. All archival references are to the UK National Archives unless otherwise stated. To be precise, DNI Rushbrooke said that war was the "fairy godmother." However, the fairy godmother is a figure latterly introduced into the story of Cinderella, the English version of Aschenputtel. In the original German version the transformation is effected by Mother Nature, in the form of birds.

2. A. J. Goodpaster, "Memorandum of a Conversation with the President," 21 Aug. 1958, box 6, Office Staff Sec., White House Office, Dwight D. Eisenhower Library, Abilene.

3. Between 1971 and 1973 this role was fulfilled by Brigadier Sir James Gow.

4. The commander-in-chief RAF Germany was also commander 2 ATAF.

5. P. Dietz, *Garrison: British Military Towns* (London, 1986), 157. This was one of the first eco-friendly military projects, with more than a million new trees being planted on the site.

6. Harding to War Office, "The Situation of BAOR," 17 Jan. 1952, WO 106/6051.

7. Hoyer Millar (Bonn) to Hood (Foreign and Commonwealth Office), 18 Dec. 1956, 11988/1/59G, FO 371/124860. Inevitably they also saw opportunities for "trying to get them to buy British equipment."

8. J. Kriendler, *NATO Intelligence and Early Warning,* Conflict Studies Research Centre, Special Series 06/13, Mar. 2006, UK Defence Academy, available at http://www.defac.ac.uk/colleges/csrc/document-listings/special/06(13)JK.pdf.

9. Little has been written on NATO intelligence; however, see P. B. Stares, *Command Performance: The Neglected Dimension of European Security* (Washington, D.C., 1991); P. J. Bracken, *The Command and Control of Nuclear Forces* (New Haven, 1983).

10. See also L. W. Cracken, *Between the Lines: Reflections on War and Peacetime* (Dallas, 1998), 161–80.

11. Confidential interview conducted in 2004.

12. Early alert systems developed in 1951 are documented in FO 371/96399 and 96400.

13. D (61) 5th Meeting (3), "SACEUR's Counter-Surprise Military System," discussing D (61) 19, 27 Apr. 1961, ADM 1/27842.

14. COMNORTHAG letter N 7985 G-3 Ops 1 of 14 Mar. 1960 to Ministries of Defense, Annex A to COS.923/14/7/60, "SACEUR'S Counter-Surprise Military System," 14 July 1960, WUN11914/36/G, FO 371/154587.

15. The best account is offered in P. Maddrell, *Spying on Science* (Oxford, 2006), 32–39.

16. Documented extensively in WO 216/949.

17. EUCOM was established at Heidelberg, Germany, in 1948. It was redesignated the U.S. Army command in Europe, making it the American equivalent of the British Army of the Rhine. In 1952 the United States established a multiservice combined command in Europe. It was given the designation of European Command, while the subordinate U.S. Army command in Heidelberg was redesignated U.S. Army, Europe (USAREUR). EUCOM was established initially at Frankfurt, Germany. In 1952 it moved to just outside of Paris. In 1967 it relocated to Stuttgart, Germany, where it remains today. USAREUR remained in Heidelberg, although as of 2012, the headquarters was in the process of relocating to Wiesbaden, Germany.

18. Short (Director of Military Intelligence) minute to Director of Staff Duties, 16 Mar. 1950, and deputy chief Imperial General Staff (IGS) minute to vice chief IGS, 26 Apr. 1950, WO 216/949. For a detailed account, see Maddrell, *Spying on Science,* 103–18 (n. 16).

19. On the British Services Security Organization and the British Services Intelligence Organization, see R. J. Aldrich, "British Intelligence, Security and Western Co-operation in Cold War Germany: The Ostpolitik Years," in *German-Dutch Intelligence Relations,* ed. B. de Graaf, B. de Jong, and W. Platje (Apeldoorn, 2007), 123–46.

20. For example, HQ NORTHAG, *Warsaw Pact Ground Forces' Weapons and Equipment,* Oct. 1972. This document had a NORTHAG cover but was produced by GS (Int & Sy) HQ BAOR.

21. Defence Operational Analysis Establishment M500, "Int. Cells and Int. Functions in I (BR) Corps," Jan. 1971, DEFE 48/817.

22. Harding to War Office, "The Situation of BAOR," 17 Jan. 1952, WO 106/6051. Minute by DMI's office, "General Harding: Appreciation," 11 Mar. 1952, WO 106/6051.

23. There were also many small stations. Hamburg, for example, had only two or three SIS officers. Confidential interview.

24. T. Bower, *The Perfect English Spy* (New York, 1995), 207–14. Confidential interview.

25. P. Maddrell, "The Western Secret Services, the East German Ministry of State Security and the Building of the Berlin Wall," *Intelligence and National Security* 21, no. 5 (2006): 829–47.

26. C. M. Andrew, *The Sword and Shield: The Mitrokhin Archive and the Secret History of the KGB* (New York, 1999), 398–401.

27. G. Blake, *No Other Choice* (London, 1990), 165–69, 206–8; O. Kalugin, *The First Directorate* (New York, 1994), 141–42.

28. U.S. Intelligence and Security Command/CIC Report, "FELFE, Heinz," III-35714, 10 June 1954, Freedom of Information Act.

29. See, for example, T. Thomas, *Signal Success* (London, 1995), 399–405; L. Woodhead, *My Life as a Spy* (London, 2005).

30. D. Stafford, *Spies beneath Berlin* (London, 2002).

31. The final phase is dealt with in S. Gibson, *The Last Mission* (London, 2005).

32. N. Wylde (ed.), *The Story of Brixmis, 1946–1990* (Arundel, 1993); T. Geraghty, *Beyond the Front Line* (London, 1996); K. Behling, *Spione in Uniform: Die alliierten Militärmissionen in Deutschland* (Stuttgart, 2004).

33. D. Ball, "Controlling Theatre Nuclear War," *British Journal of Political Science* 19, no. 3 (1989): 303–27. On the U.S. mission, see J. A. Fahey, *Licensed to Spy* (Annapolis, 2002).

34. Confidential interview, 1 Apr. 2004.

35. Directorate of Military Operations memo, "Future Requirement for SAS Type Operations," 14 July 1958, WO 32/19472.

36. 257 Signals Squadron provided the communications links from NORTHAG HQ to UK and German missile batteries. Confidential interview.

37. "Operational Directive to 23 SAS and Special Reconnaissance Squadron RAC," Annex to B 2014/10 G (Ops & Plans), 11 Sept. 1962, WO 32/19472.

38. Confidential interview, 23 Apr. 2004.

39. DOAE Project 147, "The NATO Intelligence System," June 1969, DEFE 48/496. Also confidential interview.

40. See note 17.

41. PM/62/46, "Atomic Demolition Munitions," 23 Mar. 1962, PREM 11/3990.

42. 57/Engrs/6047, Engineer-in-Chief memo, "Tactical Doctrine—Employment of Atomic Demolition Munitions," 5 Oct. 1965, WO 32/21603.

43. Bolton memo to DGGS (Ministry of Defence), "ADMs," 10 Feb. 1967, WO 32/21603; see also "Outline of Requirements for a UK manufactured ADM," 10 May 1967, WO 32/21603.

44. DOAE M7404, "Exercise Badger's Lair: The Detectability of Stay-Behind Parties," June 1974, DEFE 48/279.

45. Harding to War Office, "The Situation of BAOR," 17 Jan. 1952, WO 106/6051.

46. On GLADIO, see D. Ganser, *NATO's Secret Armies: Operation Gladio and Terrorism in Western Europe* (London, 2005).

47. DOAE Project 147, "The NATO Intelligence System," June 1969, DEFE 48/496.

48. Ibid.

49. J. Nicholls, "Unattended Ground Sensors," *Field Artilleryman* (Mar. 1971): 6–11.

50. 2 ATAF had squadrons from Belgium, Holland, Germany, and the United Kingdom.

51. DOAE Project 147, "The NATO Intelligence System," June 1969, DEFE 48/496.

52. JIC 210/66, "NATO Special Committee: Working Group on Intelligence and Other Data Exchange (Working Group No.1)," 1966, CAB 163/37.

53. "Special Committee," conclusions reached at a meeting held by Deputy Undersecretary for Policy 25 Feb. 1966, CAB 163/37.

54. "NATO Working Group on Intelligence," attached to JIC/82/108/17, Joy (UK Sec Joint Intelligence Committee) to Dillon (UK Defence Intelligence Staff), 6 Jan. 1966, CAB 163/37.

55. DOAE Project 147, "The NATO Intelligence System," June 1969, DEFE 48/496.

56. IMSM-223–68, North Atlantic Military Committee, "Terms of Reference for the Situation Center," General Ezio Pistotti (Director IMS), 17 May 1968, FCO 41/148.

57. D/DISSEC/41/4, "Visit of Captain Humphreys 8.5.1968," U.S./UK Eyes Only, FCO 41/148. The U.S./UK initiative led to the revision of MC 101, "NATO COMINT/ELINT Policy."

58. B. Schaefer and C. Nuenlist (eds.), *Parallel History Project on NATO and the Warsaw Pact (PHP): Stasi Intelligence on NATO,* PHP Publications Series (Washington, D.C./Zurich, Nov. 2003), available at http://www.php.isn.ethz.ch/collections/colltopic .cfm?lng=en&id=15296.

59. Bushell (UK NATO Deleg.) to Ashe (Security Department, UK FCO), 19 Sept. 1968, FCO 1116/39.

60. Burroughs (UK FCO) to Stewart (Secretary UK JIC (A)), "NATO Security—Nahit Imre," 28 Jan. 1969, FCO 41/441. See also Defence Planning Staff 1006/22/1/69, "Assessment of Military Damage Done to the UK as a Result of the Imre Affair," Jan. 1969, FCO 41/441.

61. Burroughs (UK FCO) to Burrows (UK Rep. NAC), EJC 10/579/4, 18 Feb. 1969, FCO 1116/39.

62. Pemberton-Piggot (UK NATO Deleg.) to Burroughs (FCO), 7 Mar. 1969, FCO 1116/39.

63. Pemberton-Piggot (UK NATO Deleg.), memo, 6 Aug. 1969, FCO 1116/39.

64. Frank Cooper (UK MoD) to Bernard Burrows (UK Rep. NAC), DSS (P)/7779, "The Roussilhe Case," 21 Nov. 1969, FCO 1116/40.

65. Richards (UK NATO Deleg.) to Holmer (Security Department, UK FCO), 11 Dec. 1969, FCO 1116/40; Richards (UK NATO Deleg.) to Holmer (Security Department, UK FCO), 16 Dec. 1969, FCO 1116/40.

66. Parsons (FCO) to Bushell (UK NATO Deleg.), 31 May 1967, FCO 41/146.

67. See, for example, Burrows (UK Rep. NAC) to Hood (FCO), "Secure Voice Link NATO H.Q. to SHAPE," 11 Nov. 1968, FCO 41/387.

68. L. Wentz and G. Hingorani, "NATO Communications in Transition," *IEEE Transactions on Communications* 28, no. 9 (1980): 1524–39.

69. MISC 71/763, "Lessons of the Middle East War," enclosing 1077/3/7, Annex B, "Lessons Relearned," 5 Feb. 1975, AIR 20/12671.

70. J. Young, *International Relations since 1945* (Oxford, 2004), 406–23.

71. V. Mastny and M. Byrne (eds.), *A Cardboard Castle? An Inside History of the Warsaw Pact, 1955–1991* (Budapest, 2005), 404, 522.

5

East German Military Intelligence for the Warsaw Pact in the Central Sector

Jan Hoffenaar

"Our military politics as a whole must . . . be based on a realistic assessment of the adversary." With this statement made in 1964, Heinz Hoffmann, the German Democratic Republic's (GDR) minister of defense, underpinned the importance of spying on the adversary.[1] As simple as this age-old logic seems, it is often very difficult to put into action. A realistic assessment of adversaries demands sufficient accurate intelligence on them. It is difficult and to an extent impossible to trace precisely how intelligence gathering, information analysis, and the respective political, strategic, and military conclusions from this analysis developed in the Eastern bloc during the 1950s and 1960s. This is because key parts of the relevant archives have remained sealed and, as yet, little research has been undertaken in this area.

The organization of intelligence gathering and the quality of the intelligence obtained are, relatively speaking, the easiest elements to research. It can be concluded from various studies that of all the intelligence services in the Warsaw Pact, the Verwaltung Aufklärung (Intelligence Service) of the Nationale Volksarmee (NVA), the armed forces of the GDR, worked the most intensively at military intelligence gathering. This took place mostly in the Federal Republic of Germany (FRG), in France, and in the Benelux countries. The military intelligence service of the Soviet Union, the Glavnoy Razvedovatel'noy Upravlenie (GRU), to which the NVA-Aufklärung reported directly, relied heavily on its findings. In the

1960s the division of intelligence tasks was more or less formalized within the Warsaw Pact.[2]

In its own country the NVA-Aufklärung—the military Aufklärung was formally a part of the Kasernierte Volkspolizei (Garrisoned People's Police) until 1956—dealt with the Hauptverwaltung Aufklärung (Directorate of Intelligence) of the all-powerful Ministerium für Staatssicherheit (Ministry for State Security), better known as the "Stasi." This division focused specifically on, among many other subjects, the foreign policies of NATO member states, and less on the specific military aspects of those policies. From the 1960s onward there was intensive cooperation and exchange of information between the two services, with the Stasi leading the way. Unfortunately, there is as yet no in-depth study into the interrelationships between the two intelligence services.[3] Nevertheless, it can be assumed safely that the NVA-Aufklärung gathered the most targeted intelligence material on the NATO armed forces in the Central Sector. It is, therefore, unfortunate that much of the archives of the NVA-Aufklärung was lost. However, enough material has been preserved, in original form or documents assessed by the Stasi Hauptverwaltung I ("Absicherung der NVA und Grenztruppen nach Innen und Aussen"), to construct a quite clear picture of their findings.[4]

One general complication that comes into play during studies of analyses made by military intelligence services in Communist Eastern Europe must be noted: the services always based their analyses on the assumption that the capitalist, "imperialist" NATO countries had aggressive intentions. Springing from Marxist-Leninist ideology, it was axiomatic that war would always start with an attack by the Western allies. The Communist leadership needed to maintain this image of fear and a clearly recognizable common enemy in order to keep the Warsaw Pact countries in line. In addition to ideological and manipulative reasons, historical experiences were at least as important for retaining this aggressive image of the enemy. Allied military support to the anti-bolshevists in 1918–1920 and the massive German invasion in 1941 had led to a permanent and deep-seated distrust among the political leadership in Moscow. Given this setting, only factual reports could provide a modicum of objectivity.[5]

Attempting to establish the measure to which the strategic and operational military planning of the Soviet Union and the Warsaw Pact was determined by intelligence is, in fact, impossible so long as the archives in Moscow remain closed. This chapter, therefore, is limited to a provisional analysis of the "yield" of military intelligence. What were they most interested in, and why? What information did they manage to gather? And what information did they not gather? And to what degree was this information correct? What were the conclusions drawn? And to what degree were those conclusions correct?

The Build-Up Phase: 1952–1958

On the basis of the available archival material, it can be concluded that prior to 1958 the gathering of military intelligence in the West had not yet taken off.[6] In senior circles there was talk of the "ongoing preparations for war in West Germany," but it did not seem that these circles were well informed.[7] Most reports were based on open sources, such as a report on the 1954 exercise BATTLE ROYAL, the largest NATO exercise held up to that time and the first exercise in which the use of tactical nuclear weapons was rehearsed.

The exercise took place under the command of General Sir Richard N. Gale, the commander of the NATO Northern Army Group (NORTHAG) and also the commander of the British Army of the Rhine (BAOR). It included the participation of all NORTHAG units and the Second Allied Tactical Air Force (2 ATAF), a total of almost 140,000 military personnel. In a concise report, the NVA analysts assessed a number of weak points that had come to light. Only three of the nine tactical nuclear weapons had been deployed with complete success; the tactical air support failed because of bad weather conditions; and the level of training of the military personnel left much to be desired. The NVA's clear conclusion was as follows: "Finally, we must conclude that the exercise has proved that a weak adversary with a sufficient number of nuclear weapons, but fewer troops, is not capable of repelling an attacker with fewer nuclear weapons but more troops."[8]

The report on SCHWARZER LÖWE, the NATO staff exercise held in March 1957, provides a further good example of how the NVA-Aufklärung during this period made relevant observations on the basis of incomplete information.[9] This exercise—the largest staff exercise to date and the first in which German divisional staffs took part—was under the command of the commander-in-chief of Allied Forces Central Europe (AFCENT), French general Jean-Etienne Valluy. The most important exercise objective was to test operational plans to deal with a surprise enemy attack from the east. The adversary was assumed to have a numerical superiority in infantry and armored units and to resort to the use of atomic weapons. According to the exercise scenario, NATO troops would succeed in repelling the attacking units and, in a counteroffensive launched four weeks after the enemy's attack, not only recapture the lost territory but also capture large sectors of the territory belonging to the Warsaw Pact's member states. The NVA analysts wrote that their report was based mainly on official statistics, the "known plans of the NATO," and poor signals intelligence.

Nevertheless, their report does contain a number of important observations, interpretations, and conclusions. For example, the extremely critical press reporting on the exercise in the West German media was noted. This would indicate something about the West German people's support for NATO and, possibly, about the morale of the West German troops. The newspapers close to the Sozialdemokratische Partei Deutschlands (SPD), then in opposition in the West German government, emphasized that the exercise had shown the defenselessness of the FRG. One newspaper reported that participating former Wehrmacht General Staff officers would have been deeply surprised by the "totally unrealistic optimism" that had been the basic assumption of the exercise. The troops had been able to move easily despite the unimaginable chaos that would have resulted from the bombardments with atomic bombs. The NVA report also mentioned an article in *Der Spiegel* magazine stating that during the exercise, a West German divisional commander had refused to request American nuclear support because, hypothetically speaking, it would have caused an enormous number of casualties among the West German population.

The NVA analysts came to the conclusion that the staff exercise was a test for NATO's real strategic and operational plans of the moment. As in the sword-and-shield concept, NATO would immediately reply to a surprise attack with the mass use of nuclear weapons. The exercise ostensibly was also a test of a forward defensive line along the Munich-Nuremberg-Kassel-Hannover-Hamburg line.[10] The NVA analysts further included a number of political interpretations in their report. According to them, the new "forward defense" concept would be used to bring pressure to bear on the FRG to field the agreed twelve divisions more rapidly. What they failed to report, however, was the fact that it was precisely the FRG that was behind the concept of moving the allied defensive line forward. According to the analysts, the exercise scenario of a deep incursion by the enemy into northern Germany was partly intended to influence Britain's government to abandon its projected reductions in troop numbers, at least until the West German divisions had been formed. Thus, the exercise was further intended to prove the necessity of equipping all NATO forces stationed in the FRG with nuclear weapons.

The NVA's final conclusion is noteworthy. First, they cited a quotation by General Nathan Twining, chief of staff of the U.S. Air Force, who purportedly said that if the United States was alerted on time and could bring its full force to bear against an attack, it could cause great damage to the Soviet Union and force it out of war. The NVA analysts then continued: "In our view, it can be concluded from this statement that the USA and NATO, within the framework of the sword-and-shield strategy and the so-called 'Forward-Defense' concept, also keep open under the cover of a 'preventive war' the possibility of delivering the first blow against the socialist camp."

Even though the sources were limited, by the end of 1957 NVA analysts were capable of making an accurate assessment of the objectives and the course of the large-scale autumn exercises in that year. As the main objectives, they recognized exercising leadership capabilities and the joint deployment of allied land, air, and sea forces in the European theater during the initial phases of a war, with the deployment of weapons of mass destruction by both sides.[11]

Tightening the Grip: 1958–1963

From 1958 onward, the NVA-Aufklärung began to increase considerably in size. This included an expanded number of *agenturische Mitarbeiter* (agent workers—persons recruited on foreign soil and working there for the Aufklärung) and so-called *Illegalen* (illegals—citizens of the GDR gathering intelligence abroad). More personnel were recruited who could speak one or more foreign languages. Signals intelligence capabilities also grew during those years.[12]

This development is understandable if we take the international political-military context into account. During this period the FRG actively began to strengthen the Western allied defense with major military units. In the eyes of the Communists of the Sozialistische Einheitspartei Deutschlands (SED, the ruling Communist Party of East Germany), this was the signal that fascists and militarists were again giving the orders on the other side. During that same year, 1958, the NATO defensive line moved farther forward toward the Weser and Fulda Rivers. The enemy was moving closer. Furthermore, NATO was determined to add tactical nuclear weapons on a large scale to its arsenal along the front line.[13] At the same time, disagreements arose within the Western alliance concerning the choice of either a rigid or a flexible strategy.[14] This development had not gone unnoticed by the politicians, military leaders, and analysts of the Warsaw Pact. Articles published in the East German magazine *Militärwesen* (Military Science) continuously drummed into its readers that NATO was in a political and military crisis.[15] This observation of on the one side the potentially threatening Western defensive build-up and on the other side the Western perception of its own weakness led the Soviet leadership to take a more assertive, often even a more aggressive military stance toward the West. This stance was the basis for the successes with the Sputnik earth satellite and intercontinental ballistic missiles. Within this framework the NVA was incorporated into the military structure of the Warsaw Pact, and the pact was transformed into a military alliance.[16]

Under these circumstances not only the size but also the importance of the NVA-Aufklärung increased. It became for the GRU the main source of military intelligence concerning the Western Theater of War.[17] The weight of the NVA-Aufklärung is also illustrated by the fact that from 1958 on, the political and military leadership in the GDR (the details for the Soviet Union are not available) linked East Germany's defense plans directly to its own observations of its adversary.[18]

The four general targets the NVA-Aufklärung focused on were as follows: (1) NATO as a military organization; (2) the armed forces of the FRG (the Bundeswehr); (3) the Western theatre, including the armed forces stationed and operating there; and (4) the armament of the NATO armed forces. There is, furthermore, a clear list of priorities discernable with regard to the armed forces that had the full attention of the Aufklärung.[19] First and foremost, they were interested in the developments surrounding the Bundeswehr. This was followed by the American forces on West German territory; the BAOR; and the French, Belgian, and Dutch forces stationed in the FRG. According to the Aufklärung's analysts, Bonn was trying to drag the United States and NATO into a nuclear war against the Soviet Union and its allies.[20] They found that NATO member states were pushing through the weapons program that had been set out in the Military Committee (MC) 70 document *The Minimum Essential Force Requirements, 1958–1963*.[21] Specific attention focused on the American nuclear weapons that had been allocated to the European allies' armed forces as part of the "preparations for aggressive action against the Socialist camp."[22]

During 1958–1963 the NVA-Aufklärung's intelligence position was not yet optimal. Various summaries and analyses were based on outdated information or had other shortcomings. For example, a 1960 summary of the locations of major NATO headquarters, command posts, communications centers, and national headquarters was partially based on observations made during the autumn maneuvers carried out three years previously. At that time, the exact locations of the Belgian and Dutch army corps headquarters were unknown.[23]

Another example of the initial inaccuracy of the intelligence gathered concerns the location of the first Dutch nuclear field artillery battalion equipped with the MGR-1 Honest John free-flight rocket. In August 1960 the NVA-Aufklärung pinpointed the battalion in the village of Elspeet, instead of in 't Harde, the actual location of the battalion.[24] A few years later the Aufklärung corrected that mistake.[25] As of 1962 East German intelligence officers were still basing a large part of their information for a report on the order of battle and missions of NATO air forces in Central Europe on a document originating in 1955.[26] Considering the rapid developments during this period, the information was outdated.[27] The intelligence collected for an adequate analysis of the NATO autumn maneuvers of 1962 and 1963 was also incomplete—but the analysts themselves did report that.[28]

An Excellent Intelligence Position: 1963–1968

From 1963 onward, the NVA-Aufklärung was in an excellent intelligence position. It was capable of following closely the planning, the exercises, and the armed forces build-up of NATO in the Central Sector. It obtained a more prominent position within the intelligence exchange network in the Warsaw Pact, which was slowly being established during those years. From 1964 on, the heads of the national military intelligence services met annually.[29] The NVA-Aufklärung even knew everything about the nuclear forces in the Central Sector. It had detailed information on the organization and the location of the units, the capabilities of the various weapon systems, and the storage locations of the nuclear warheads. There was, however, one very important area that remained unknown to the GDR intelligence services. That was the operational planning and the prewar targeting of the Western nuclear weapons. Until the end of the Cold War they were able to present only hypotheses on the subject, based on analyses of various exercise scenarios.[30] It cannot—as already mentioned—be precisely determined to what degree there was an exchange of information between the Stasi's Hauptverwaltung Aufklärung and the NVA-Aufklärung. Whatever may have been the case, the NVA-Aufklärung's reports and analyses were detailed and correct.

When studying the many remaining documents, one aspect becomes apparent immediately. In line with Communist thinking, the greatest interest by far was in identifying military indicators warning that the enemy was actually preparing for a war in the very short term and could possibly launch an attack. At the end of 1966 this focus was specified as follows in the Aufklärung's task description: "The main task consists of a timely and continuous surveillance and rapid and goal-specific collection of factual information concerning the plans and concrete measures of the representatives of West German militarism and NATO commands, with regard to the preparation and execution of a war of aggression against the GDR and the Warsaw Pact. The main objective is to provide an early warning signal in the event of a surprise attack."[31] This was completely consistent with the military-strategic principles formulated at the beginning of 1964 by Soviet marshal Vasily D. Sokolovsky, who emphasized the increased importance of the initial phase of a war as the determining factor for its outcome.[32]

The NVA-Aufklärung, therefore, endeavored to develop as exact a picture as possible of the available personnel and material resources, as well as the peacetime locations of those resources.[33] A great amount of energy was expended on breaking down NATO's phased and interconnected alert system into the smallest details, including the related alert systems in the separate member states. Each alert phase was accompanied by a large number of special indicators. The observation of a number of indicators connected to a certain phase would be a sign that preparations for war were being stepped up. For example, increased activity at enemy signals centers, restrictions on holiday and day leave, and the discharge of ambulatory patients from hospitals were clear signs that the "State of Military Vigilance" was in effect. Air defense artillery units taking up their prepared positions and military personnel being recalled from leave were indicators that NATO assessed the situation as being more serious and that "State Orange" was in effect. If military aircraft were being dispersed among airfields and noncombat units were being deployed over a wide area, then "State Red" was in effect and NATO assumed that war was an imminent possibility.[34]

During this period of rising tension, measures were taken to ensure that all NATO armed forces and economic and political bodies would adapt rapidly from a peacetime posture to a wartime posture, including the various protective measures. In principle, this process would take place in three phases: (1) Simple Alert; (2) Reinforced Alert; and (3) General Alert. Each phase was accompanied by a series of measures that would be clearly discernable to the NVA-Aufklärung. During the course of the 1960s, the service developed an ever clearer picture of which units would be alerted and where their concentration areas would be on the basis of analyses of many alert exercises.[35] The NVA analysts endeavored to extend their thinking and visualize the possible actions that NATO troops would carry out during the initial phase of a war.[36]

The NVA-Aufklärung could draw from a small number of rich sources of information in order to follow developments as closely as possible and maintain an up-to-date picture of its adversary. The two most important were the many large and small military exercises conducted each year by NATO, and from 1962 on, the large amount of information about the biennial, highly classified FALLEX NATO command post exercise—the predecessor of the later WINTEX exercises. The latter provided the military-strategic big picture, while the various exercises gave more-detailed operational information. The intelligence officers sought contact with persons able to provide them with information. These *agenturische Mitarbeiter* could be persons working on military staffs who could gather relatively simple material during the preparation phase for an exercise. Military personnel participating in the exercise were obviously suitable, as were military personnel acting as evaluators during the exercise. Drivers of high-ranking military officers and other support personnel could also become valuable informants. Journalists reporting on the exercises were in a separate category. By seeking close relations with commanding officers, they could obtain the answers to detailed questions. Finally, there was the category of *Beobachter* (observers), outsiders who were to keep certain important locations such as air fields, entrances to barracks, and supply depots under surveillance. The most difficult assignment for all of these operatives was obtaining any information concerning the deployment and effects of nuclear weapons.[37]

The biennial FALLEX exercises were the richest seams of information for the NVA analysts.[38] During these exercises, senior NATO officials studied the possible scenarios that could arise during the course of a possible war. In addition to military personnel, ministers and other civilian officials often also took part in the exercises. The exercises provided the NVA-Aufklärung with a great deal of insight into the NATO perception of the balance of power between the two power blocs, as well as into the considerations for the use of nuclear weapons and anticipated casualties and damage on both sides. Thus, access to such highly classified information meant that NATO held almost no secrets from the enemy. With the exception of nuclear targeting information, the alliance was an open book.

NATO Attacks First

This again raises the issue of the distorted representation of the anticipated NATO actions. The NVA-Aufklärung was very well informed on the capabilities and the intentions of NATO. In general, all reports provided a correct picture of the plans. NATO would repel a Warsaw Pact attack by following a clear operational doctrine and subsequently would launch a counteroffensive.

Purely defensive intentions included a number of offensive elements, such as in-depth bombing of enemy nuclear missile positions and communications junctions, as well as launching a counterattack. These observations were not, however, consistent with the politically correct assumption that NATO was preparing to attack the Warsaw Pact, probably by a surprise offensive. This inconsistency could lead to unusual lines of reasoning, such as "the NATO leadership bases its strategic exercises concerning defensive operations at the beginning of a war on the grounds of transparent political propaganda."[39]

Sometimes a further step was taken. A good example of this is the three-hour lecture held in December 1965 on the displacement, mobilization measures, possible starting points, and potential actions of NATO forces in Central Europe.[40] The audience probably consisted of high-ranking military officers and party officials.[41] "The nature of the strategy of imperialism," the speaker following the Soviet minister of defense announced, was "the preparation for the preventive war, for the surprise nuclear attack."[42] The beginning of such an attack would immediately take on a global character, with strategic forces and combined and joint operations, as they are currently called, in various theaters of war. The speaker subsequently gave a summary of all resources available to NATO for a nuclear attack in Central Europe. It is striking to note the importance he attached to atomic demolition munitions (ADM). According to him, "the construction of nuclear blockade belts" was one of the most important actions in the event of a nuclear attack.[43]

NATO, according to the NVA speaker, was counting on a force ratio to its advantage of from 1.3:1 to 2.3:1 for operations, which was completely contradictory to NATO's own estimates. The NVA estimated the ratios to be 1.8:1 in the NORTHAG area of operations; 1.5:1 in the Central Army Group (CENTAG) area; and 2:1 in Jutland, the area of an advance. According to the speaker, NATO estimated the ratio for the number of divisions in Central Europe to be 1.7:1 to its own advantage. NATO would thereby depend on its clear superiority in the area of nuclear weapons of all types—an analysis that the speaker disputed. Furthermore, the NATO allies purportedly estimated the combat power of some of its available divisions, especially those of the United States, to be twice as strong as the Warsaw Pact's divisions. Taking all of these factors into account, the NATO leadership considered offensive operations in the important directions of the theater of war to be feasible, at least at the beginning of the war. The speaker further reasoned that the objective of the offensive operations could be considered as the complete destruction of the first strategic echelon of the Warsaw Pact's forces, including the simultaneous in-depth destruction of the supporting reserve forces. The

NORTHAG units would probably attack in two main, parallel, directions, with the objective of defeating the enemy units of the first echelon, forcing their way over the Elbe, moving on to Szczezin and Eisenhüttenstadt, and subsequently developing operations on Polish territory. The commander of CENTAG could possibly receive a similar mission, such as rapidly penetrating the territories of the GDR and Czechoslovakia and continuing the attack into Poland. The speaker provided a breakdown of these possible operations down to the level of the various army corps.

While the main part of this lecture was based on the dogma that NATO would attack first, the final part included an explanation of the expected NATO defensive actions and the opposition that Warsaw Pact forces could expect in the first days of its own offensive operations. This part of the lecture was realistic and largely in accordance with official NATO plans. The entire lecture was a mixture of prejudice, perceptions, and consciously created images of the enemy. It contained the ingredients for the rationalization of the Warsaw Pact plans for preventive offensive operations that were drawn up at the beginning of the 1960s.[44] As early as 1959, Marshal Ivan S. Konev, the first commander of the Unified Warsaw Pact Forces, defended this change of course with the following, somewhat distorted, line of reasoning: as NATO based its exercises on the incorrect assumption that the Warsaw Pact had plans to attack, the Warsaw Pact itself had to conduct its exercises based on the assumption that NATO would attack.[45]

Flexible Response

The Cold War of spying and being spied on, of (self) imagery and assumptions, became no less nebulous during the 1960s. This made the NVA-Aufklärung's analyses more and more interesting. The strategy of Flexible Response in particular created much confusion and uncertainty on both sides. In the autumn of 1963 the NVA analysts had already noticed that NATO, in contrast to previous years, no longer based its exercises on the premise that both camps would use nuclear weapons from the first day of hostilities. The change of strategy was interpreted as a sign of the weakness of the West, and especially the United States, as the United States had become vulnerable to the Soviet Union's intercontinental ballistic missiles. The Aufklärung's analysts took the view that NATO initially intended to limit a war to within Germany or Europe, and preferably to the lowest level of force possible. In the meantime, additional American units would be flown in (as was being practiced in the exercise designated BIG LIFT) and NATO would then from an improved position resort to the use of nuclear weapons.[46] This line of reasoning soon appeared in specialist military journals, which gave maximum exposure to the fact that the change of strategy initiated by the United States had been met by major political and military objections in the FRG and France.[47]

As the 1960s progressed, the NVA analysts adopted a sharper tone. They constantly criticized the Flexible Response doctrine. According to them, the weak point of this strategy lay in the fact that the adversary had to be prepared to "keep to the rules" and not, for example, make immediate use of nuclear weapons. They regarded the new strategy as a cunning plan by the imperialists to divert attention from their own weaknesses and make a virtue of necessity. Their conclusion was that NATO was becoming not stronger, but more aggressive. In the NVA analysts' opinion, the increase in the number of American nuclear weapons indicated only one thing: NATO and the United States were still preparing for a total nuclear war. All preceding phases (the analysts distinguished between a period of political tension; a "hidden" psychological war aimed at eroding the willpower of the enemy; and a limited war, initially excluding but subsequently including the use of tactical nuclear weapons) were intended for gaining time and reinforcing positions. In this way NATO could capture an important area to use for trade-off during later negotiations. NATO command, however, realized that in the event of war it would quickly have to use tactical nuclear weapons, and that a total nuclear war was ultimately inevitable.[48]

The situation was dangerous and demanded the utmost effort from the NVA-Aufklärung. It observed how NATO forces were reorganized into smaller, more mobile and independent units, which conducted small- and large-scale exercises in the FRG. The Aufklärung had to be extremely alert, because exercises as part of Flexible Response could transmute into an actual attack more unexpectedly and rapidly than previously had been the case. As the eyes and ears of the NVA and the Warsaw Pact, the NVA-Aufklärung had to recognize the enemy's intentions as early as possible in order to facilitate an offensive counteraction as described by the minister for national defense, Heinz Hoffmann: "With the assistance of the Unified Armed Forces, which have been trained and equipped for special rapid and deep initial operations, push through along the entire length of West Germany, which is NATO's main link in Europe, and, by restricting the choices available to the political and military leadership for deploying nuclear weapons, prevent a decision by NATO to start a general nuclear war."[49] The enemy could, at any moment, resort to the use of nuclear weapons. "For that reason, most attention must be paid, both in peacetime and wartime, to gathering intelligence regarding nuclear weapons and their logistics bases."[50]

After the Arab-Israeli Six-Day War of June 1967, and especially after the Warsaw Pact's invasion of Czechoslovakia in August 1968, the tone of the GDR's politicians and military analysts hardened. Forward Defense, it was reasoned, again made *Blitzkrieg* a real possibility. The rapid advance of Israeli forces showed how it could be done successfully. The Israelis had executed lightning-fast actions with their Western weapon systems and created faits accomplis.[51] The implicit line of reasoning was that this was an indication of how NATO might operate in Europe.[52] The NVA analysts aimed their arrows especially at the FRG, which they consistently called West Germany, claiming that it pursued a policy of "revenge," as part of the "global strategy of U.S. imperialism." What Germany was also aiming for was the "restoration of the imperialist Greater German predator state." Allegedly, Bonn and Washington consciously were creating periods of tension. The developments in Czechoslovakia leading up to August 1968 were the clearest evidence. West German *Ostpolitik* was also branded a "counterrevolutionary, subversive activity."[53]

However much importance was attached to intelligence work, the only inescapable and somber conclusion that could be reached after the invasion in Czechoslovakia and the FALLEX '68 NATO command post exercise was that the NVA-Aufklärung had failed badly. Much of the information had been reported belatedly and had therefore lost its value. Information that was received on time was often too general and incomplete, and only a small number of objectives had been observed systematically on a day-by-day basis by *Beobachter*. The Aufklärung had failed at the moment it really mattered. It had not been capable of providing a "real time" picture of the developments.[54]

Regarding the Imperialistic Enemy of the Classes without Illusions

The Cold War—or rather, the military preparations for a potential real war—continued relentlessly. The Berlin crisis and the building of the Berlin Wall had clearly established the borderline of the spheres of influence in Europe for many years to come. The Cuban missile crisis had shown the world the limits to the possibilities of a direct military confrontation between the two superpowers. But there was no noticeable relaxation at the NVA-Aufklärung. The new, more complex and ambiguous NATO strategy even seemed to reinforce suspicion. This course of developments had the net result that both camps continued to build up enormous armed forces equipped with state-of-the-art weapons along the Iron Curtain. The Aufklärung's personnel had to continue their work with redoubled vigor, because, as one staff member put it: "As socialist military servicemen, we have the duty, as our class consciousness compels us, to regard our imperialistic enemy of the classes without illusions and to watchfully distinguish between words and actions."[55]

Notes

1. "Unsere Militärpolitik als Ganzes muß . . . von der reale Beurteilung des Gegners ausgehen." Quoted in Bodo Wegmann, *Die Militäraufklärung der NVA: Die zentrale Organisation der militärischen Aufklärung der Streitkräfte der Deutschen Demokratischen Republik,* 2nd rev. ed., Beiträge zur Friedensforschung und Sicherheitspolitik, vol. 22 (Berlin, 2006), 21.

2. The most recent and extensive study on the NVA-Aufklärung is in Wegmann, *Militäraufklärung.* This is mainly a history of the organization. For a summary of the historical research, see also Helmut Müller-Enbergs, "Forschungen zur DDR-Spionage in der Bundesrepublik Deutschland: Stand und Perspektiven," *Horch und Gluck* 39 (2002): 38–46. Much information is to be found in Walter Richter, *Der Militärische Nachrichtendienst der Nationalen Volksarmee der DDR und seine Kontrolle durch das Ministerium für Staatssicherheit: Die Geschichte eines deutschen Geheimdienstes,* 2nd rev. ed., Europäische Hochschulschriften, ser. 31 Politikwissenschaft, vol. 439 (Frankfurt am Main, 2004), and also in Georg Herbstritt and Helmut Müller-Enbergs, *Das Gesicht dem Westen zu: DDR-Spionage gegen die Bundesrepublik Deutschland* (Bremen, 2003). See also Andreas Kabus, *Auftrag Windrose: Der militärische Geheimdienst der DDR* (Berlin, 1993), and Helmut Göpel, "Aufklärung," in *NVA: Anspruch und Wirklichkeit,* ed. Klaus Naumann (Berlin, 1993), 221–39.

3. For information on the relations between the Stasi and the NVA-Aufklärung, see Bernd Schaefer, "The Warsaw Pact's Intelligence on NATO: East German Military Espionage against the West," International Relations and Security Network (ISN), http://www.isn.ethz.ch/; Wegmann, *Militäraufklärung,* 532–74; and Richter, *Militärische Nachrichtendienst.* Also informative (among others) is Heinz Busch, "Die Militärspionage der DDR-Staatssicherheit," *Europäische Sicherheit* (1993): 617–21.

4. The archive of the Verwaltung Aufklärung is located at the Bundesarchiv-Militärarchiv (BA-MA) in Freiburg im Breisgau and is easily accessible. It is not known which parts of the archive were destroyed.

5. For this subject, see Horst-Henning Basler, "Operatives Denken und Plannen in der NVA," in *Ein Staat—Eine Armee: Von der NVA zur Bundeswehr,* ed. Dieter Farwick (Frankfurt am Main, 1992), 58–60; Göpel, "Aufklärung," 237; and Torsten Diedrich's chapter in this volume.

6. For the Communist side, it definitely was not the case. See Matthias Uhl and Armin Wagner, "Pullachs Aufklärung gegen sowjetisches Militär in der DDR: Um-

fang, Potential und Grenzen der *order-of-battle-intelligence* von Organisation Gehlen und Bundesnachrichtendienst," *Deutschland Archiv* 40 (2007): 49–67.

7. BA-MA, Bestand DVW 1 (Nationale Volksarmee, Ministerium für Nationale Verteidigung, Verwaltung Aufklärung), 25805, "Laufende Kriegsvorbereitungen in Westdeutschland im Dezember 1953." From the outset, the political and military leadership in the GDR endeavored to follow military exercises in Western Europe as closely as possible. BA-MA, Bestand DVH 3 (Kasernierte Volkspolizei/Stab), 2050, Nationaler Verteidigungsrat, Minutes 14 Oct. 1952. The NATO exercise HOLD FAST and various exercises in Scandinavia are mentioned here, as well as the use of Patton and Centurion tanks.

8. BA-MA, DVW 1, 25809/d, "Bericht über das NATO-Manöver 'Battle Royal.'"

9. BA-MA, DVW 1, 25768/g, "Bericht über die NATO-Stabsübung 'Schwarzer Löwe.'"

10. See Bruno Thoss's chapter in this volume.

11. BA-MA, DVW 1, 25804, "Die NATO-Herbstmanöver 1957."

12. Wegmann, *Militäraufklärung,* 201, 221, and 439 (in 1960 a personnel member was appointed who spoke fluent Dutch); Richter, *Militärische Nachrichtendienst,* 221.

13. See Bruno Thoss's chapter in this volume.

14. See Lawrence Kaplan's chapter in this volume.

15. See, among other things, "Zur politischen und militärischen Krise der NATO," *Militärwesen: Zeitschrift für Militärpolitik und Militärtheorie* 2 (1958): 280–99.

16. Vojtech Mastny and Malcolm Byrne (eds.), *A Cardboard Castle? An Inside History of the Warsaw Pact, 1955–1991* (Budapest, 2005), 12–15.

17. Wegmann, *Militäraufklärung,* 435–36.

18. Ibid.

19. See, for example, BA-MA, DVW 1, "Bericht über die Mobilisierungs- und Entfaltungsmöglichkeiten der vereinigten Landstreitkräfte der NATO auf dem zentraleuropäischen Kriegsschauplatz" (as per 1 Apr. 1958).

20. BA-MA, DVW 1, 25859/e, "Einschätzung der militärpolitischen militärischen Lage in Westdeutschland am Ende des 1. Halbjahres 1961," 1 July 1961.

21. BA-MA, DVW 1, 25826/c, "Information über die Kampfausbildung der Vereinigten Land- und Luftstreitkräfte der NATO auf dem Zentraleuropäischen Kriegsschauplatz im Jahre 1961" (as per 15 Nov. 1961), and 25815/c, "Information über den Kräftezuwachs der NATO-Land- und Luftstreitkräfte in Zentraleuropa bis zum Jahre 1963" (as per 15 Feb. 1962).

22. BA-MA, DVW 1, 25826/b, "Information über die Verstärkung der vereinigten NATO-Streitkräfte in Europa mit Massenvernichtungsmitteln" (as per 1 Aug. 1961). For further reading, see, for example, BA-MA, DVW 1, 25785/5, "Bericht über die Reorganisation des I. belgischen und I. niederländischen Armeekorps und die Pläne zur Ausrüstung mit Raketen und Kernwaffen" (as per 1 July 1961).

23. DWV 1, 25823/I, 30 July 1960.

24. BA-MA, DVW 1, 25821/g, "Information über die Organisation, den Person-

al- und Kampfbestand, Bewaffnung und Ausrüstung sowie den Stand der Kampfvorbereitung der niederländischen Land- und Luftstreitkräfte" (as per 15 Aug. 1960). For nuclear artillery in the Netherlands, see Jan Hoffenaar, Joep van Hoof, and Jaap de Moor, *Vuur in beweging: 325 jaar veldartillerie 1677–2002* (Amsterdam, 2002), 153–62.

25. BA-MA, DVW 1, 25781/h, "Aufstellung über die Gruppierung und Dislozierung der NATO-Streitkräfte des NATO-Kommandos Zentraleuropa" (as per 15 Jan. 1963).

26. DVW 1, 25815/l.

27. For the establishment of an integrated NATO air defense, see Dieter Krüger, "Die Entstehung der NATO-Luftverteidigung und die Integration der Luftwaffe," in *Die Luftwaffe 1950 bis 1970: Konzeption, Aufbau, Integration,* Bernd Lemke, Dieter Krüger, Heinz Rebhan, and Wolfgang Schmidt (Munich, 2006), 485–556.

28. DVW 1, 25776/d and 25768/f.

29. Wegmann, *Militäraufklärung,* 505.

30. Busch, "Militärspionage," 620.

31. BA-MA, DVW 1, 25764/c, "Aufklärungsaufgaben über die Streitkräfte Westdeutschlands und die in Westdeutschland dislozierten NATO- und französischen Streitkräfte für die Jahre 1967–1969," 10 Dec. 1966.

32. See Viktor Gavrilov's chapter in this volume.

33. See, for example, BA-MA, DVW 1, 25781/h, "Aufstellung über die Gruppierung und Dislozierung der NATO-Streitkräfte des NATO-Kommandos Zentraleuropa" (as per 15 Jan. 1963); 32660/a, "Einige Angaben über den politisch-moralischen Zustand der Bundeswehr und der in Westdeutschland stationierten ausländischen NATO-Streitkräfte"; 25784/d, "Bericht über die Kampfbereitschaft, den Ausbildingsstand und die Dislozierung der Kernwaffeneinheiten der NATO-Land- und Luftstreitkräfte in Westdeutschland" (as per 1 July 1964), and a speech on the subject: "Der Stand und die Perspektiven der Ausrüstung Westdeutschlands und des operativen Ausbaus des westeuropäischen Territoriums als Aufmarschbasis der NATO-Streitkräfte für einen neuen Weltkrieg."

34. BA-MA, DVW 1, 25781/e, "Information über das NATO-Alarmsystem und über Anzeichen, die auf eine Erhöhung der Kriegsgefahr und auf unmittelbar bevorstehende militärische Aggressionshandlungen hindeuten," 2 Jan. 1962; 25783/f, "Bericht zu einigen Fragen des Alarmsystems und der Alarmkonzentrierungsräume der NATO-Landstreitkräfte in Westdeutschland" (as per 1 Oct. 1963); and 25780, "Bericht über das NATO-Alarmsystem und die mögliche Lage der Auflockerungs- und Alarmkonzentrierungsräume der NATO-Landstreitkräfte Zentraleuropa und des NATO-Kommandos Ostseeausgänge" (as per Sept. 1965).

35. Dutch units first had to go to assembling (concentration) areas in the eastern parts of the Netherlands, and then from there to their deployment areas in the GDR. See annotation n.34.

36. See, for example, BA-MA, DVW 1, 25816/n, "Information über den mögli-

chen Einsatz der westdeutschen Streitkräfte im Rahmen der operativen NATO-Gruppierung in der Anfangsperiode eines Krieges auf dem zentraleuropäischen Kriegsschauplatz" (as per 1 Sept. 1962); 94294, "Bericht über den möglichen Einsatz der NATO-Seestreitkräfte in der Anfangsperiode eines Krieges" (as per 1 Sept. 1963); and 32659/j, *Lektion,* "Die Dislozierung, Mobilmachungsmöglichkeiten, mögliche Ausgangsgruppierung und warscheinliche Handlungen der NATO-Streitkräfte auf dem Zentraleuropäischen Kriegsschauplatz der NATO und im Bereich des NATO-Kommandos Ostseeausgänge in der Anfangsperiode eines Krieges" (as per Sept. 1965).

37. BA-MA, DVW 1, 32658, *Lektion,* "Die Aufklärung von Manövern und Übungen der NATO-Streitkräfte Zentraleuropa und Ostseeaugänge durch den militärischen Aufklärungsdienst der DDR."

38. BA-MA, DVW 1, 25776/d, "Kurze Einschätzung der Anlage, der Thematik, der Ziele und der Ergebnisse der NATO-Herbstübungen 'FALLEX 62'" (as per 20 Dec. 1962); 25798, "Bericht über die NATO-Kommando-Stabsübung 'FALLEX 64'"; and 25739/a, "Bericht über die NATO-Kommando-Stabsübung 'FALLEX 66.'"

39. DVW 1, 25768/f.

40. BA-MA, DVW 1, 32659/j, *Lektion,* "Die Dislozierung."

41. Almost all lectures were attended or at least the lecture notes were read by members of the political and military elite, as appears from name listings present in the archives.

42. "Das Wesen der Strategie des Imperialismus [ist] die Vorbereitung zum Präventivkrieg, zum überraschenden Kernwaffenüberfall."

43. Literally, "die Schaffung atomarer Sperrgürtel."

44. See Torsten Diedrich's chapter in this volume.

45. Analysis by Marshal Ivan Konev of a Czechoslovakian army exercise held early April 1959. Included as document no. 9 in Mastny and Byrne, *A Cardboard Castle?,* 97–99.

46. DVW 1, 25768/f.

47. See, for example, J. Kleine, "Die imperialistische Theorie des 'begrenzten Krieges,'" *Militärwesen* 7 (1963): 671–82, and "Die Unhaltbarkeit imperialistischer Spekulationen auf Begrenzung eines Krieges in Deutschlands," *Militärwesen* 7 (1963): 859–70.

48. BA-MA, DVW 1, 32659/j, *Lektion,* "Die Dislozierung." BA-MA, DVW 1, 32658/q, "Einsatzgrundsätze und Einsatzmöglichkeiten von Kernmitteln und Kernwaffeneinsatzmitteln der NATO-Streitkräfte" (speech, 22 Apr. 1967). W. Lehmann, "Was heißt 'Eskalation'?," *Militärwesen* 10 (1966): 415–16, and "Zur Theorie und Praxis der imperialistischen 'Eskalation,'" *Militärwesen* 10 (1966): 801–11, 933–42, and 1079–88.

49. BA-MA, DVW 1, 25715, "Die wichtigsten Ziele der operativ-strategischen NATO-Kommandostabsübung 'Fallex 68,' der gegenwärtige Stand der Aggressionsvorbereitungen Westdeutschlands und Schlußfolgerungen, die sich für das System

der Landesverteidigung der DDR ergeben" (speech by the minister for national defense for the National Defense Council of the GDR; as per 15 Nov. 1968).

50. "Darum ist im Frieden wie im Krieg die Hauptaufmerksamkeit auf die Aufklärung der Kernwaffeneinsatzmittel und ihren Versorgungsbasen zu richten." BA-MA, DVW 1, 32658/q, "Einsatzgrundsätze."

51. BA-MA, DVW 1, 25715, "Referat des Chefs der Verwaltung Aufklärung zur Einweisung der operativen und Informationsoffiziere in die Aufgaben zur Aufklärung der NATO-Übung 'Fallex 68,'" and "Beitrag der Verwaltung Aufklärung zu den Ausführungen des Genossen Walter Ulbrichts auf der Beratung des politisch-beratenden Ausschusses der Warschauer Vertragsstaaten" (25 Nov. 1968).

52. See also Mastny and Byrne, *A Cardboard Castle?*, 33.

53. BA-MA, DVW 1, 25715, "Referat des Chefs." BA-MA, DVW 1, 25741/f, "Entwurf einer Analyse über die Rolle und Bedeutung der Spannungsperiode in de NATO-Strategie" (as per Aug. 1967); 25798/a, "Sonderinformation Nr. 1 über die operativ-strategische NATO-Kommandostabsübung 'Fallex 68'" (18 Sept. 1968); 25753/b, "Der Stand und die Perspektiven der Aufrüstung Westdeutschlands und des operativen Ausbaus des westeuropäischen Territoriums als Aufmarschbasis der NATO-Streitkräfte für einen neuen Weltkrieg" (speech, 27 Sept. 1968), "Die sogenannte neue Ostpolitik Bonns und die Konzeption zur weiteren Entwicklung der Bundeswehr—Ausdruck der revanchistischen pläne des westdeutschen Imperialismus zur Überwindung des Status quo in Europa" (speech, 15 Oct. 1968), "Die hauptsächlichsten Aufklärungsmerkmale, die die Herstellung der erhöhten und vollen Gefechtsbereitschaft der NATO-Streitkräfte in Westdeutschland—besondere der Bundeswehr—und die Überführung Westdeutschlands vom Friedens- in den Kriegszustand charakterisieren" (speech, 29 Nov. 1968), and "Einige wichtige Folgerungen aus der Truppenübung 'Schwarzer Löwe' des II. Westdeutschen Armeekorps und der NATO-Kommandostabsübung 'Fallex 68'" (speech, 15 Feb. 1969); 25715, "Einschätzung der wichtigsten Ergebnisse der NATO-Übung 'Fallex 68'" (21 Feb. 1969); and 25729, "Bericht über die NATO-Übung 'Fallex 68'" (Apr. 1969). H. Hoffmann, "Die Brüsseler NATO-Tagung zur Strategie der 'flexibelen Reaktion,'" *Militärwesen* 12 (1966): 30–36.

54. BA-MA, DVW 1, 25715, "Kurze Einschätzung der operativen Meldungen (Objektbeobachtung), die in der Zeit der Ereignisse in der CSSR und bei 'Fallex 68' übermittelt wurden" (20 Jan. 1969).

55. BA-MA, DVW 1, 25710/a, speech by Lieutenant Colonel W. Wolf during an attaché meeting (probably held in 1970).

6

Waste and Confusion?

NATO Logistics from the Dutch Perspective

Herman Roozenbeek

Within NATO, logistics was and still is a national responsibility, which reflects practical, political, and economic considerations. Every country that provided troops to an operation was expected to provide the necessary logistic support as well. That included both the preparation in peacetime and the actual support of operations in wartime. Every country had to provide for proper equipment, adequate materiel, and the build-up of sufficient stock levels necessary to maintain the combat readiness of its forces. Effective and robust logistics organizations and procedures had to be established, and the logistics units in particular were to be skilled and trained to perform their assigned tasks, even under great pressure.

In addition to the principle of national responsibility, allied logistics had a second characteristic. The architects of the alliance were well aware that circumstances might arise in which a country—even if only locally and temporarily—could not meet its logistics obligations, which in turn would place the operational task itself at risk. Vital harbor installations or munitions depots, for instance, could be destroyed by conventional aerial bombardment or attack by nuclear weapons. A combat division might have to deploy for operational reasons far from its national supply lines. In such cases, the member states committed themselves to mutual support, through the provision of materiel or supplies, or by providing services, such as transportation.

Situations requiring mutual support arose primarily in crisis conditions. At such moments, simple procedures, short lines, and clear command structures were a matter of life and death. International consultations at high political or military levels were in no way an appropriate response. An additional complication was that mutual support was more difficult because every country had different equipment and its own logistics procedures. As early as 1950, NATO was aware that the principle of national responsibility hampered a common solution to logistical problems.

Identifying the logistics problem was easier than solving it, however. A Dutch memorandum in 1957 noted: "There is waste and confusion in NATO's present logistics supply system. The principal causes of this waste and confusion are lack of coordination and inadequate cooperation resulting from the fact that logistics are a purely national responsibility. The Netherlands government is convinced that, through effective logistical collaboration and with the resources available, the efficiency of our defense can be greatly increased." The Netherlands looked for a solution that leveraged "integrated lines of supply," "coordinated storage of ammunition and other supplies," "joint use of maintenance facilities for heavy equipment and electronics," and "a coordinated procurement system for spare parts." But what did all this mean precisely? As it turned out, the author of the memorandum had no clear idea how to achieve the goal, and he definitely could not foresee its implications. Most important, was the government of the Netherlands itself prepared to make the financial sacrifices that undoubtedly would be required to implement all of those measures? This question was never really put to the test. The Netherlands ultimately softened its memorandum by weakening the original concrete proposals, which were given a much less radical interpretation. "Integrated lines of supply" and "coordinated storage of ammunition and other supplies," for example, were said to mean nothing more than establishing storage sites on the territory of another member state.[1] Far-reaching logistics integration and standardization implied that countries would have to surrender some of their autonomy, even in peacetime, which could provoke far-reaching economic and financial consequences. In fact, most of the NATO countries were not prepared to go that far.

Establishing an integrated logistics system also would have taken a long time, and NATO felt already that its preparations were running behind those of the Soviet Union. The supreme allied commander, Europe (SACEUR), therefore, concluded in 1954: "The attainment of a completely integrated logistics support system within NATO, although militarily desirable, is from a practical point of view considered to be too remote in point of time to provide an acceptable solution to the immediate problem of overcoming present deficiencies."[2] No progress was made beyond striking a compromise between what was desirable from the perspective of military operations and what was feasible in political and economic terms.

It should come as no surprise that discussion concerning logistics integration primarily took place in the Central Sector, since that area of operations would be defended by a variety of forces from different member countries. Most of those forces, moreover, would also operate outside their own national borders, relying on lines of communications that extended over the territory of at least one other member state.

Supply Lines

At the beginning of 1950 American and British forces in Germany were organized as occupation troops. Based on that mission they used supply lines that ran north-south. Bremen was the import harbor for U.S. forces, and Hamburg for the British. Those supply lines were, however, not suitable for defense against an enemy advancing rapidly from the east. A west-east axis was essential. Even before the outbreak of the Korean War, the Americans began shifting their lines of communications to the southern French port at Bordeaux. At the same time, the British were preparing to have their supplies run through the northern French port at Le Havre or the Belgian port at Antwerp. Both the Americans and British had to build up stocks and establish logistics installations directly behind the Rhine—NATO's main line of defense—and in the more westerly support areas. France was already using west-east supply lines.[3]

Except for the lines of communications, logistics for the U.S., British, and French armed forces remained a national responsibility. This was different for the smaller allies, and Belgium and the Netherlands in particular. At the beginning of the 1950s their armed forces were still developing and they were dependent to a large extent on outside support for materiel and supplies. In wartime, the Benelux countries provided troops to NATO's Northern Army Group (NORTHAG), the greater part of which consisted of the British Army of the Rhine. It may have been natural to embed the logistics support for the Belgian and Dutch troops into the British army logistics system, but in keeping with NATO philosophy, both contingents relied on their own national channels. Without supplies from abroad, however, neither country would be able to sustain itself in combat for a long period of time. That the Belgian and Dutch armed forces, which had originally been organized and equipped by the United Kingdom, were increasingly furnished with U.S. materiel under the Mutual Defense Assistance Program rendered their situation even more complex.

Inasmuch as the Americans and the British could not be expected to deliver spare parts and stocks directly in Belgium or the Netherlands during wartime, the Benelux countries themselves had to pick up the goods that were destined for them in the U.S. and British base areas in France. The supply routes the two countries had to establish crossed the American and British lines of communications. The Benelux forces would have competed, too, with their American, British, and French allies for access to the scarce transport capacity on the continent. According to the guidelines developed since 1950, both the supplier nation and the host nation were required to provide support "as far as possible." The Netherlands was particularly doubtful whether this requirement could have been met. The supply lines over land were long and vulnerable and consumed a great deal of the available transport capacity. In addition, it was not entirely certain that the allies would lend the promised helping hand in times of crisis. "That means," according to a staff officer in The Hague, "that one is entirely dependent on the goodwill of others. At critical moments, however, one tends to think of one's self and that's the end of all the good intentions!"[4] Confidence in mutual logistic support grew but slowly as the years passed.

The recalcitrant attitude of the Netherlands on this point had everything to do with the fear that it would not be possible to long defend a "firm base Holland" protected by water lines, without assured supplies from overseas. The chief of the naval staff, Vice Admiral E. J. Jonkheer Van Holthe, believed that "logistic resupply of the Armed Forces of the Netherlands would come too little, too late, if it would have to be done over the proposed lines of communications by land." "It will, therefore, be doubtful," he continued, "whether the Arnhem North front can be held, and as a result, the consequence of accepting such a solution will be that, with this decision, the evacuation of the Netherlands above the big rivers is being sanctioned, or at least made necessary."[5] It was unacceptable for the Netherlands to give up such a large and vital part of its national territory. The country, therefore, worked on incorporating the harbors of Antwerp and especially Rotterdam, the two largest harbors in Europe, in the alliance defense plans. Minister of War Cornelis Staf formulated the matter concisely: "Without Rotterdam, the IJssel front will be left swinging in the wind."[6] The status of a military supply harbor made it possible to use it as a civilian harbor, too.

In the 1950s, however, the allied plans assumed that the harbor facilities of both cities would be completely destroyed early in any conflict, possibly by nuclear weapons. The Netherlands did everything to compensate for the potential loss of Rotterdam by preparing emergency harbors and anchorages in the Scheldt River and the Wadden Sea that would provide protective anchorage for seagoing ships. Barges would transfer cargoes to the many smaller harbors in the area or to improvised unloading sites. From there, further transport would be carried out via inland waterways, railways, and road. The emergency sites would be manned by harbor workers transferred from Rotterdam and Amsterdam. On paper, there was sufficient capacity to compensate for the loss of the Rotterdam and Amsterdam harbors, and the dispersal of the anchorages over a wide area theoretically would reduce the risk from enemy nuclear weapons.[7] To the south of Rotterdam, near Rockanje, enormous underground fuel storage tanks would be built to contain enough fuel to supply the military and civilian needs of the Netherlands in wartime for thirty days. That plan proved to be a bridge too far, however, partly because of a lack of interest from the civilian side.[8]

Stock Levels

The question of the supply lines was not the only problem that gave the NATO planners headaches. During the early 1950s the alliance was preparing for a long war with heavy losses, including serious damage to infrastructure, materiel, and stocks. The conversion to a wartime economy and the establishment of overseas supply lines would take a long time. Such assessments became increasingly pessimistic with the increase in the number of atomic weapons expected to be deployed during the initial phase of the conflict. To ensure survival until supply from overseas could be established and was operational, Supreme Headquarters Allied Powers Europe (SHAPE) directed all NATO member countries to build up a transitional reserve of spare parts and stocks to cover war requirements for a period of sixty days. That was in addition to the regular working stocks that were based on thirty days' wartime consumption. Establishing and maintaining sufficient wartime stocks for ninety days was difficult for many NATO countries to achieve, both financially and economically. The Netherlands concentrated initially on the thirty-day supply. There was little that SHAPE could do about it. Many countries fell even more seriously short in the stocks build-up, especially in ammunition.[9]

NATO chose a different strategy for dealing with fuel supplies. World War II had demonstrated that fuel supplies were crucial in modern warfare. Since then, the thirst for fuel had increased. Building large storage facilities—such as those intended in the Dutch Rockanje Plan noted previously—would not be sufficient. In contrast with ammunition, fuels are not suitable for long-term storage. Furthermore, a large shortfall in transport capacity was expected during wartime, and the means of transportation with the greatest capacity, via water and rail, were also the most vulnerable. The air forces, which played a leading role in the NATO strategy, faced the most urgent problems. Air force squadrons from different countries, all of which required previously unheard-of quantities of jet fuel to execute their assigned tasks, were stationed at countless air bases on the European continent. Whereas the land forces could still draw on large civilian fuel supplies in the initial phase of a war, that was not the case for jet fuel. Enormous military stocks of jet fuel had to be established together with associated installations, while the transportation problem also had to be addressed. To cope with that challenge, NATO decided at the end of 1952 to construct underground pipeline systems that linked the supply harbors with the air bases. The pipelines were financed by the so-called Common Infrastructure Program. A year later the alliance decided to use those systems to supply gasoline for the land forces as well, and they were expanded to handle the additional demand.[10]

The Central European Pipeline System (CEPS), which in 1961 consisted of eight thousand kilometers of pipes and thirty-one fuel depots in France, Belgium, the Netherlands, and Germany, was far and away the most extensive system. A complicated structure in which international and national levels could be distinguished was developed to administer that system. The infrastructure itself was common, but that did not apply to the stocks stored within it. In principle, every country could use only the stocks that it had contributed itself. After all, the pipeline system itself had to fit into the general philosophy of NATO, which was based on the principle that each country should be responsible as much as possible for its own logistics.

Although the standards imposed by SHAPE in the 1960s continued to be based on supply levels sufficient for ninety combat days, the stocks needed to meet that requirement in absolute terms had grown explosively since the 1950s. Not only had the NATO armed forces grown significantly larger in the intervening years, they often had more and more modern equipment. In wartime, that would lead to substantially higher rates of consumption of spare parts, fuel, and especially ammunition. In 1955 the standard day of supply for the Dutch I Army Corps was 900 tons of ammunition. Ten years later that had increased to 1,500 tons. In addition, SHAPE in 1964 introduced a new method of determining the required stock levels. According to the new calculations, at least twice as much ammunition would be fired off in the first thirty days of a conflict. Thereafter, the expenditure rate would be lower because the armed forces on both sides were expected to have been thinned out considerably by then. The introduction of the attrition rates was bad news for those countries, such as the Netherlands, that had built up their stock levels based only on the first thirty days. They had to make major expenditures to bring their stocks in line with the new consumption rate standards.

It was not sufficient, however, that the NATO member states simply increased their war stocks. The logistics units equally had to improve their capability to handle this increased load under the conditions of mobile and flexible modern warfare. In 1964 a representative of the commander, Land Forces Central Europe (COMLANDCENT), at the Allied Command Europe (ACE) Logistics Conference noted that the possibilities and the capabilities of the logistics units of NATO had remained at more or less the same levels since World War II, while the combat units had been modernized substantially over the same period.[11] There also were significant differences among the NATO countries in this area. American forces in particular had taken a lead. During the 1960s the implementations of such methods as bulk supply and mechanical transshipment increased within NATO, but it would take many years before the logistics area had caught up with progress in other areas of the armed forces.

An Operative Logistics System

The usually inadequate supply levels, the vulnerability of supply lines over sea and land, and the expectation that substantial stocks would be lost to nuclear attacks and conventional bombardment all contributed to the concerns of NATO commanders at all levels about the logistical support for their operations. The principle of national responsibility further limited their control over logistics. In 1952, for example, SACEUR noted that although he was permitted to draw up guidelines for national logistics support, he had virtually nothing to say about the implementation of that support, during neither peacetime nor wartime. Although the NATO member states shared his concern and agreed at the summit in Lisbon at the end of that year to take steps to create an "operative logistics system" that would override the shortcomings by pragmatic solutions, the member states were still not prepared to go along completely.[12] The principle of national responsibility had to be maintained, especially during peacetime, but SACEUR was not given a free hand in wartime either. As a general guideline the NATO commanders were allowed to intervene in logistics matters only if there were an "emergency in war," and even then the preferred course of action if at all possible was to get the approval of the national authorities concerned. Within the confines of those parameters, the NATO commanders had authority over the logistics support for their operations and they had the logistics resources—units and stocks—of the different contingents under their command. They could restrict the use of so-called critical items, and in emergencies, start rationing and redistributing stocks.

The practical implementation of those general principles was not an easy matter, as COMLANDCENT discovered in 1955 when he attempted to formalize procedures for mutual support. A couple of countries had the agreed amounts of stocks for ninety days; others could not even provide for more than eight to fifteen days, especially ammunition. LANDCENT noted that the countries whose stocks were as they should be feared that "any accord on their part to measures for mutual support may cause those nations with low stock-levels to tend to slacken their efforts to correct such a dangerous situation in the expectation that their deficiencies will be made good in war through mutual support."[13] That mutual distrust complicated the development of effective regulations, more so because it was also necessary to work out in detail when and at what level NATO commanders were authorized to redistribute stocks. Although LANDCENT had asked the countries from the beginning to evaluate the problem "in the mental attitude of wartime when purely national interests may perhaps have to be subordinated . . . in order to further the common cause," many more years passed before the procedures took effect formally in 1960.[14]

There also was concern at the army group commander level. The commanding general of NORTHAG sounded the alarm in 1955. The logistics assets available to him in the combat zone were insufficient to meet the planning requirements of his operations. Those assets were intended to sustain the units in combat for ten days, but the planning horizon for the army group was longer, extending preferably to thirty days. How could he command operations if he was not sure the stocks required were available in sufficient quantities in the national depots? To ensure the progress of the operations, the army group commanders claimed authority over a portion of the spare parts that had been stored in the communications zone under national responsibility. The member states concerned demonstrated full understanding of the wishes of the commander, Northern Army Group (COMNORTHAG). That did not mean, however, that those countries agreed to the proposal. The principle of national responsibility for logistics was too strongly embedded in the alliance to make such agreement possible. Under the compromise achieved and finally accepted by the army group commanders, the national authorities committed to inform the NATO commanders if there were shortfalls in their stock levels.[15]

Some confusion resulted from the terminology used in the NATO documents to refer to the stocks to which NATO commanders could lay claim. Such stocks were called "logistics resources made available," but there was no definition of that phrase anywhere in writing. It was, therefore, not clear whether in an emergency the NATO commanders were authorized to release to other contingents the basic stocks that were stored in national depots and were intended for the resupply of the respective national NATO contingents. Many member states were inclined to answer that question in the negative, because they reserved the right to use those stocks under certain circumstances for their own national requirements. The Netherlands took the position that the desire of NATO commanders for authority to redistribute the "resources made available" in an emergency "is completely understandable and acceptable to us *as long as* 'made available' means what the National Authority has determined as having been made available." NATO, therefore, could not trust that all of the stocks reported during peacetime and that were the basis of NATO planning would actually be available for alliance use in wartime. If NATO were to disagree with the Dutch position, the Netherlands could modify its logistic reports, or in the worst case, insist on changes to the mutual support regulations.[16]

Exercising and testing mutual support during NATO exercises did not amount to much. Usually, such exercises did not last long enough for logistics problems to arise and then to be resolved. During Exercise FLASH BACK II in 1960, for example, the acting commander of the Netherlands Logistics Support Command, Colonel Gerhard H. de Kleijn, noted: "Considering the Exercise FLASH BACK II from a logistical point of view, only a five-day exercise is insufficient to let pass by and bring to an end all main problems which may arise during wartime." There was, therefore, insufficient reason and opportunity for "cross-servicing" between the participating countries, among other things.[17]

Integrated Depots

To avoid irritating all manner of sensibilities concerning authority over stocks, SHAPE since 1952 had been making plans to develop integrated depots under the authority of the NATO commanders. Such depots were desirable at various points along the logistics chain. In addition to the ten days of tactical stocks that the army corps had at their disposal, the army group commander also would gain access to intermediate depots under his command, which would contain tactical stocks for thirty-five days. According to these plans, the remaining forty-five days of stocks were stored in base depots that fell under national control as far as those stocks came from local production, such as combat rations. Other so-called common-user supplies that were furnished from overseas, such as fuel and ammunition, would fall under joint authority and would be stored in base areas in the United Kingdom or in northwestern France. The problem was that NATO could not compel the member countries to establish such integrated depots and had to rely instead on bilateral and multilateral agreements. The establishment of the integrated depots, therefore, was seen as "the most important feature and the biggest problem of the SHAPE plan." Initially, the Netherlands greeted this plan with enthusiasm, but when it became clear the combined depots for the Central Sector would not be in the United Kingdom but in northwestern France, the enthusiasm cooled immediately.[18] Other countries also registered objections, primarily because the implementation of the SHAPE plans was very expensive. In 1955 the plans for integrated base areas were definitely scrapped. In their stead, SHAPE emphasized the importance of establishing national depots on the territory of other member states.[19]

That change of course by SHAPE resulted from more than just the lack of cooperation. The plans for the common base areas had been made obsolete by new developments, one of which was the impending adoption of the forward strategy. Beginning in 1958 the defense of the alliance shifted in several steps from the Rhine and IJssel Rivers to the Inner-German Border. The supply lines became substantially longer and crossed several water obstacles. The expected use of tactical nuclear weapons increased their vulnerability further. To ensure the supply of NATO forces, a tactical supply had to be established in the rear combat zone to enable the forces to engage for a period of thirty days.[20] Small, dispersed depots were the most suitable for that role. Every country needed to develop the required depot space for its own forces, supported by the host country's civilian and military authorities. Sometimes, because West Germany had a requirement for storage options farther to the rear, there was an option to trade depots.

Despite the high priority Allied Forces Central Europe (AFCENT) gave to this issue, the development of the depot system took a great deal of time. Suitable locations often proved difficult to find, and expropriation procedures took a long time. Furthermore, the CEPS had to be extended eastward. In the meantime, it would be necessary to initiate procedures to transfer tactical stocks to the combat zone as quickly as possible in times of crisis, which would certainly be a time-consuming and risky operation. Because the forward strategy was not implemented in one stroke, this complex and difficult process was repeated in several stages. Since 1958 the Netherlands had been building depots to provide logistics support for its army corps, first in depots in the Netherlands to the east of the IJssel River, and later at an acquired depot site near Cloppenburg, west of the Weser River. Later the Netherlands could continue the search for depot space to the east of the Weser. Logistics could hardly keep pace with the forward strategy.[21]

Because of the difficulties that many NATO countries had in establishing their depots, SHAPE in 1966 took the initiative by establishing so-called forward defense depots, which were later renamed forward storage sites. Those sites would be financed by common funding and would promote interoperability. Although the NATO Military Committee had already acknowledged in 1967 that establishing the forward storage sites was "an essential military requirement in support of the forward defense concept," the project was delayed for years.[22] Many of the planned forward storage sites were not yet ready when the fall of the Berlin Wall in 1989 heralded the end of the Cold War.

Another logistics challenge that presented itself in 1966 and continued to resound for years afterward was the decision of France to withdraw from the integrated military command structure of NATO. Inasmuch as the American and British lines of communications ran through French territory, the CEPS was largely on French territory, and the most important supply ports were French, the logistic impact was severe. Both the Americans and the British began to investigate the possibilities of using Belgian and Dutch territory, but it was not until 1970 that tangible results appeared.

The Extent of the Possibilities

During the 1950s and 1960s there was no lack of attempts to promote logistical integration within NATO and to increase the authority of the NATO commanders over logistics. Little came of those efforts, however. When push came to shove, the NATO member states allowed national interests to prevail and held firm to the principle that logistics was a national responsibility. Although an American proposal in 1958 resulted in the establishment of the NATO Maintenance Supply Services System, which was responsible for the administration and issue of specific categories of spare parts, participation in that system was voluntary and noncommittal.[23] Other initiatives, such as a Dutch initiative in 1957 and one from West Germany in 1960, also ran aground. To improve logistics cooperation and promote harmonization in the area of operations, the ACE Logistic Coordination Center (ACE-LCC) was established in the 1960s. The center's ambitions were modest. According to one speaker during the ACE Logistics Conference in May 1964, "The success of the center will depend primarily on how willing the nations are to cooperate and on the mutual benefit they and SACEUR may derive from discussing their common problems."[24] That was about the extent of the possibilities.

Notes

1. Semi-static archive Royal Netherlands Army, NATO archive CGS/BLS, NAS 4365/195, Memorandum, submitted by letter from the chairman of the Dutch Joint Chiefs of Staff, no. 7000 A (NAS 4365/195), 29 Nov. 1957.

2. Semi-static archive RNLA, archive MPA HKGS 1948–1955, inv. no. 832, Memorandum "Logistic System Allied Command Europe" no. AG 1228.08/P92/54 LOG, 16 Feb. 1954.

3. Semi-static archive RNLA, archive MPA HKGS 1948–1955, inv. no. 824, "Draft report" from Western Union Defense Organization (WUDO)/Western Union Chiefs-of-Staff Committee/Principal Administrative Planning Committee "Logistical arrangements in the event of war in Western Europe" no. WQ (50) 29 (1st Draft), 12 June 1950.

4. Semi-static archive RNLA, archive MPA HKGS 1948–1955, inv. no. 471, "The principles governing the maintenance on the Continent, in war time, of the Benelux forces" report of the Principal Administrative Planning Committee no. WQ(P) (50) 17 (Draft), submitted [presented 6 Apr. 1950] with commentary added.

5. Semi-static archive RNLA, archive MPA HKGS 1948–1955, inv. no. 471, Letter "Maintenance of Benelux forces" from the chief of the naval staff, Vice Adm. E. J. Jhr. Van Holthe to the chairman of the Joint Chiefs of Staff, Gen. H. J. Kruls, no. 5M/100/244, dated 25 Mar. 1950.

6. Semi-static archive RNLA, archive MPA HKGS 1948–1955, inv. no. 811, Draft letter from the Dutch Joint Chiefs of Staff to SHAPE, submitted by letter from the chairman of the Joint Chiefs of Staff no. 7451a/1911-110-130 Top Secret, dated 29 May 1952; Draft memorandum for the General Defense Council, submitted by letter from the minister of war to the Joint Chiefs of Staff no. NAP 52/1173 Top Secret, dated 11 Sept. 1952. Semi-static archive RNLA, archive MPA HKGS 1948–1955, inv. no. 831, Draft letter from the chairman of the Joint Chiefs of Staff to the head of the Netherlands detachment Allied Land Forces Central Europe Col. Holle, submitted by letter from the chairman of the Joint Chiefs of Staff to chiefs of staff no. 7451x/110-100-1907 Top Secret, dated 10 Sept. 1952. Semi-static archive RNLA, archive MPA HKGS 1948–1955, inv. no. 832, Notes by Harmsen (G4-HKGS) dated 24 Feb. [1955]; Letter from SHAPE chief of staff (COS) Lt. Gen. C. V. R. Schuyler to Netherlands National Military Representative no. AG 2503/Mv-133/55 LOG NATO Secret, dated 18 Apr. 1955.

7. Semi-static archive RNLA, archive MPA HKGS 1948–1955, inv. no. 832, "Memorandum concerning the insights of the Netherlands in respect of the study designed by SHAPE concerning 'Operative and Logistic Supply system in support of NATO Defense'" Secret, undated; Notes by Harmsen (G4-HKGS) dated 24 Feb. [1955]. Central Archives Depot Ministry of Defense (CAD), Transportation Inspection Archives, box 37, "The use of emergency anchorages in the waters of Zeeland and the Wadden Sea with the associated secondary harbors in wartime," by the minister of highways and water management, no. DGS 1/55 Secret, 1955.

8. Semi-static archive RNLA, archive MPA HKGS 1948–1955, inv. no. 614, Memorandum "Study of military wartime POL transportation requirements and capabilities for SACEUR forces in Central Europe" from the chief of the General Staff to the chairman of the Joint Chiefs of Staff no. MPA 1420 CA/150-950 Secret, dated 23 Mar. 1953. CAD, Archives of the Ministry of War/Navy 1946–1955, inv. no. 6282, Letter from the chairman of the Joint Chiefs of Staff to the minister of war no. 4317 Top Secret, dated 14 Aug. 1954.

9. Semi-static archive RNLA, archive MPA HKGS 1948–1955, inv. no. 476, Draft report "Definition and allocation of stocks of war material" from the Administrative Planning Division, WUDO, no. WQ(50) 31 (1st Draft), dated 22 June 1950, Draft report "Stock piling in peacetime to meet maintenance needs at the start of war in respect of equipment from outside sources" from the Principal Staff Officers Committee, Western European Regional Planning Group, NATO, nr. WQ(50) 51, dated 6 Nov. 1950. Semi-static archives RNLA, archive MPA HKGS 1948–1955, inv. no. 832, Memorandum "Initial levels of reserves in Allied Command Europe" SHAPE nr. LOG 6002/Sup-119/53, dated 21 Feb. 1953, submitted by letter from the chairman of the Joint Chiefs of Staff to the chiefs of staff no. 8141 h/100–101 NATO Secret, dated 18 Mar. 1953.

10. Semi-static archive RNLA, archive MPA HKGS 1948–1955, inv. no. 927, Various documents from the Working Group on Bulk Inland POL Transport from Planning Board for European Inland Surface Transport, incl. the memorandum "Wartime Inland Transport Deficit in Central Europe," dated 24 Aug. 1953; Semi-static archive RNLA, NATO archive CGS/BLS, NAS 4764/277, Address by Maj. Cail and Lt. Col. Milton in the report of the ACE Logistics Conference, May 1964.

11. Semi-static archive RNLA, NATO archive CGS/BLS, NAS 4764/277, Address by Maj. Gen. Holle in the report of the ACE Logistics Conference, May 1964.

12. Semi-static archive RNLA, archive MPA HKGS 1948–1955, inv. no. 832, Minutes of the meeting of the SHAPE Logistics Briefing Team with Dutch representatives concerning "Operative logistic and supply system in support of NATO defense" in The Hague on 13 Jan. 1954, submitted by letter from the chairman of the Joint Chiefs of Staff to the minister of war and the navy et al. no. 4240d NATO Secret, dated 21 Jan. 1954.

13. Semi-static archive RNLA, archive MPA HKGS 1948–1955, inv. no. 838, LANDCENT Standing Logistic Procedures for War—Mutual Support, ns. 6001/6/LOG/S&M/405, 18 Oct. 1955.

14. Semi-static archive RNLA, archive MPA HKGS 1948–1955, inv. no. 838, Memorandum "Standing Logistic Instructions for War, Central European Land Forces. Arrangements in Wartime for the provision in certain circumstances of logistic support by one nation to the forces of another" of ALFCE no. ALFCE/1112/B4/54, 15 June 1954.

15. Semi-static archive RNLA, archive MPA HKGS 1948–1955, inv. no. 838, Letter from COMLANDCENT no. 6001/9/LOG/S&M/211 NATO Secret, dated 1 July 1955; Letter from COMLANDCENT no. 6001.9/LOG/S&M NATO Secret, dated 19 Sept. 1955; Letter from CGS to COMLANDCENT no. NATO 2423 AC/100, dated 8 Dec. 1955; Notes by Maj. J. P. Scheltens (G4-HKGS) dated 13 July, 18 July, 25 Oct., and 18 Nov. [1955]; Notes by Maj. F. E. A. H. de Jong (G4-HKGS) dated 12 Nov. [1955].

16. Semi-static archive RNLA, archive MPA HKGS 1948–1955, inv. no. 832, Notes by Maj. F. E. A. H. de Jong (G4-HKGS) dated 20 Oct. [1955] and Maj. J. P. Scheltens (G4-HKGS) dated 6 Dec. [1955]; Letter from the chairman of the Joint Chiefs of Staff to the minister of war and the navy no. 5240 AQ Secret, dated [26 Nov. 1955]; Letter from the minister of war and the navy to the chairman of the Joint Chiefs of Staff no. NAP 55/343b-11 Secret, dated 13 Dec. 1955. Semi-static archive RNLA, archive MPA HKGS 1948–1955, inv. no. 838, Notes from G4-HKGS, attached to letter "Standing Logistic Instructions for War, Land Forces Central Europe. Critical supplies" from ALFCE no. ALFCE/1173/B4/54 Cosmic Secret, dated 29 June 1954; Letter from CGS to COMLANDCENT no. MPA 2423 F/100, dated 20 Aug. 1954; Notes by Maj. J. P. Scheltens (G4-HKGS) dated 25 Oct. [1955] and Maj. F. E. A. H. de Jong (G4-HKGS) dated 12 Nov. [1955]; "LANDCENT Standing Logistic Procedures for War—Mutual Support," no. 6001/6/LOG/S&M/405 NATO Secret, dated 18 Oct. 1955.

17. CAD, archive National Logistic Support Command/RCZ, inv. no. 14, Final Report Flash Back II by NLSC (NL), submitted by letter from acting C-Netherlands Logistic Support Command Col. G. H. de Kleijn no. 10072/V Secret, dated 27 Oct. 1960. CAD, archive NLSC/RCZ, inv. no. 16, Report on Exercise Gentleman's Relish by NLSC (NL), submitted by letter from C-NLSC Brig. Gen. W. M. Berkhout to COMNORTHAG no. 048/G NATO Secret, dated 6 May 1961.

18. Semi-static archives RNLA, archive MPA HKGS 1948–1955, inv. no. 832, Minutes of the meeting of the SHAPE Logistics Briefing Team with NLD representatives concerning "Operative logistic and supply system in support of NATO defense" at The Hague on 13 Jan. 1954, submitted by letter from the chairman of the Joint Chiefs of Staff to the minister of war and the navy et al. no. 4240d, dated 21 Jan. 1954; Letter from SHAPE deputy chief of staff (DCOS) Logistics and Administration Lt. Gen. O. Poydenot to the chairman of the Joint Chiefs of Staff no. AG 1228.08/P-134 LOG/54 NATO Secret, undated [Feb. 1954]; Memorandum "Logistic System Allied Command Europe" no. AG 1228.08/P92/54 LOG NATO Secret, dated 16 Feb. 1954; Notes by de Jong (G4-CGS) dated 10 Mar. [1954]; Letter from AFCENT assistant DCOS Logistics to Ministry of Defense dated 15 June 1954; Memo from the acting head NLD Liaison Mission SHAPE Lt. Col.—aviator F. J. A. Lutz to the chairman of

the Joint Chiefs of Staff dated 7 July 1954; Letter from the chairman of the Joint Chiefs of Staff to CINCENT no. 5250 D NATO Secret, dated 16 Feb. 1955; Notes from Capt. J. P. Scheltens (G4-HKGS) dated 22 Feb. [1955]; Memorandum from SACEUR Gen. Alfred M. Gruenther no. LOG 1228.08/P521/55 LOG dated 3 Sept. 1955.

19. Semi-static archive RNLA, archive MPA HKGS 1948–1955, inv. no. 832, Notes by Maj. J. P. Scheltens (G4-HKGS) dated 20 Oct. [1955]; Letter from the chairman of the Joint Chiefs of Staff to the minister of war and the navy no. 5240 AQ Secret, dated [26 Nov. 1955].

20. Semi-static archive RNLA, NATO archive CGS/BLS, NAS 4764, Memorandum "Central Europe Logistic Concept. Depot system east of the Rhine-IJssel" from AFCENT no. 6000.12/JLA/LOG/290/58 (NATO Secret), dated 9 June 1958; Report "Central Europe Logistic Concept. Depot system east of the Rhine-IJssel" from AFCENT no. 6000.12/JLA/LOG/383/58 (NATO Secret), dated 4 Aug. 1958.

21. See Herman Roozenbeek (ed.), *In dienst van de troep: Bevoorrading en transport bij de Koninklijke Landmacht* (The Hague, 2008), 153–84.

22. See semi-static archive RNLA, NATO archive HKGS, NAS 9072/529, MC 32/46, "A Report by the Military Committee to the Defense Planning Committee on Common Funding of Forward Storage Sites."

23. Semi-static archive RNLA, NATO archive CGS/BLS, NAS 4764/277, Address by Air Commodore Smith in the report of the ACE Logistics Conference, May 1964.

24. Semi-static archive RNLA, NATO archive CGS/BLS, NAS 4764/277, Address by Colonel Castelbon in the report of the ACE Logistics Conference, May 1964.

7

The Logistics System of the Soviet and Warsaw Pact Armed Forces in the 1950s and 1960s

Dimitri N. Filippovych

During the 1950s and 1960s the strength and organizational structure of the strategic operational logistics system and the unit trains of the Soviet armed forces and the Warsaw Pact members underwent essential changes. Starting during the second half of the 1940s and the first half of the 1950s, the changes to the logistics system resulted from both the reduction and accompanying reorganization of the Soviet armed forces, and the formation of the Soviet Groups of Forces outside the territory of the Soviet Union.[1] The major objective of modernizing the logistics structure was to increase the ability of its components to support the missions of independently operating units and major formations.

Among the most important initial changes was the replacement of pack and cart transport by automotive transport at all levels of logistical support. The exception was for the mountain infantry corps and divisions, where the older means of transport continued to be used for carrying weapon systems and equipment. By 1950 this process was complete. The result was a major surge in the carrying capacity of the transportation units. This process was accompanied by increases in the logistical and mobility capabilities that improved the supply of the ground forces and naval units, and expedited medical and other evacuations, and an increased mobility of the major logistics units and facilities, particularly the combat service support elements.[2]

Obviously the logistical structures and capabilities increasingly were determined by the organizational structure of the forces supported, the requirements of the operational art, the character and scope of operations, the increased maneuverability of major combined-arms units, and the capability to switch from one operation to another without significant interruption. This process implied a significant growth in the material and other logistical support tasks in favor of large-scale unit operations on the one hand, and an increase in the influence of logistics on the success of an operation on the other.[3]

Nevertheless, the concentration of forces and logistics resources in the decisive operational directions continued to remain one of the basic principles of the operational art. Most exercises, including those conducted in the early 1950s by the Group of Soviet Forces in Germany, were characterized by a noticeable rise in the combat and personnel strength of the major units and an increased complexity of the required logistics tasks. The major problem to be resolved was how to achieve larger logistical autonomy of the groupings of forces and increased mobility of the logistics support assets.[4]

First of all, the forces required more and more equipment, thus straining the supply and maintenance capabilities of the logistics system. Hence, by late 1953 the daily ammunition requirement for a division was 2.5 times what it had been in 1946; for petroleum, oil, and lubricants (POL) the increase was almost 10 times. In 1953 one volley of fire from a rifle corps— minus tanks, self-propelled guns, and antiaircraft artillery—amounted to more than thirty-seven metric tons, which was seven times the amount fired by a single Soviet corps at the end of the Great Patriotic War (World War II). The quantity of daily supplies required by the subordinate units had also almost doubled, as verified during exercises. The scope of the military supplies consumed by the ground forces and naval units was also widening.[5] The increasing amounts of material supply and force deployment and relocation tasks, together with the steady tendency toward highly dynamic and deep operations, rapidly intensified the movement of transportation and other assets along the forward main supply and evacuation routes and the other major military roads. The result was much higher requirements on the installation, technical management, security, and repair and maintenance of the major military roads. Simultaneously, the demands grew for transport services via the rail, water, and aerial lines of communications (LOC). The development of operational-level logistics at the army or front (army group) level developed along two major lines: (1) the establishment and operation of the inherited system of logistical support, as was common during times of war and peace; and (2) the development of optimum structures for logistics units and facilities and efficient procedures for operating logistics assets in future wartime operations.[6]

Operational Logistics in the 1950s

By late 1953, wartime operational logistics consisted of frontal- and army-level logistics based on the logistics systems of the military districts and armies. A few years later frontal-level logistics in the armed forces of the Warsaw Pact member states included forward support units and facilities that were directly subordinate to the front. Forward depots were established for all classes of equipment and supply, including ordnance (armaments and ammunition), automotive and armored equipment, chemical warfare supplies, engineer explosives and equipment, signal equipment, POL, rations and grain, clothing and train supplies, medical and veterinary supplies, political educational material, quartermaster and war booty items, topographic charts, and scrap. Separate battalions and companies for labor, security, transport, and services were placed under the authority of the respective regional commanders responsible for operating those forward depots. A close look at the composition of the frontal logistics organization indicates a considerably increasing demand on the depots for receiving, consolidating, storing, issuing, and dispatching material. This also included the means of transporting the supplies to and from the depots. The ongoing process of motorization and equipment upgrades of the forces with new and complex systems resulted in the requirement to augment the fronts significantly with specialized units for maintenance, evacuation, and repair. The increases in casualties likely suffered during operations also required expansions in the medical network and the capacities of the frontal hospitals, new specialized medical treatment facilities, medical transport, and other medical support.

In contrast to the logistics structures during the Great Patriotic War, the number of logistics units and facilities available to the front increased significantly, along with motorization and enhanced technical capabilities and tactical and productive capacity. During wartime, front-based logistics may have totaled four hundred to six hundred units and facilities, with some 120,000 to 150,000 personnel and 20,000 to 25,000 motor vehicles. Between 1949 and 1953 field-army-level logistics included the army forward logistics base; automotive and road battalions; signal, medical, and veterinary units; and service support units. The logistics system of a field army consisted of up to fifty units and facilities.[7]

Extended Scope of Material Support Tasks

At the end of the 1950s radical changes in the fundamentals of the military craft occurred that had a great impact on the conditions of providing logistical support to the armed forces. First of all, the quantity of required material multiplied. Whereas during World War I the amount of supplies required to support a single soldier was six kilograms daily, the rate had reached forty kilograms by the mid-1950s. During one hour of flight, a single jet aircraft now consumed twenty to thirty times the amount of fuel that one aircraft consumed during the period of the Great Patriotic War. The total amount of kerosene, gasoline, and diesel fuel required by an aviation regiment was now about as much in weight as a combined-arms army consumed back then.

Furthermore, the scope of material support tasks expanded, owing to the modern equipment of the major combined-arms units, which now included nuclear missiles and large numbers of powerful conventional armaments. Hence, during the second half of the 1950s the combat ammunition basic load for a motorized rifle division was 1,927 metric tons, and for a tank division 1,014 metric tons, while fuel totals reached up to 600 metric tons.[8] To support the march movement of a motorized rifle division for one hundred kilometers, up to 450 tons of fuel were required; and for a tank division, up to 530 tons.[9] As a consequence, the sustainability of forces provided through standard army-level supply stocks decreased. Whereas before the Great Patriotic War the basic supply load of a field army was sufficient to sustain that army for fifteen days of operations, by the end of the war it was sufficient for five days, and in 1959, as exercises showed, only for two days. Meanwhile, the field army's supply stocks had become fully mobile.

During the 1960s the supply requirements continued to rise at an annual rate of 5 to 6 percent, which inevitably caused an increase in the strength of the logistics organizations and, consequently, the material and financial resources to sustain them. This situation was a function of the state of the manufacturing, storage, repair, and transportation technologies of the period. The material requirements of the armed forces of the Warsaw Pact increased not only in quantities, but also in scope. New categories of supplies emerged, including missiles, nuclear warheads, rocket fuel, electronic devices of all sorts, special equipment, and new protective gear. The pattern of material requirements changed significantly as well. Whereas during World War II the primary supply requirements were food, clothing, and ammunition, now the top item on the sustainment list was fuel.[10]

The character of logistical support substantially transformed, as reflected in the quantities and methods in which stockpiles were distributed in depth. Because of the changes in the quality of military equipment and armaments, operational art and the theory of offensive operations also evolved. A new operational concept emerged, characterized by deep nuclear strikes combined with forces thrusting forward along major avenues of attack, without a contiguous front line. Thus, not only did the dimensions of operations expand—depth of five hundred to seven hundred kilometers, mean speed of advance of fifty to eighty kilometers per day, and duration of seven to ten days—but the personnel and material strength of the major units increased accordingly. Consequently, the workload placed on the logistics system to support the operations of the combat of forces and naval units increased under the evolving conditions of warfare.[11] The weight of a front's unit of fire (minus aviation) in the 1960s amounted to 18,500 tons, and fuel servicing exceeded 22,000 tons. Calculations indicated that during the immediate period of preparation and for the first eight to ten days of an offensive operation at the speed of advance of eighty to one hundred kilometers per day, the troops of a front could expend upward of 240,000 tons of fuel and about 120,000 tons of various types of ammunition.[12]

Coping with the New Challenges

Traditional approaches seeking to improve logistics by increasing quantities were not adequate. Such measures increased the volume of the forward and rear operational logistics and expanded the logistics facilities to huge dimensions, thus hampering the mobility of the forces. The traditional measures also contrasted sharply with the new trends in the development of the forces that emphasized increasing combat capabilities by improving the qualitative performances of weapons and equipment. The rise in the strength of the logistics system increased its proportion of the overall personnel strength in the major operational units to 15 to 25 percent at the battalion, regimental, and divisional levels; up to 10 percent at the field army level; and from 25 to 35 percent at the front level.[13] The mechanization of the operational logistics elements, while maintaining the old organizational structures, only partially allowed for increasing their mobility and making the rear support organizations less dependent on the railways.

Warsaw Pact exercises held during the 1950s and 1960s showed clearly that conducting operations with either a very short operational pause or none at all to prepare for the follow-on phase of the battle made it very difficult to concentrate and bring up the necessary logistics assets as well as ensure the uninterrupted logistical support of the forces. The dependence of the fronts' major logistics systems on the railways was in stark contrast to the required mobility and maneuverability of the support, as well as the necessary logistical autonomy of the major operational units. Hence, the quantitative upgrade of logistics, as progressive and favorable as it had been during the period of the Great Patriotic War, did not meet the evolving basic requirement of force planning, which was to improve the qualitative parameters of the units of all the armed services, branches, and specialized forces. The major emphasis, therefore, had to be on improving the qualitative characteristics of the logistics units and facilities.

The following main criteria were established to facilitate practical solutions:

- The support organization must correspond to the organizational principles of the armed forces.
- A certain percentage of the logistics support elements have to be maintained at the various main organizational levels in order to preserve logistical autonomy and increase logistical sustainability.
- The logistical support assets of the higher echelons must be coordinated with those of the lower echelons as quickly as possible.
- All transportation means should be used fully and efficiently, ensuring the uninterrupted flow of supplies.
- Uninterrupted medical care for the injured and sick must be guaranteed.
- The logistics units and command and control elements must be organized with modern equipment.

These criteria expressed the essence and the main directions of the reorganization of the logistics system. The primary objective was to overcome the imbalance between the structure and capabilities of the combat units on the one hand, and those of the logistic units and facilities supporting them on the other. By this time the field army capable of conducting combined-arms warfare had developed into a highly maneuverable major operational force. On the basis of this premise, measures also were taken to increase the mobility of the field army's logistics components. In particular, the frontal level of command relieved the armies of the responsibility for operating certain railway sections, and the requirements for supplies stored in army-level depots also were reduced. The new supply standards gave the forces more autonomy to accomplish their combat missions as part of an army-level offensive of up to seven days' duration. The mobility of the army-level support elements significantly increased because a large amount of material supplies had been moved up and placed under the control of the front. The army-level logistics structure was relieved of the medical hospital bases, which were replaced by independent medical groups that could be attached to the forward divisions, either to reinforce their organic medical assets or to operate independently.

These measures caused pertinent changes in the logistics organization of the front. To facilitate the timely concentration of the logistics effort at the army level, a mobile echelon of forward logistics bases was established at the frontal level, the quantity of automotive assets for transporting supplies was increased, and new road and traffic management brigades and battalions were established.

The results were a reduction in the total number of logistics units and facilities, making a percentage of them independent of the railway network; a boost in the mobility of the operational logistics elements; and an increase in the reliability of uninterrupted supplies to meet the forces' requirements during ongoing operations. The availability of a mobile logistics echelon at the front level facilitated a continuous concentration of effort of army-level logistics, which in turn significantly increased the logistical autonomy of the groupings of forces. Thus, the changes in the structure of operational logistics helped catch up with the increasing capabilities of the forces and provided a more efficient utilization of resources and support to uninterrupted combat action during an operation. During the 1960s the tendency developed to adapt the organizational structure in logistics more and more to those of combined-arms units, especially at the company, battalion, and brigade levels.[14]

Logistics Support under the New Operational Conditions

The preparation for operations and the functions of logistics support elements during operations was based on the logistics support principles that had been developed to that point:

- Ensure high combat readiness of the logistics elements.
- Be ready to accomplish logistic support tasks in the case of a sudden outbreak of hostilities, even with the limited peacetime assets on hand.
- Facilitate the logistical autonomy of groupings of forces and ensure sustained logistical support for the forces in operations without operational pauses.
- Shape the logistics support organization in accordance with the theater

of operations, the availability and status of logistics assets, the mission of the forces, and the specific operational and strategic environment.

- Concentrate the logistics effort on supporting the forces at the center of gravity.

These principles were the basis for improving logistical support of operations under the new conditions of warfare.

When organizing logistical support it was necessary to take into account the fact that the depth of offensive operations had increased some 1.5 to 2 times, compared with the final stage of the Great Patriotic War. Also, the tempo of operations was now much higher. A combined-arms army with modern weapons and equipment, for example, could easily advance twenty-five to forty kilometers in twenty-four hours, and a tank army could advance up to fifty kilometers. This high speed of attack significantly shortened the duration of operations, in particular those at front level. Instead of a duration of fifteen to twenty days, an operation could now require only twelve to fifteen days. The preparation and conduct of operations of such huge dimensions complicated the task of the logistics support organization. Logistics had to be highly mobile and capable of providing comprehensive support to the forces at very short notice during the initial stage of an operation, and then continuously build up the logistics effort to be ready to shift the operational direction, if the situation so required.[15]

Lessons learned from exercises conducted during the second half of the 1950s in the German Democratic Republic (GDR) indicated the following requirements for the logistics system:

- Unit trains—i.e., the forward organic support echelon—had to be fully mobile with all of the supplies stored on automotive transport assets for a minimum of three to five days of combat.
- The logistics of a combined-arms army had to be as light and mobile as possible, immediately capable of following the advancing forces. These logistics elements had to be equipped with all-terrain vehicles and have vehicle-based supplies available sufficient to support combat for at least two days.[16]
- Front-level logistics should be interconnected with army-level logistics through forward logistics support bases (material and medical) capable of supporting the combat action of the front for two days.
- All means of transport had to be used comprehensively for both the forces themselves and their support elements. Special attention was

paid to the extensive application of new and powerful technologies for ensuring POL supplies, field pipelines, and highly mobile means of transport, including rotary and fixed-wing transport aircraft.

- The table of organization and equipment (TO&E) of logistics units and facilities had to be augmented to include all-terrain, multipurpose vehicles and road trains; highly efficient loading and unloading equipment; modern nuclear, biological, and chemical (NBC) protective equipment; and communications and automation equipment for optimizing logistical command and control.[17]

In the event the enemy employed nuclear barriers, the resources, capabilities, supplies, and support assets within the theater of operations had to be dispersed among several echelons to ensure a reliable link between the forces and the supporting logistics elements. This required considerations about how to organize the logistics support to the groupings of forces in case they were cut off from one another. Also considered quite important were the possible ways to improve logistics sustainability, flexibility, reliability, command and control, and the effectiveness of medical support in mass casualty situations. Finally, there was a requirement to establish in peacetime independent and mobile groupings of strategic logistics assets in the theater of operations, while increasing the mobility of certain elements of the centralized logistics system.

The Proof of the Pudding

During the 1950s and 1960s the main questions concerning logistical support organization were studied and the possible solutions tested in Warsaw Pact exercises. These questions included the following:

- How should the immediate preparations of the logistics elements be organized and put into practice?
- How should they be moved up and concentrated in the specified sectors?
- How should they be redeployed during an ongoing operation?
- How should the broad range of logistical support for the forces be organized and effected, as well as the defense and security of the logistics organization itself?

During the exercises much attention was paid to the command and control of the logistics assets. Joint and combined exercises were conducted according to the planning of the Warsaw Pact Unified Staff. The largest joint military exercises of the allied armies included OCTOBER STORM (1965), VLTAVA (1966), RHODOPES (1967), DNEPR (1967), SUMAVA (1968), NORTH or SERVER (1968), NEMAN (1968), and ODER-NEISSE (1969).[18] In addition to the topics discussed previously, the complex tasks of ensuring the transport and deployment for operations of the Warsaw Pact allied armies were exercised. Road and railway forces, for example, participated in constructing high-water bridges and ferries across the Vistula, Oder, and Danube Rivers. In the course of these exercises, special emphasis was placed on organizing movement with comprehensive utilization of all means of transport, in order to exercise thoroughly the interaction between the military transportation agencies and units of the allied armies.[19]

During the 1960s a number of basic regulations were issued that specified the general approach to the preparation and conduct of operations and the respective logistical support of the forces. These included *USSR Armed Forces Field Service Regulation* (1963), *Operational Logistics Military Manual* (1963), *Recommendations on Front and Army Staff Procedures for Attack Operations* (1964), and *Forward (or Tactical) Logistics Military Manual* (1964).[20] These documents significantly increased the role of the logistics staffs as the basic command organization for both peacetime and wartime logistics. The logistical support plan had developed into a serious and complex document. Fragmentary orders on the various aspects of logistical support, as well as the employment of specialized forces and logistic elements, had become a component of practical staff work.

The material basis and the composition and organizational structure of the logistics system were shaped essentially by the formation of the Strategic Missile Forces, as well as the equipment of the other services and forces with nuclear missile systems and the modernization of conventional weapons. It is mainly because of these developments that at all echelons of the armed forces of the Soviet Union and the other Warsaw Pact members there emerged many new units and facilities of specialized services, resulting in large logistics structures. Further research is required to analyze how far all these measures succeeded in meeting the far-reaching Soviet and Warsaw Pact logistical goals.

Notes

1. See V. A. Zolotarev, O. V. Saksonov, and S. A. Tyushkevich, *Voennaya istorya Rossii* (Moscow, 2002), 619–21.

2. See *Razvitie Tyla Sovetskikh Vooruzhennykh Sil 1918–1988*, ed. V. N. Rodin (Moscow, 1989), 219–22.

3. See *General'nyj shtab Rossijskoj armii: Istoriya i sovremenost'*, ed. Ju. N. Baluevskiy (Moscow, 2006), 295.

4. See Ivan M. Golushko, *Soldaty tyla* (Moscow, 1988), 74–88.

5. See *50 let Vooruzhennykh Sil SSSR*, ed. M. W. Zacharov (Moscow, 1968), 483; *Razvitie Tyla Sovetskikh Vooruzhennykh Sil*, 218.

6. See A. A. Babakov, *Vooruzhennye sily SSSR posle vojny* (Moscow, 1987), 59.

7. See "Reorganizatsiya shtaba tyla i razvitie tyla vooruzhennykh sil SSSR," http://www.tyl.mil.ru/page355.htm (accessed 13 Apr. 2008).

8. See "Razvitie tyla vooruzhennykh sil v usloviyach nauchno-tekhnicheskoj revolyutsii," http://www.tyl.mil.ru/page339.htm (accessed 13 Apr. 2008); I. I. Anureev, *Nauchno-tekhnicheskij progress i revolyutsiya v voennom dele* (Moscow, 1973), 118.

9. See Ya. Shchepennikov, "Support of the Strategic Concentration and Deployment of the Armed Forces in Respect to Transport," *Military Thought—Special Collection*, no. 3 (1961): 7, in "Lt. Col. Oleg Penkovsky: Western Spy in Soviet GRU" (document collection), http://www.foia.cia.gov/penkovsky.asp (accessed 14 Apr. 2008).

10. See *50 let Vooruzhennykh Sil SSSR*, 513.

11. See "Razvitie tyla vooruzhennykh sil v usloviyach nauchno-tekhnicheskoj revolyutsii."

12. See F. Malykhin, "Some Problems in the Preparation of the Rear Area for Support of the Armed Forces in the Initial Period of a War," *Military Thought—Special Collection*, no. 2 (1960): 5, in "Lt. Col. Oleg Penkovsky: Western Spy in Soviet GRU," http://www.foia.cia.gov/penkovsky.asp (accessed 14 Apr. 2008).

13. See "Razvitie tyla vooruzhennykh sil v usloviyach nauchno-tekhnicheskoj revolyutsii," http://www.tyl.mil.ru/page340.htm (accessed 13 Apr. 2008).

14. See ibid.

15. See *Istoriya voennoj strategii Rossii*, ed. V. A. Zolotarev (Moscow, 2000), 457–73.

16. See Malykhin, "Some Problems in the Preparation of the Rear Area," 9.

17. See "Razvitie tyla vooruzhennykh sil v usloviyach nauchno-tekhnicheskoj revolyutsii," http://www.tyl.mil.ru/page342.htm (accessed 13 Apr. 2008).

18. See *Istoriya voennoj strategii Rossii*, ed. Zolotarev, 406.

19. See "Dal'nejshee razvitie i sovershenstvovanie tyla vooruzhennykh sil v obstanovke voenno-strategicheskogo pariteta," http://www.tyl.mil.ru/page370.htm (accessed 13 Apr. 2008).

20. See *Rossijskie predpriyatiya—Tylu Vooruzhennykh Sil*, ed. V. A. Isakov (Moscow, 2005), 5.

8

Soviet Union Military Planning, 1948–1968

Viktor Gavrilov

1948–1953

Immediately after World War II the 12-million-man Soviet army was reduced to a strength of 2.8 million. The most capable forces at the time were concentrated in the occupation zones in Germany, Austria, and Hungary. Along with the reconstruction of the Soviet economy, more attention was paid to the military. Within seven to eight years following the end of the war the Soviet armed forces were reequipped with advanced automatic rifles, artillery systems, engineering equipment, radar systems, and other modern types of weapons and arms. The "Uranium Project" had been successfully completed. New and intensive research was conducted in the area of missile weapons. Great attention was paid to the modernization of battle tanks and aviation. The Soviet Ground Forces (Army) were completely motorized and mechanized. The development of doctrine on the use of mobile troops and aviation received further attention. Strategic offensive was considered the primary form of operations, which intended to reach successively intermediate strategic objectives through the coordinated actions of all services and branches of the armed forces.

This key element of Soviet military doctrine of that time was well known in the West, although it had not yet been published. Western planners also knew that according to the Soviet doctrine, the primary forms of strategic offensive operations were envelopment and the destruction of the enemy forces. Unlike Washington, whose favored approach placed the priority on the destruction of the enemy's economic potential, the Soviet military primarily relied on the destruction of the enemy's armed forces. Recently declassified documents also show clearly that at that time the Soviet Union had no plans to attack the Western democracies. The strategic offensive was a concept to be used only as a response to critical situations.

In 1946–1947 a document called *USSR Territory's Active Defense Plan,* which established the missions of the armed forces, was prepared and approved. A so-called Rebuff Force, based in fortified positions, had the mission of defeating any enemy attack within the defensive zone adjacent to the national boundaries and establishing the conditions for launching a counteroffensive by the main forces concentrated on the western boundaries of the Socialist bloc. Air force and air defense units that were components of the Rebuff Force were assigned the mission of providing air cover. The High Command Reserve Force, supported by the Rebuff Force units, was assigned the mission of defeating the enemy's main forces and launching the counteroffensive. The scale and depth of the counteroffensive were not specified in the plan.[1]

Western leaders knew about the concentration of the Soviet forces along the western boundaries of the Socialist bloc as well as the recently improved capabilities of Soviet troops compared with the modest military potential of the West European countries. They therefore supposed that if the United States started an aerial-atomic war, the Soviet tank armadas would breach the European defenses and reach the English Channel within two weeks. West Europe and the NATO European countries, therefore, were hostages in the case of war between the United States and the Soviet Union. When, at a press conference on 30 November 1950 (during the Korean War), President Harry S. Truman declared American readiness to undertake "all necessary measures which the military situation will require," and added that the use of the atomic bomb was always under active consideration, British prime minister Clement R. Attlee flew urgently to Washington to meet him. In the course of the negotiations Truman said he "would not consider the use of the bomb without consulting with the United Kingdom."[2]

It is therefore not an exaggeration to conclude that the American leadership was deterred from unleashing an aerial-atomic war against the Soviet Union only by the powerful Soviet tank armies based in the center of Europe. The Soviet Five-Year Plan (1946–1950) provided for the production of 38,250 tanks and self-propelled guns, including 9,450 heavy tanks, 22,800 medium tanks, and 6,000 light tanks. Special plans also were developed for their use in case of war.[3]

In 1949 the Soviet Union became an atomic power, with the delivery means of attacking with nuclear weapons targets in the depth of the Western European defenses, as well as Alaska. The 1946–1950 Plan also provided for the production of 25,765 military aircraft, including 5,700 jets. By 1948–1953 the Soviet military was developing a new generation of bombers, including the Tu-4, Tu-16, and Il-28.

Stalin did everything in his power to put the large numbers of the new Il-28 jet bombers into service. Only a few people knew about Stalin's order issued in the spring of 1952 to raise one hundred bomber divisions equipped with the Il-28. Soviet air force senior officers scratched their heads after receiving that order.[4] It is impossible to predict the end of that process if the more capable Tu-16 jet bomber had not been successfully test flown in 1952. That aircraft had a speed of one thousand kilometers per hour and a range of four thousand kilometers. Stalin ordered the start of the Tu-16 series production even before the completion of its final tests. The previous order to build up a huge Il-28 air fleet lost its significance, and after Stalin's death the program was canceled.

Simultaneously, Soviet military planning made great advancements in the field of missile construction. The first missiles with a range up to six hundred kilometers were designed in 1948–1951. Great attention also was paid to air defense, as active research started to develop air defense missile systems based initially on captured German models.

The Soviet navy was supposed to play a defensive role only, although just after World War II a large-scale and ambitious ten-year program of military shipbuilding was approved. Speaking at a Kremlin meeting on 27 September 1945, Stalin declared that the main striking power of the navy would be based not on battleships and aircraft carriers, but rather on submarines and heavy cruisers. Addressing the admirals, he said: "During the next ten to twelve or even fifteen years our squadrons will wage only littoral warfare. It's quite different if you want to go to America. Then you should have quite a different ratio of ship classes. Since there is no need to go to America, then there is no need to overload our industry. I prefer heavy cruisers."[5]

Thus, at the start of the Cold War the Soviet Union, challenged by the United States and later by NATO, decided to oppose them with military power. In response to Washington power politics, Moscow initiated its own program of power politics. Increasingly, new types of weapons and armament entered into the service of the army, the air force, and the navy. At the end of the 1940s, after the establishment of NATO, the Soviet Union started to expand the strength of its armed forces.

1954–1960

Washington always reacted negatively to any Soviet action to secure its "spheres of interest" in Eastern Europe, for which it had paid a great price during World War II. The American government relied on military power and was absolutely confident in its victory in any future war. Without hesitation it challenged the Soviet Union and drew it into the arms race.

Under these circumstances the Soviet Union began atomic and missile weapons projects and developments in the field of jet aviation and air defense. During that period Soviet military planning was dominated by the new possibilities of nuclear missiles. While the Americans at that time were relying on aerial delivery systems for nuclear and conventional weapons, the Soviet Union was developing operational and tactical missiles—and later strategic missiles.

After the Soviet Union acquired atomic weapons delivery systems—missiles and aircraft—the Soviet armed forces entered a new stage of development. The operational capabilities of the army, air force, and navy increased sharply. That allowed the Soviet Union to reduce its large and costly army. In 1955 the armed forces were reduced by 640,000 men; in 1956 by 1.2 million; and in 1957 by 300,000. During that period 63 divisions and brigades and some military schools were inactivated, and 375 ships were converted to the reserve fleet.

The success in creating an atomic bomb, jet aviation, and missiles with nuclear warheads allowed the Soviet military to rearm its units, increase their efficiency, and train servicemen under simulated conditions of atomic war. In September 1954 a major military exercise at the Totsk range near the town of Buzuluk was one of the remarkable events of those years. During the course of that exercise an RDS-3 nuclear bomb was dropped. After 2.5 hours the leading units of the attacking troops approached the detonation area. Servicemen using the individual protective equipment passed within five hundred to six hundred meters of ground zero. The radiation dose received by the infantry personnel was about 0.02 to 0.03 roentgen, while the dose of the tank crews was four to five times less. The troops got the experience of operating under realistic wartime conditions—as they were thought to be at that time.[6]

Soviet military planning increasingly rested on developments in the field of nuclear weapons. During that period the Soviet Union tested its first thermonuclear bomb and made the first underwater nuclear explosion. The Soviet Union, however, still lagged significantly behind the United States in

nuclear weapons development. In 1958, for example, the United States detonated approximately eighty nuclear warheads, the Soviets seventy-two. The
most powerful nuclear weapon, which was detonated by the United States,
was a fifteen-megaton device exploded on Bikini Island in 1954.

The successful development of missile technology also shaped the new
features of Soviet military planning. An especially vivid example is the Suez
crisis of November 1956, when the Soviet government issued an ultimatum
to Great Britain, France, and Israel to stop their invasion of Egypt. If they did
not, Khrushchev threatened, he would use missiles.

The most important task, however, was the establishment of an effective
air defense system to counter any possible American massive nuclear aerial
strike. Air defense developed in multiple directions. Jet fighter interceptors,
radio-controlled antiaircraft guns, new radar and radio equipment, antiaircraft missiles, and the newest means of radio electronic warfare all were
added to the Soviet armory. By 1955 the S-25 BERKUT air defense system
came into service. Organized in two air defense rings around Moscow, the
system was capable of engaging simultaneously twenty targets at altitudes
ranging between three thousand and twenty-five thousand meters. Each air

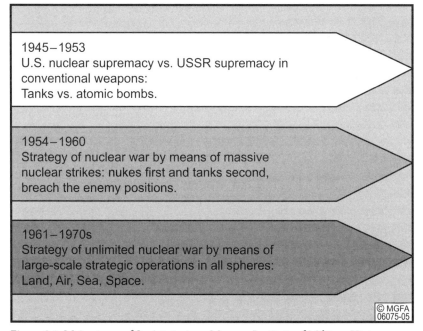

Figure 8.1. Main stages of Soviet strategy. Moscow Institute of Military History.

defense regiment had a separate zone of responsibility. Moscow, therefore, was quite well protected from any possible aerial attack. As in previous years, the air space beyond Moscow was protected by fighters and advanced air defense artillery systems. These systems were effective against propeller-driven strategic bombers and jets of the first generation, such as the American B-36, but they were not effective against high-speed (one thousand kilometers per hour) and high-altitude (sixteen thousand to seventeen thousand meters) targets. A key weak point in Soviet air defense was the poorly equipped radar units, particularly in the Soviet Union's northern regions.

The revolution in military affairs of the 1950s had a strong impact on Soviet military planning. At that time plans provided for launching nuclear air and missile first strikes throughout the depth of the enemy's defenses. Following those strikes tank divisions would breach the enemy positions with the mission of reaching their assigned objectives at the highest possible speed.

1961–1968

The end of the 1950s was marked by a reduction in international tensions. On 14 January 1960 Soviet leader Nikita Khrushchev proposed to reduce further the Soviet armed forces by 1.2 million men. Meanwhile, the development of nuclear-armed missiles proceeded steadily. In 1959 the R-12 missile came into service and the R-14 missile successfully passed its operational tests. These new missiles could be fired from stationary launching positions, such as silos. The Soviet military thus began the intermediate planning to use the new missiles against predetermined targets. A draft field manual issued in 1959 specified that in case of war, missile units were not to be attached to or made operationally subordinate to the fronts (army groups); only the Supreme Command was to decide how to use them. In 1959 the Soviet armed forces established the Strategic Missile Troops as a separate branch of service.

The intercontinental ballistic missiles (ICBMs) that had been developed further after the R-12 and R-14 missiles were tested in Operation ANADYR (the Cuban missile crisis) as an instrument of power brinksmanship. That experience made the Soviet military face up to some unpleasant conclusions. The maneuverability and survivability of the newer missiles had been greatly decreased because of the overall increases in the sizes of the accompanying transport and fueling equipment. That problem was resolved by the introduction of solid fuel missiles. By 1966 the RT-15 solid fuel missile on a mobile launcher had been developed.

Military planning more and more rested on the operational efficiency of the Strategic Missile Troops in general and their operational readiness in particular. The primary advantages of missile weapons included their practically unlimited range, their high and constantly maintained operational readiness, their pinpoint strike accuracy, their minimum flight time to distant targets, their operational functionality in any weather and time of day, and their invulnerability while in their flight trajectory.

Research and development efforts also attempted to develop antisatellite defenses and space reconnaissance systems. During the period from 1957 to 1962 the Soviet space program conducted 166 launches carrying a variety of orbital vehicles, 92 of which were military. During the same period the United States conducted 348 orbital launches.

The development of nuclear weapons continued. After a yearlong moratorium on nuclear testing, the Soviet Union in October 1961 detonated its largest nuclear devices at the Novaya Zemlya test range. Those tests of thirty and fifty-eight megaton thermonuclear warheads got the world's attention, but they did not stop the nuclear arms race.

The 1964 book *Military Strategy,* edited by Marshal Vasily Danilovich Sokolovsky, was considered the essence of Soviet military-theoretical thought of that time and a kind of original Soviet military doctrine. It outlined the long-term main features of Soviet military planning. The key concepts of the book included the following:

1. In a future war the belligerents will widely use the most decisive means of conducting the war, including the first use of nuclear missiles to destroy the enemy or to force him to surrender as quickly as possible. The main military-strategic objective of war under such conditions is to defeat the enemy and destroy and disorganize his rear area facilities.
2. The importance of the initial period of any war will increase substantially, and that initial period will determine the course and the outcome of the entire war.
3. The center of gravity of the armed struggle will move from the forward engagement zones to the enemy's depth, including his most remote facilities. As a result, the scope of warfare will increase to an incredulous level.
4. In a future war the direct engagement with the enemy will be infrequent. The war will be waged with strategic offensive means at vast distances and depths against those enemy objectives making the backbone of his military power and his economic and politico-moral potential.

5. In the land theaters of the war there will be multiple zones of total destruction and radioactive contamination resulting from nuclear missile strikes. Operations will be characterized by maneuver and be conducted simultaneously or in series in separate zones at different operational depths to seize and hold vital regions and centers. Force maneuver by air will be of decisive importance.

6. Defense will rely on the rapid maneuver of highly mobile forces and counterattacks conducted in combination with the stubborn holding of the main defensive zones along the probable directions of the enemy's advance.

7. In the maritime theaters the era of battles between large formations of surface ships will pass away, as will the large surface ships themselves. Submarine-launched missiles in coordination with missile-armed aviation will strike the main blows and execute the strategic missions at sea.

8. One of the most important missions of Soviet military strategy will be the defense of the hinterland by means of airpower and antimissile defenses.[7]

The Soviet theory of military strategy articulated the following types of strategic actions by the armed forces in any future nuclear war:

1. Nuclear missile strikes to destroy and demolish the objectives that make the basis of the enemy's military-economic potential, the disruption of his military and political command and control system, and the destruction of his strategic nuclear capabilities and his main forces groupings

2. Strategic offensives in the land theaters of war to destroy completely the enemy's forces

3. Protection of the country's hinterlands and forces from the enemy's nuclear strikes

4. Maritime theater operations to destroy the enemy's naval forces.[8]

The Cuban missile crisis, however, came as a severe shock. That crisis was the highest point of the armed confrontation between the Soviet Union and the United States—between the Warsaw Pact and NATO. That crisis made it clear that the hopes of any belligerent to win a victory in a global nuclear war were a complete illusion, and that any such war would ruin both the victor and the loser. In military planning, then, the primary object was seen as not winning the nuclear war, but rather deterring the enemy through force supremacy, to force the enemy to believe that he was the weaker side, and thus to undermine his ability to strike first. Thus, the struggle for strategic nuclear parity started.

Soviet military planning relied on ICBMs in land silo launchers, missile submarines, and strategic aviation. By 1967, however, the United States had achieved absolute supremacy with the establishment of its Strategic Triad, which included 1,054 land-based ICBMs, 41 missile submarines armed with 656 missiles, and 615 B-52 heavy bombers. The United States was actively developing ICBMs with multiple individually targeted reentry vehicles (MIRVs), as well as antimissile defense systems. The Soviet Union's nuclear potential at that time totaled only about 600 nuclear delivery systems, including two nuclear submarines with 32 launchers.[9] The Soviet government had no alternative but to speed up its Nuclear Strategic Program. By the early 1970s the Soviet Union and the United States had reached parity, and that in turn resulted in agreements on limitations of strategic arms and antimissile defense systems.

Notes

1. See A. A. Kokoshin, *Армия и политика* [Army and politics] (Moscow, 1995), 207.

2. J. Newhouse, *The Nuclear Age: From Hiroshima to Star Wars* (London, 1989), 84.

3. See S. N. Khrushchev, *Никита Хрущев: Кризис и ракеты* [Nikita Khrushchev: Crisis and missiles], vol. 1 (Moscow, 1994), 160.

4. See N. N. Ostroumov, "Армада, которая не взлетела" [Armada that had never flown], *Военно-исторический журнал* [Journal of Military History], no. 10 (1992): 39–40.

5. Russian State Archive of Economics, f. 8899, op. 1, d. 1485, pp. 11–12.

6. V. N. Mikhailov, *Ядерные испытания ССР* [The nuclear tests of the USSR] (Moscow, 1997), 254–87.

7. Marshal Sokolovsky (ed.), *Военная стратегия* [Military strategy], 3rd rev. ed. (Moscow, 1968), 244–48.

8. Ibid., 344.

9. *Откуда исходит угроза миру* [Whence the threat to world peace comes] (Moscow, 1982), 8, 34.

9

War Games in Europe

The U.S. Army Experiments with Atomic Doctrine

Donald A. Carter

At the end of World War II the U.S. Army assumed a new mission. The emergence of the Soviet Union as a hostile power and the threat posed by substantial Soviet armed forces in Eastern Europe forced American military leaders to reexamine their strategic policy. For the army, this meant developing the equipment, organization, and doctrine to meet and defeat a numerically superior opponent. Atomic weapons seemed to offer a means of evening the odds in the event of a Soviet attack. Throughout the 1950s, the U.S. Army experimented with ways to integrate the new and powerful weapons into its plans for the defense of Western Europe.

Of course, the army's experiences with tactical atomic weapons in Europe must be placed into the larger context of the service's role in American national security. One of the cornerstones of President Dwight D. Eisenhower's "New Look" strategic policy was strength through a sound national economy. His administration looked for a "bigger bang for the buck," as it emphasized atomic weapons, the Strategic Air Command, and massive retaliation at the expense of the army's conventional forces. Throughout the 1950s, the army faced a series of personnel and budget cuts that threatened its existence as an organization. As one senior army general explained it, "The Army literally struggled for survival."[1] Through its development of an atomic weapons doctrine in Europe, the army hoped to prove that it had a role to play on the modern battlefield and in the national security policy of the United States.

Setting the Stage

As it had after every war it had ever fought, the army demobilized after World War II. The eight-million-man force that ended the war evaporated, leaving by 1948 slightly more than five hundred thousand troops to carry on with occupation duties in Germany and Japan.[2] For a brief period, Americans expected that the atomic bomb would guarantee security and deter Soviet aggression. President Harry S. Truman and Secretary of Defense Louis A. Johnson made extensive cuts in the U.S. defense budget on the basis of that expectation. The U.S. atomic monopoly, however, ended on 23 September 1949, when the Soviet Union detonated its own nuclear device.

The explosion of the Soviet atomic bomb in 1949 and the start of the Korean War in 1950 ended American demobilization. Despite the fighting in Korea, the threat of Soviet expansion into Western Europe continued to pose the greatest challenge to American security. The Red Army had solidified its gains in Eastern Europe and had turned Poland, Hungary, and the Balkans over to Soviet-backed governments. The Soviets also solidified control of their portion of occupied Germany, with Communist officials molding a government in their own image. American intelligence estimated that the Red Army retained as many as two hundred divisions under arms, more than half of which were poised to attack Western Europe. In this environment, containment of Soviet expansion became the centerpiece of American strategic policy.

That threat prompted the formation of NATO in 1949 and the beginning of an American commitment to defend the region. To that end, in November 1950 the United States activated Seventh Army in Europe, to consist of the V and VII Corps. In addition to the 1st Infantry Division, the only division remaining in Europe at the time, Seventh Army prepared to receive the 4th, 28th, and 43rd Infantry and the 2nd Armored Divisions. These new organizations deployed to Europe by the end of 1952, supported by ample artillery, engineer, and antiaircraft artillery units. Planners reorganized the Constabulary that had performed most of the occupation duties into three armored cavalry regiments: the 2nd, 6th, and 14th. The 1st and 4th Infantry Divisions, the 2nd Armored Division, and the 14th Armored Cavalry Regiment composed V Corps, centered on Frankfurt. The 28th and 43rd Infantry Divisions and the 2nd and 6th Armored Cavalry Regiments made up VII Corps stationed farther south in the area of Stuttgart.[3]

Although the initial deployments to Seventh Army were completed by the end of 1952, the demand for replacements to support the war in Korea stripped the force of most of its trained and experienced troops. Almost all of the national guardsmen who had deployed with the 28th and 43rd Infantry Divisions on two-year call-ups returned to the United States, to be replaced by inexperienced troops. The 4th Infantry Division experienced an almost 100 percent turnover of personnel during 1952, losing more than twelve thousand trained soldiers. The other divisions reported similar personnel turbulence. Commanders indicated that the excellent training their units had undergone during the first year of the deployment was largely undone by the extreme turnover. Although all major subordinate units reported that they were operationally ready in 1952, subsequent training programs had little to build on and had to start over from scratch.[4]

Initial War Games, Early Doctrine Developments

Although it represented a formidable combat force, Seventh Army never matched the numerical superiority of the Soviets. Red Army forces within striking distance of Germany outnumbered U.S. and NATO units in personnel, tanks, and almost all other major combat systems. As a result, Seventh Army from its inception had to develop battle plans that would enable it to fight and win while outnumbered. Leaders planned to do this by building on the service's World War II organization and doctrine. Divisions retained their traditional triangular structure, providing for a maneuver element, a base of fire, and a reserve. The *Report of the General Board, European Theater of Operations* and other studies conducted by the Historical Section of Army Ground Forces reflected the serious and diligent effort the army made to learn from and build on its experience in World War II.[5]

The deployment to Europe also prompted army leaders to look to the German experience in World War II for doctrinal guidance. Military historians invested considerable effort in studying Germany's campaigns on the eastern front and cataloging the lessons to be learned. Former Wehrmacht officers encouraged this study, promoting a belief that their operational concepts had been sound and had been defeated only by Adolf Hitler's inept strategic leadership. In that line, and confronted by a lack of training areas suitable for large-scale maneuvers, Seventh Army compiled training guidance that highlighted the German army's strong emphasis on small unit tactics. Seventh Army's plan for the defense of Western Europe began to resemble the German doctrine of mobile defense. It abandoned fixed linear defense concepts in favor of a more active resistance, with tanks replacing antitank guns and tank destroyers as the primary antitank weapon.[6]

The conflict in Korea also provided lessons in defeating a numerically superior foe, but the nature of that war made army leaders in Europe reluctant to study seriously the developments in tactics, organization, and equipment that it seemed to suggest. Neither the North Korean nor the Chinese army employed the type of mechanized assault force the Americans expected to face in Europe. Although Korea demonstrated the killing power of massed field artillery, a lesson not lost on those planning for combat in Europe, the country's mountainous terrain channeled forces into narrow valleys and offered few opportunities for the war of movement emphasized by the Germans. Instead, it bore a bleak resemblance to the trench warfare of World War I.

The operational doctrine that began to emerge within Seventh Army in 1951 thus combined many of the elements gleaned from the army's most recent experiences. General Manton Eddy, the Seventh Army commanding general, for example, embraced the German concept of the mobile defense. He deployed his armored cavalry regiments forward to provide early warning, to force the attackers to deploy into assault formations, thus indicating the main directions of an attack. They would then continue to harass the advancing formations, inflicting casualties as they withdrew. Instead of fighting from fixed, fortified positions, armor and infantry along the main line of resistance would defend from successive positions, trading space for time and the ability to inflict maximum casualties as the enemy advanced. Meanwhile, massed artillery and mortar fire would break up enemy assault formations and inflict casualties. As it had in Korea, their artillery gave U.S. commanders a considerable battlefield advantage. They could call upon thirty-nine battalions of field artillery and eighteen battalions of antiaircraft artillery in addition to the mortars organic to their infantry battalions.[7] The ability of American gunners to mass fire on a single target and to deliver it in a single, simultaneous volley (the time-on-target technique) had made them the most proficient in the world during World War II. Seventh Army's plans for the defense of Western Europe depended on maintaining that level of fire support.

Field exercises began in 1951 to train new arrivals and to refine battle plans. Almost immediately, observers noted that much of Seventh Army's training seemed too closely related to World War II tactical experiences.[8] The most frequent issue raised in exercise critiques, for example, was an unrealistic assumption of air superiority. Ground units assumed that they would have the same virtually unlimited air support they had enjoyed during the campaign across Europe at the end of World War II. Even so, air-ground coordination was poor throughout the maneuvers. To some extent that reflected the postwar military reorganization and the formation of an independent U.S. Air Force fixated on the concept of strategic bombing. Air Force commanders placed a much lower degree of emphasis on training and equipping for ground support missions than their Army Air Forces predecessors had during World War II, and often canceled such training because of weather conditions. Despite these concerns and against the background of severe personnel turbulence, Seventh Army units demonstrated considerable operational skill during a two-sided, multidivision maneuver in October 1951 known as Exercise COMBINE.[9]

Up through the end of 1951, Seventh Army planned for only a conventional defense. The army had yet to consider atomic weapons as firepower available to support war on the ground. Korea was a case in point. Until then, not only were there too few nuclear weapons available to risk depleting the stockpile reserved for general war with the Soviet Union, but North Korea also offered little in the way of suitable targets, and potentially lucrative sites in China were off-limits for political reasons. Although massed formations of Chinese infantry might have warranted an atomic strike, American intelligence lacked the ability to identify and locate them with enough precision to justify that kind of attack.

Throughout this period, however, there were army officers who were beginning to consider the use of atomic weapons in support of conventional battlefield maneuver. Army professional publications, such as *Military Review* and *Army Information Digest,* printed several articles on the subject. In November 1951 the army published *Field Manual 100–31: Tactical Use of Atomic Weapons,* which formalized many of the ideas posed in the professional journals into the service's first attempt at a tactical atomic doctrine. The new manual and the concepts it presented, however, remained mostly speculation through the end of 1951. None of Seventh Army's training highlights or exercise scenarios at the time reflected consideration of atomic weaponry beyond an occasional radiological decontamination drill.

Integrating Atomic Weapons into Existing Conventional Doctrine

From 2 January through 20 February 1952, the army conducted a two-sided tactical exercise employing the 3rd Armored Cavalry Regiment, the 11th Airborne Division, and the 278th Regimental Combat Team. Exercise SNOWFALL, held in upstate New York, was the first maneuver to include the simulated tactical usage of atomic weapons. Both friendly and aggressor forces employed atomic bombs dropped from aircraft to break up enemy formations and to facilitate maneuvers on the ground. Commanders experimented with procedures for target selection and the effects of atomic explosions on troops and equipment. Lieutenant General Willis D. Crittenberger, the maneuver director, indicated after the exercise that the effort's main value was to set in motion the thought and planning necessary for the production of sound nuclear doctrine.[10]

At the same time, the army also began to conduct a series of tests at Yucca Flats, Nevada, to study the effects of an atomic detonation on troop behavior. Known as the DESERT ROCK exercises, the project exposed troops under varying degrees of protection to atomic explosions. The researchers also placed military equipment, vehicles, and tethered animals at varying distances to assess the blast and heat effects. Besides becoming conditioned to the concept of atomic combat, the participants in the effort learned that, properly dispersed and protected, they could survive an atomic explosion and continue their mission. On the basis of these tests, dispersion became a key element in all subsequent doctrine involving atomic weapons. Although the tests included periodic checks to determine levels of radioactive fallout, however, they demonstrated a lack of understanding of radioactivity's long-term effects. Army training literature and films tended to treat the matter rather lightly. It remained for further tests and experiments to confirm the implications of radiation exposure.[11]

Throughout 1952, training and tactical exercises in Europe continued to focus on conventional warfare. *Seventh Army Training Circular Number 2* for 1952–1953 encouraged emphasis on preparing individual and small unit leaders, fire support, air defense, night operations, mines and demolitions, physical fitness, concurrent integrated training, equipment maintenance, and tactical offensives in delaying action. There was no mention of, let alone emphasis on, atomic warfare. Command post exercise GRAND ALLIANCE, conducted in 1952, was a case in point. It tested Seventh Army's ability to establish communications with European Command, the British Army of the Rhine, and the First French Army without any reference to the nuclear option. NORTH WIND, a VII Corps command post exercise conducted in January 1952, did include an enemy atomic strike in its scenario, but that event had little impact on the scheme of maneuver for either side. Its primary purpose was to prompt units to exercise appropriate radiological decontamination measures.[12]

Seventh Army conducted Exercise ROSE BUSH as its major field training for 1952. This short maneuver, running from 4 to 9 September, served to test training objectives for the year. ROSE BUSH was a free-maneuver, two-sided exercise that included elements of the U.S. V Corps, the French II Corps, and the U.S. Twelfth Air Force. Most of it emphasized individual and small unit skills. The scenario and after-action critiques again contained no mention of concern for atomic weapons.[13] Later that year, V Corps conducted BELL HOOK (13–18 October) and VII Corps conducted BLOW TORCH (27–31 October). Both were also two-sided maneuvers driven by a prearranged operational plan that required units to deploy and execute both offensive and defensive missions. These tasks reflected the existing doctrine of mobile defense and included assaults across a defended river and a river line defense. Post-exercise critiques indicated that the most significant weaknesses the operation revealed were to be found in the coordination of tactical air support and air-ground communications. Observers and umpires directed additional criticism toward problems with movement, security, and individual soldier skills. As with ROSE BUSH, there was no indication of any concern for the employment of atomic weapons.[14]

In 1953 the U.S. Army in Europe took its first steps toward integrating atomic weapons into its operational doctrine. The Eisenhower administration's New Look strategic policies made it quite clear that the United States would use atomic weapons in any general war with the Soviet Union. The Strategic Air Command would have the primary responsibility to drop atomic bombs on targets deep within the Soviet Union. Without any means of delivering atomic munitions on their own, Seventh Army leaders had to rely on whatever bombs the air force was willing to divert to tactical support. Some within Seventh Army were skeptical regarding any level of air force support. In a critique of atomic weapons play in U.S. Army, Europe (USAREUR), exercise SPRING TIDE in May 1953, for example, one observer questioned the use of atomic weapons in support of frontline operations, noting that the army and air force in Korea had been unable to identify suitable atomic targets near the front lines.[15] Whatever their doubts, the Seventh Army's commanders began planning to use the nuclear option.

Later that year, some of the ideas officers had expressed in the service's doctrinal literature found their way into Seventh Army's training program. A NATO-sponsored Special Weapons Orientation Course, for example, revised its curriculum so that all classes would include instruction on the use of atomic weapons in support of the land battle.[16] Seventh Army also designed maneuvers to include the use of atomic weapons to support ground forces on the attack and in the defense.

In September USAREUR conducted Exercise MONTE CARLO to evaluate the level of training in Seventh Army units. More than 182,000 U.S. and allied troops participated in this maneuver, the largest in Europe since the reactivation of Seventh Army in 1951. The exercise also focused on the development of atomic warfare techniques, its mission statement included the objective to instill in participating soldiers an "atomic mindedness" and to dispel misconceptions about the use of atomic weapons. The maneuver tested the ability of ground forces to communicate with air units capable of delivering atomic munitions. Ground elements also demonstrated their ability to concentrate swiftly from widely dispersed positions and to coordinate their movements with the fire support provided by atomic weapons, since timely and accurate delivery of those weapons could completely disrupt an attacking armored formation. Once Seventh Army units moved to the offensive, atomic weapons could also rupture the strongest defensive line at the point of the attack. Since ground units still depended on the air force to blast open the enemy's defenses, they attempted to synchronize their maneuver to take advantage of that support. Observers labeled the exercise a success because it demonstrated the progress that had been achieved during the training year while indicating areas that required further work.[17]

In October 1953 the first unit equipped with the M-65 280-millimeter atomic cannon arrived in Europe, where army leaders made a great show of displaying the ordnance for the American and European press. The message implicit in the delivery of such weapons was every bit as important as the tactical capabilities they represented. The atomic cannons symbolized the Eisenhower administration's reliance on nuclear weapons to defend Europe. They also provided Seventh Army with the ability to provide its own atomic fire support without having to rely on the air force. Although the cannons lacked the range and flexibility of aircraft-delivered munitions, they provided a far greater measure of accuracy and reliability. The subsequent arrival of air force B-61 Matador missile units provided yet another means of supporting the ground forces with atomic firepower.[18]

By 1954 atomic weapons were firmly established as essential components of any proposed defense in Western Europe. In its annual training guidance, USAREUR directed Seventh Army to emphasize those weapons throughout division-, corps-, and army-level maneuvers. In response, Seventh Army developed standing operating procedures that integrated atomic fire support into its battle doctrine.[19] The 280-millimeter cannon battalions dragged their big guns all over Germany as they participated in field exercises from divisional to NATO-level maneuvers. Army technicians constructed pyrotechnics that simulated atomic detonations for use in training. In September,

V Corps participated in NATO exercise INDIAN SUMMER, which emphasized the use of atomic weapons and guided missiles against an enemy similarly armed. Observers of this maneuver commented on the increased level
of concern for camouflage and dispersion, recognizing that their own atomic
forces were high-priority targets for the other side's weapons. Division-level
exercises for the rest of the year included extensive atomic play.[20]

At the end of 1954, the first MGR-1 Honest John rocket and MGM-5 Corporal guided missile units began to arrive in Europe. Although these weapons
were capable of firing both conventional and atomic warheads, their limited
range and relative inaccuracy made them poorly suited for nonnuclear use.
They did, however, provide Seventh Army with another option for atomic
fire support. The command assigned the Honest John batteries to the V and
VII Corps headquarters as part of their artillery support assets. The Corporal
missiles had a longer range than the Honest John rockets and could reach
targets well beyond the corps boundaries, and therefore remained under
Seventh Army control. Lack of available firing ranges, however, hampered
training with the new weapons. By the middle of 1955, Seventh Army had
launched only two Honest John rockets (both with conventional warheads),
using firing ranges at Grafenwöhr, the largest training area in Germany. By
the end of the year, USAREUR and U.S. European Command were still ne-
gotiating to obtain suitable range facilities. As a result, although the addition
of the rocket and guided missile units increased Seventh Army's options for
atomic firepower, the lack of firing ranges limited the command's ability to
train its soldiers to use and support the weapons.[21]

The increasing role of atomic weapons in Seventh Army's operational doc-
trine raised questions about command and control. While the president of the
United States retained authority for their initial release, military officers in
Europe grappled over custody issues within the theater. The Supreme Allied
Commander, Europe (SACEUR), an American general officer, directed the
employment of the atomic weapons once authorized by the president. Seventh
Army commanders, however, pressed for a more decentralized authority over
atomic assets available for use in theater. They argued that once the weapons
were released, control should be vested in the field army commander.

While SACEUR retained operational control over NATO's international
military units, U.S. Seventh Army also required a means of coordinating allied access to atomic weapons. To facilitate this coordination, USAREUR established atomic liaison units in all subordinate elements at corps level and
above. The liaison units supported allied commanders with access to allocated atomic weapons and provided advice on how to employ them.[22]

USAREUR and Seventh Army headquarters also recommended the establishment of a special weapons division at Supreme Headquarters Allied Powers Europe (SHAPE) to be the primary staff advisor for atomic weapons issues. Up until then, the Special Air Staff had performed that function, but commanders at Seventh Army and USAREUR headquarters believed that the air force officers failed to acknowledge their concerns about how many weapons should be allocated to ground support missions and how those communications would be controlled. Unwilling to participate in the interservice rivalry, SHAPE tabled the recommendation, and Seventh Army leaders remained skeptical about the level of support they would receive from the air force–dominated section.[23]

The year 1955 was an important transition point in the evolution of atomic doctrine for USAREUR. The 280-millimeter artillery battalions, Honest John rocket batteries, and Corporal missile battalions had by then arrived in sufficient numbers to give real credence to Seventh Army's emerging atomic capability. In September, the army announced plans to replace the 280-millimeter guns with smaller 8-inch howitzers, greatly improving the mobility of its atomic artillery.[24] After two years of field training and command post exercises that emphasized reliance on atomic weapons, units in Germany began to demonstrate real proficiency in the execution of an operational doctrine based on their use. General William M. Hoge, the retiring USAREUR commander, reported that U.S. forces in Europe had reached their highest level of training since World War II.[25]

As Seventh Army's skill increased, many of the NATO allies began to consider the implications of an atomic war for them and their people. The West Germans in particular recognized exactly where any major conflict would take place. If any doubt remained, NATO exercise CARTE BLANCHE in June 1955 erased it. In what was predominantly an air maneuver designed to test communications, command and control, air defense, and counterstrike doctrine, opposing forces dropped 335 atomic bombs throughout the battle on West Germany, France, Belgium, Luxembourg, and the Netherlands.[26] Exercise umpires estimated that the simulated attacks resulted in almost 2 million dead and 3.5 million wounded even before the effects of radioactive contamination came into account. Up until CARTE BLANCHE, there had been little public comment about the implications of a potential defense of Western Europe based on tactical atomic weapons. After it, however, the floodgates opened. Substantial commentary began among the European allies and in the international media on what would occur.[27] Fritz Erler, the opposition speaker in the German parliament, questioned the relevance of

German participation in Western Europe's defense if Germany were going to be devastated by atomic weapons anyway. German chancellor Konrad Adenauer called the report of CARTE BLANCHE "frightening" and felt he had been stabbed in the back by his potential allies as he worked to make German participation in NATO a reality.[28] In critiques of subsequent NATO exercises, the Germans questioned the excessive use of atomic weapons against what they considered inappropriate targets. They expressed particular concern about their use in areas where NATO policy had encouraged civilians to remain in their homes to prevent large flows of refugees.[29]

The German response raised important new issues concerning the army's plans for surviving an atomic exchange. U.S. military units in Europe relied on civilian labor to provide much of their administrative support, for tasks such as clearing away rubble to facilitate movement and retrieving the dead and wounded. Since any civilians who survived the initial attacks would be reluctant to reenter the stricken area, let alone assist in the recovery, commanders would have to strip out soldiers from their own units to perform those basic support tasks.[30]

Army chief of staff General Matthew B. Ridgway alluded to CARTE BLANCHE's results when he distributed *Department of the Army Pamphlet 21-7 The Role of the Army,* in June 1955. In it Ridgway wrote that no one could "ignore that man may now possess the means of annihilating life on this planet." He continued: "To retain the full support of our allies, the United States must continue to offer reasonable hope that civilization will survive; that hope is best promoted by policies which demonstrate that in any future war there will be a maximum effort to achieve a controlled application of atomic destructive power." He concluded that the army was the service with the most experience and ability to selectively employ such power.[31] In effect, Ridgway was attempting to improve the army's position in the Eisenhower defense hierarchy by underscoring its ability to limit the collateral effects of atomic war, because of the smaller, more accurate warheads its artillery could deliver.

Lieutenant General James M. Gavin, the army's director of research and development, amplified European concerns in testimony before the Senate Subcommittee on the Air Force in June 1956. In responding to a question on potential casualties in an atomic war, he indicated that current estimates ran toward several hundred million, depending on the strength and direction of the prevailing winds.[32] Coming on the heels of the CARTE BLANCHE exercise, his testimony hardened European attitudes against tactical atomic warfare.

The Pentomic Division Comes to Europe

While Seventh Army's battle plans emphasized the use of atomic weapons, through 1956 they still reflected a conventional doctrine. Commanders intended to use atomic weapons in support of traditional maneuver forces in the defense and counterattack. The organization of the divisions and armored cavalry regiments supported a conventional scheme of maneuver. At the same time, President Eisenhower's support for a doctrine of Massive Retaliation expanded the U.S. Air Force's capability to deliver atomic weapons to strategic targets within the Soviet Union. Eisenhower perceived the ground forces in Europe as a trip wire, any substantial violation of which would trigger a decisive response from the bombers and missiles of the Strategic Air Command. This policy appealed to the NATO allies much more than did a ground-oriented defense that would toss atomic weapons at Soviet formations after they had already crossed friendly borders.

By the end of 1956, army leaders believed that they were engaged in a struggle for their service's survival. The Eisenhower administration's doctrine of Massive Retaliation and its reliance on strategic nuclear forces left the service with a steadily decreasing portion of the national defense budget. Secretary of Defense Charles E. Wilson rejected requests to replace or update stocks of conventional weapons, vehicles, and equipment and encouraged army chief of staff General Maxwell D. Taylor to submit requests for modern weaponry that reflected the administration's strategic outlook. Taylor concluded that the only way his service could survive the bureaucratic infighting was to demonstrate that it had a role to play on the atomic battlefield. He set out to redesign the service's organizational structure in a way that would shrink overall manpower requirements while retaining the existing number of divisions and emphasizing the army's readiness to wage an atomic war.[33]

Taylor's experience during the Korean War had caused him to consider potential changes in the army's organizational structure. He now faced the dilemma of maintaining as much of the army's combat strength as possible in the face of looming budget and personnel cuts. Instead of the traditional triangular organization from World War II, or the older four-regiment square division from World War I, he envisioned a structure made up of five self-contained formations called battle groups. Smaller than a regiment but bigger than a battalion, each battle group would consist of four rifle companies, a 4.2-inch mortar battery, and a company combining headquarters and service support elements. Later revisions increased the group to five rifle companies, mirroring the five-sided structure of the division. Titled the Pentomic

Division, the new organization consolidated the division artillery into one 105-millimeter howitzer battalion with five batteries and one mixed-artillery battalion that included two 155-millimeter howitzer batteries and two nuclear elements; an 8-inch howitzer battery; and an Honest John rocket battery. The two nuclear systems provided the division its primary offensive punch. One of the most important principles of the restructuring was the elimination from division control of all nonessential elements by removing much of the force's support base, including transportation, supply, and aviation assets, which became the responsibility of corps and higher headquarters. Given the army's anticipated personnel reductions, perhaps the most important result, in General Taylor's view, was that the new structure reduced the authorized strength of an airborne division by six thousand men and that of an infantry division by five thousand. Because army leaders believed that the current capabilities of the armored divisions already met the requirements of the atomic battlefield, the strength and organization of those units changed little.[34]

Taylor saw the Pentomic organization as ideally suited for fighting an atomic war. The five subordinate battle groups in each of its divisions enabled the force to disperse in width and depth rather than in a single, linear formation. Companies within the battle groups could disperse even further, so that no single element presented a lucrative target for atomic attacks. Taylor believed that improved communications equipment allowed division commanders to exert more direct control over their separated units than in the past. He also contended that new armored personnel carriers shortly to join the force would provide the mobility to enable the formations to converge rapidly and to exploit opportunities provided by atomic fire support. Although many senior officers in the army questioned whether the new technologies could deliver the required capabilities, General Taylor pushed on with his plans for reorganization.

By the end of 1957 the army had reorganized all five divisions in Europe under the Pentomic concept. After a series of unit rotations, Seventh Army consisted of the 11th Airborne, the 3rd and 4th Armored, and the 8th and 10th Infantry Divisions. The 3rd, 11th, and 14th Cavalry Regiments composed the border patrol and forward screen.[35]

In 1958 Seventh Army prepared to put the new organization to the test with another training cycle. Beginning 10 February 1958, Exercise SABRE HAWK sent more than 125,000 soldiers to the field for the largest maneuver yet in the history of Seventh Army. V Corps maneuvered against VII Corps in a series of attack, defend, delay, and withdraw scenarios. The maneuvers tested atomic weapons employment, target acquisition, resupply, and aerial troop movement while emphasizing individual and small unit training in cold-weather conditions.[36] During the critique of the exercise, the Seventh Army's Operations and Planning Staff identified training deficiencies that could be traced to flaws in the new organization. Divisional transportation and support assets were insufficient to ensure timely delivery of atomic weapons to forward artillery units. When asked to assess the combat effectiveness of the new organization, division commanders complained that the force also lacked adequate conventional artillery support. They requested increased artillery assets at the earliest possible time.[37]

In March 1958 Seventh Army units down to divisional level participated in command post exercise LION BLEU, which focused attention on atomic response capability throughout NATO. The exercise identified conflicting priorities between Seventh Army and higher headquarters elements, particularly between the army and the air force. Air commanders favored an early employment of most of their atomic weapons allocation, leaving very little for subsequent support of the ground component. LION BLEU also demonstrated that ground units needed to spread out to a far greater width and depth than they had originally planned to avoid presenting tempting targets for the enemy's atomic weapons.[38]

Overall, if the test demonstrated the capability for dispersion inherent in the Pentomic units, it had also exposed serious communications difficulties. Even with improved equipment, the extended distances between units and staffs and the frequent movement required under the Pentomic doctrine rendered communications problematic. The lack of intermediate headquarters, moreover, forced division staffs to monitor the communications of as many as sixteen subordinate elements at once.[39]

Later exercises and maneuvers identified more flaws in the Pentomic organization. In June 1958, for example, Seventh Army participated in Exercise FULL PLAY, which evaluated all elements involved in the logistical support of atomic weapons. The effort revealed that ordnance and transportation units responsible for supporting the delivery of atomic weapons to Seventh Army were unprepared to carry out those assignments. As SABRE HAWK had already indicated, moreover, the divisions continued to lack the capability to augment logistical support from their own resources.[40]

In September USAREUR conducted QUICK SERVE, a command post and maneuver exercise designed to test the capability of atomic munitions support units to deploy rapidly and to retrieve, transport, guard, and deliver atomic weapons to delivery units at the expenditure rate expected in a tactical atomic conflict. The scenario planned for the detonation of 123 atomic weapons during a three-day period, but the exercise itself soon indicated that release procedures were too cumbersome and that ammunition supply points were too far from firing units for support units to deliver munitions forward in a timely manner. The final exercise report recommended that ammunition supply points be located along readily accessible road networks and closer to the units they supported. It also encouraged SHAPE to authorize Seventh Army to use atomic weapons at the earliest possible moment in any nuclear confrontation.[41] Overall, the exercise proved so valuable as a gauge of the logistical readiness of atomic support units that Seventh Army made plans to conduct similar exercises on a regular basis.

At the end of September 1958 Seventh Army reported twenty-one of its atomic delivery and support weapons units operationally ready, twenty-two marginally ready at reduced capability, and six unready. Although technically competent, most units lacked sufficient personnel and suffered shortages in required electronics, spare parts, and essential communications equipment. The army devoted funds to research and development that it might have spent to alleviate these shortages. In his Annual Historical Report, the commander-in-chief of USAREUR, General Henry I. Hodes, reported that the continuous development of new missile systems made it very difficult to maintain a strong capability on a day-to-day basis.[42]

That being the case, the reorganization was nonetheless serving its major purpose. For if the Eisenhower administration continued to cut conventional forces and the army's role in national security policy, it also continued to fund the service's experimental programs involving long-range missiles, rockets, and air defense weapons. It seems clear, in that light, that the army's leaders had sacrificed the operational readiness of units in the field in order to fund the research and development necessary to strengthen their hand in the nation's larger strategic and bureaucratic debates. Army chief of staff General Maxwell Taylor alluded to the political nature of the Pentomic division in his book *Swords and Plowshares*, published in 1972.[43] In comments to General Bruce Palmer Jr., then assistant secretary of the General Staff, Taylor defended his brainchild: "You know if I hadn't done that, what might have happened. I had to do something to show that the Army was innovative, and forward looking, and recognized the atomic era."[44]

The final big command post exercise of 1958, BOUNCE BACK, reflected the approach that the army was beginning to take. The scenario depicted an initial aggressor strike against NATO military installations employing forty-nine separate atomic warheads with yields ranging from five to one hundred kilotons. What had started as an honest attempt to understand the realities of atomic warfare in the early 1950s was, by the end of 1958, beginning to resemble the plot of a Hollywood B-movie science fiction thriller. Much of the exercise seemed to involve mathematical calculations of how much of the force would remain after the initial strikes.[45] Evaluators noted in their reports that personnel were no longer taking the training seriously. Following one simulated atomic strike, commanders ordered a hospital to evacuate because it was in the middle of a contaminated area. When the Seventh Army command surgeon countermanded the order, controllers declared the hospital and all its personnel lost to overexposure.[46] The V Corps distributed a booklet at that time titled *Tips on Atomic Warfare* that reduced atomic tactics to comic-book form. The booklet depicted soldiers who, after surviving an atomic strike, rallied those who remained and continued the mission as the ghosts of their dead comrades waved farewell in the background.[47]

By 1959 it was clear that the Pentomic organization and the atomic training and doctrine that accompanied it were neither realistic nor appropriate responses to the military threat in Europe. In July 1958 USAREUR deployed two airborne battle groups reinforced with artillery and armor to Lebanon as a show of force and to assist in peacekeeping efforts there.[48] Planning also began for a similar deployment to secure U.S. installations in Morocco.[49] When the Soviets indicated their intent to abrogate agreements on American, British, and French access to Berlin, a response planned but never executed involved the movement of tactical units armed with conventional weapons through the traditional access corridors to Berlin. While the atomic organization and doctrine had some utility in deterring a major war, it was becoming clear that it was of much less use in dealing with the smaller confrontations that the army faced on a regular basis.

The Pentomic concept continued to unravel with each successive training exercise. Under the new organization the infantry divisions retained sufficient armored personnel carriers to move only one reinforced battle group at a time. For an organization whose very existence depended on mobility, this was an extraordinary deficiency. Additionally, since armored personnel carriers were consolidated at division level and parceled out as required, drivers never consistently trained with the companies and squads they supported. Communications and command and control assets were inadequate to manage so many dispersed subelements. With no intervening headquarters between the company and the battle group, there were too few experienced mid-level leaders. Without them, it was impossible for the commander to maintain effective control.[50] As General Hamilton H. Howze, a former deputy chief of staff for plans in Seventh Army who also had been a Pentomic division commander, remarked:

> The battle group of five companies . . . didn't make much sense. In other words a square structure is . . . much better than a pentomic structure and perhaps a triangular structure is the best of all. . . .
>
> In actual fact what it amounted to was a structure so deficient in support units at the division level that it was necessary to rob the line units in order to beef up the others. Therefore, it was not possible to run the division and not cheat on the structure as respects support versus combat units.[51]

As the 1950s ended, the Pentomic division had served its purpose. It had allowed the army to survive President Eisenhower's strategic policies and to maintain its divisional and corps structure in Europe.

Reassessment, Flexible Response, and ROAD

The early 1960s brought a new president, John F. Kennedy, into office in the United States and new challenges in Europe, centered particularly on Berlin. In response, the U.S. Army in Germany continued to test organizations and doctrinal concepts in order to maintain and improve its readiness for combat. Training exercises often involved company- and battle-group-sized elements to achieve limited objectives. In May 1960, for example, FLECHER D'OR (GOLDEN ARROW) involved an airborne assault by two battle groups to seize an airfield.[52] In FER DE LANCE the 8th Infantry Division experimented with a series of airborne assaults by reinforced rifle companies.[53] These exercises reflected the army's growing interest in air mobility and an increased use of helicopters in a tactical role.

Seventh Army continued the process in larger exercises such as WINTERSHIELD in February 1960, but it also emphasized atomic weapons employment, Pentomic organization and doctrine, and logistical support procedures.[54] For although the army had been quietly working on a replacement for the Pentomic organization since 1959, actual change would not occur until after the Eisenhower administration had left office. The new administration of President Kennedy had campaigned for office by openly challenging President Eisenhower's strategic policies. Both Kennedy and his secretary of defense, Robert S. McNamara, wanted to have military options short of nuclear war. Kennedy accepted much of the military philosophy that former army chief of staff Maxwell Taylor had expressed in his book *The Uncertain Trumpet* (1960). Indeed, he found himself so impressed with Taylor's ideas concerning a more flexible military response that he offered the retired officer a spot on his staff as special military advisor to the president. Seizing the opportunity, the army wasted little time following Kennedy's inauguration before moving to rid itself of the atomic albatross. In March 1961, less than two months after the new president took office, army chief of staff General George H. Decker approved a plan for restructuring the service titled Reorganization Objectives Army Division (ROAD) 1965. The president publicly announced the conversion in May 1961.[55]

ROAD reduced the emphasis on atomic weapons and tactics, returning to many of the concepts of the World War II triangular division and its subordinate regimental combat teams. The new concept restored the brigade headquarters to the division as command and control elements while assigning separate battalions to the brigades as mission required. Most brigades inherited a mix of armor and infantry units to encourage a combined-arms approach. ROAD also increased conventional artillery support by allocating a direct support artillery battalion for each maneuver brigade while retaining at least one additional general support battalion in support of the division as a whole. The division base regained many of the support assets it had lost under the Pentomic structure. Most of the commanders in Seventh Army regarded ROAD as a substantial improvement over the Pentomic division because it gave them the firepower, flexibility, and sustainability to face a significant conventional threat without having to resort to nuclear war.[56]

The units in Europe did not complete their conversion to the ROAD organization until October 1963. Throughout 1961 and 1962, however, Seventh Army received modernized equipment and weapons that increased its combat readiness. In 1961 units began to receive the new M-14 rifle, which replaced the M-1 rifle, the M-1 carbine, and the Browning automatic rifle. That same year M-60 tanks began to replace the heavier, slower M-48s. Later, in 1962, updated helicopters and other support aircraft also appeared on the scene. Perhaps most significant, M-113 armored personnel carriers arrived in quantities sufficient to create entire divisions of mechanized infantry. This corrected the lack of mobility inherent in the Pentomic organization.[57]

In 1961 one of the last vestiges of the army's atomic fixation, the Davy Crockett atomic projectile and recoilless launcher, deployed to Europe. The M-28 102-millimeter launcher or the M-29 155-millimeter launcher fired a seventy-six-pound atomic projectile to a range of 1.2 miles or 2.5 miles, respectively. Planners assigned two and later three Davy Crocketts to each infantry battalion and each reconnaissance squadron, with battalion commanders controlling their employment once the president authorized an atomic release. The new weapons were not popular with commanders because of the security, training, and support problems they posed. Few relished the idea, moreover, that junior and noncommissioned officers would be riding around a combat zone with atomic weapons under their direct control. Most welcomed the elimination of the Davy Crockett sections when the army deployed W-48 nuclear 155-millimeter howitzer rounds to Europe in 1965.[58]

Maneuvers and exercises in the early 1960s continued to have an atomic orientation, but they increasingly emphasized conventional warfare. The commanding general of USAREUR, General Bruce C. Clarke, accelerated the trend in 1961 by directing Seventh Army to eliminate large-scale training exercises and to focus on division-level maneuvers and below. He believed that individual and small unit training was more important than combined operations with larger units.[59] In January 1962 NATO conducted Exercise LONG THRUST II, which airlifted three battle groups of the 4th Infantry Division from Fort Lewis, Washington, to Germany. A test of strategic mobility and of the use of prepositioned equipment stocks, this effort presaged REFORGER (Return of Forces to Germany) deployments that would follow in the 1970s.[60]

The period beginning with the start of the Eisenhower administration thus represents an important transition in the way military leaders perceived their nuclear options. In 1952, with the United States only seven years removed from the actual use of atomic weapons in wartime, the World War II generation of officers not only accepted nuclear weapons as a viable wartime option, it had already employed them. By the early 1960s, however, most of the senior leadership from World War II had left the service and its successors had come to regard atomic weapons with a much higher degree of skepticism.

Ultimately, the reliance on the nuclear expedient in Europe became more of a political issue than a military one. President Eisenhower's strategy encouraged the army to develop its doctrine under the assumption that nuclear weapons would be used. Once Seventh Army began to receive atomic munitions it could deploy under its own operational control, they became the foundation of its doctrine. When NATO allies in Europe considered the implications of such a defense, however, a political impetus grew to develop alternatives. Seventh Army exercises throughout this period stressed the use of atomic weapons and indicated an honest attempt to develop a viable approach to their employment, but the speed with which army leaders moved away from the concept once the opportunity arose indicated a lack of comfort with the whole idea. Although army units in Europe continued to receive modernized weapons throughout the 1960s and 1970s, they integrated those weapons into a doctrine that remained firmly grounded in conventional tactics. Ultimately, atomic weapons had more value as deterrents than as implements of war.

Notes

1. Interview with General Bruce Palmer, 1976, U.S. Army Military History Research Collection, Senior Officers Debriefing Program, U.S. Army Military History Institute, Carlisle Barracks, Pennsylvania, p. 375.

2. Russell Weigley, *History of the United States Army* (Bloomington: Indiana University Press, 1984), 600.

3. Headquarters EUCOM/USAREUR Command Report, 1952, U.S. Army Center of Military History, Historical Manuscripts Collection (hereinafter USACMH, HMC), 8-3.1 CH5, p. 193.

4. Ibid., pp. 192–98; Seventh Army Command Report, 1952, National Archives II, College Park, Maryland, Record Group 549, U.S. Army, Europe, General Correspondence 1952–1954, pp. 141–54.

5. *Report of the General Board, ETO,* Army Ground Forces Studies, Historical Section, 1946, Combined Arms Research Library, U.S. Army Command and General Staff College, Fort Leavenworth, Kansas.

6. Kevin Soutor, "To Stem the Tide: The German Report Series and Its Effect on American Defense Doctrine, 1948–1954," *Journal of Military History* (Oct. 1993): 653–88.

7. "Seventh Army Artillery," September 1952, Seventh Army Command Report 1952, Report of the Artillery Section, National Archives II, Record Group 549, U.S. Army, Europe, General Correspondence, 1952–1954.

8. Drew Middleton, "Seventh Army in Line to Beat off Attack by Aggressor from East," *New York Times,* 4 Oct. 1951.

9. Drew Middleton, "Spirit of Allied Soldiers Acclaimed after Field Exercises in Germany," *New York Times,* 13 Oct. 1951.

10. Jean Moenk, *History of Large Scale Maneuvers in the United States: 1935–1961* (Fort Monroe, Va.: U.S. Continental Army Command, 1969), 167.

11. "Troop Performance on a Training Maneuver Involving the Use of Atomic Weapons," Operations Research Office Report T-170, 15 Mar. 1952, *Medical Effects of Nuclear Radiation,* U.S. Army Training Film, 23284DA, 1951.

12. "Exercise North Wind," VII Corps Command Report 1952, National Archives II, Record Group 338, VII Corps, 1953–1966.

13. "Exercise ROSE BUSH," V Corps Command Report 1952, Supporting Documents, National Archives II, Record Group 338, V Corps, 1949–1966.

14. Headquarters EUCOM/USAREUR Command Report, 1952, USACMH, HMC, 8-3.1 CH5, pp. 205–7.

15. "Memorandum for General Ferenbaugh, SUBJ: Critique of Spring Tide CPX [command post exercise]," 3 Jun. 1953, National Archives II, Record Group 549, U.S. Army, Europe, Assistant Chief of Staff, G3 Operations, General Correspondence, Decimal File.

16. "Memorandum for SAC, SUBJ: Revision of NATO Special Weapons Orientation Course," 23 Oct. 1953, National Archives II, Record Group 549, U.S. Army, Europe, G3 General Correspondence, Decimal File (Schools).

17. USAREUR Annual Historical Report, 1 Jan. 1953–30 June 1954, USACMH, HMC, 8-3.1 CK1, p. 249.

18. Ibid., pp. 220–21.

19. Letter from Gen. Hoge to Gen. Moore, 19 Dec. 1953, National Archives, Record Group 549, U.S. Army, Europe, G3 OPS General Correspondence, Decimal File 1953–1955.

20. USAREUR Annual Historical Report, 1 July 1954–30 June 1955, USACMH, HMC, 8-3.1 CL, pp. 215–29.

21. Ibid.

22. Letter from Gen. Hoge to Gen. Moore, 19 Dec. 1953, National Archives, Record Group 549, U.S. Army, Europe, G3 OPS General Correspondence, Decimal File 1953–1955.

23. "Memorandum Subject: Guidance on Atomic Matters," 4 Aug. 1953, National Archives II, Record Group 549, U.S. Army, Europe, Assistant Chief of Staff, G3 Operations.

24. "Army May Scrap Big Atomic Cannon," *New York Times,* 11 Sept. 1955.

25. "Efficiency of GI in Europe Lauded," *New York Times,* 27 Dec. 1954.

26. Thomas Brady, "Atomic Air War Ends in Confusion," *New York Times,* 28 June 1955.

27. Drew Middleton, "Soviet Peace Drive: Impact on West Europe," *New York Times,* 10 July 1955.

28. Alfred Grosser, *The Western Alliance* (New York: Random House, 1982), 167.

29. "USAREUR Annual History 1956–1957," USACMH, HMC, 8-3.1 CN2, p. 195.

30. "Composite Report, Exercise Sidestep," 22 Oct. 1959, National Archives II, Record Group 549, U.S. Army, Europe, Training Operations Files, 1958–1969.

31. Matthew Ridgway, *The Role of the Army,* DA Pamphlet 21-7, 29 June 1956, p. 16.

32. *New York Times,* 28 June 1956.

33. Maxwell Taylor, *Swords and Plowshares* (New York: W. W. Norton, 1972), 171.

34. John Wilson, *The Evolution of Divisions and Separate Brigades* (Washington, D.C.: U.S. Army Center of Military History, 1998), 270–78.

35. "Operation GYROSCOPE in the United States Army," USAREUR Historical Division, 1957, USACMH, HMC, 8-3.1 CN1, pp. 44–45.

36. USAREUR Annual Historical Report 1957–58, USACMH, HMC, 8-3.1 C02, p. 171.

37. "Actions to be taken as a result of FTX Sabre Hawk Critique," 12 Mar. 1958, National Archives II, Record Group 338, Seventh Army G3 Plans, 1954–1965, Organization Planning Files. (Also, 10th ID Response to USAREUR Msg "Request for Recommendations for major ROCID changes," dated 30 Jan. 1958, in the same box.)

38. USAREUR Annual Historical Report 1957–58, USACMH, HMC, 8-3.1 C02, pp. 169–70.

39. Andrew Bacevich, The Pentomic Era (Washington, D.C.: National Defense University Press, 1986), 134.

40. USAREUR Annual Historical Report 1957–58, USACMH, HMC, 8-3.1 C02, pp. 170–71.

41. "Final Report, Exercise QUICK SERVE," 25 Nov. 1958, National Archives II, Record Group 549, U.S. Army, Europe, G3 OPS, Training Operations Files.

42 USAREUR Annual Historical Report 1957–58, USACMH, HMC, 8-3.1 C02, pp. 176–77.

43. Taylor, Swords and Plowshares, 171.

44. Interview with General Bruce Palmer, 1976, U.S. Army Military History Research Collection, Senior Officers Debriefing Program, U.S. Army Military History Institute, Carlisle Barracks, Pennsylvania, p. 375.

45. "Exercise BOUNCE BACK," December 1958, National Archives II, Record Group 549, U.S. Army, Europe, Assistant Chief of Staff, G3 Operations, Troop Operations Branch, Training Operations Files, 1958–1960.

46. "Preliminary Report, Exercise BOUNCE BACK," 4 Dec. 1958, National Archives II, Record Group 549, U.S. Army, Europe, G3 Training Files.

47. Tips on Atomic Warfare, National Archives II, Record Group 338, Seventh Army, 1954–65, G3 Plans, Organizational Planning Files.

48. USAREUR Annual Historical Report 1958–1959, USACMH, HMC, 8-3.1 CP1, pp. 33–36.

49. Ibid., p. 45

50. John Wilson, The Evolution of Divisions and Separate Brigades (Washington, D.C.: U.S. Army Center of Military History, 1998), 270–85.

51. Interview with General Hamilton Howze, 1976, U.S. Army Military History Research Collection, Senior Officers Debriefing Program, U.S. Army Military History Institute, Carlisle Barracks, Pennsylvania, p. 7.

52. "Message from CINCUSAREUR to CINCNELM, USCINCEUR," 9 May 1960, National Archives II, Record Group 549, U.S. Army, Europe, Assistant Chief of Staff, G3 Operations, Troop Operations Branch, Training Operations Files, 1958–1960.

53. Quarterly Training Status Report, Forecast of Training Exercises FY 61, Na-

tional Archives II, Record Group 549, U.S. Army, Europe, Assistant Chief of Staff, G3 Operations, Organization and Training Branch, Training Operation Files.

54. Quarterly Training Status Report, 26 Oct. 1960, National Archives II, Record Group 549, U.S. Army, Europe, Assistant Chief of Staff, G3 Operations, Organization and Training Branch, Training Operation Files.

55. Robert Doughty, *The Evolution of U.S. Army Tactical Doctrine, 1946–1976* (Fort Leavenworth, Kan.: Combat Studies Institute, 1979), 30.

56. Lieutenant Colonel William Glasgow, "Attitude of USAREUR Commanders and Troops toward the ROAD Organization," USAREUR Historical Section, 1964, USACMH, HMC, 8-3.1 CU5.

57. Report of Stewardship, October 1960–April 1962, Headquarters, U.S. Army Europe, pp. 117–18.

58. Stephen Schwartz (ed.), *Atomic Audit: The Costs and Consequences of US Nuclear Weapons since 1940* (Washington, D.C.: Brookings, 1998), 156; Glasgow, "Attitude of USAREUR Commanders and Troops toward the ROAD Organization."

59. Report of Stewardship, October 1960–April 1962, Headquarters, U.S. Army Europe, p. 106.

60. Ibid., p. 81.

10

Fighting for the Heart of Germany

German I Corps and NATO's Plans for the Defense of the North German Plain in the 1960s

Helmut Hammerich

"Who actually knows about Jassy?"[1] A few years ago Bernd Wegner raised this question to broach the issue of the ignorance of a growing number of historians who dedicate themselves to the history of the military using a quite remarkable variety of methods.[2] But not knowing that the Soviet major offensive launched near Jassy and Kishinev in August 1944 resulted after a few days in the encirclement and destruction of the German Sixth Army, and even in the destruction of an entire army group, thus putting an end to German supremacy in southeastern Europe, would make it difficult to write a history of World War II. Individual and collective war experience can be reconstructed only through the mirror of battles and combat, especially if the preparations for and the effects of the bloody conflicts are taken into consideration. In this context the political, economic, technological, psychological, and social influences on the military decision-making process are equally important as the effects of those decisions on the combat actions of the soldiers.[3] The stigmatization of the history of campaigns and battles and of the art of military leadership as "drum and trumpet history" is hardly helpful for modern military history and war studies.[4] The history of modern military campaigns, therefore, must include and interpret both the complexity and order as well as the chaos of military and civilian transfers, interaction, effects, and environmental impacts.[5] The extensive analysis of military operations commonly practiced by Anglo-Saxon historians should also include social and psychological aspects such as historical anthropology or cultural history.[6] The history of campaigns and battles, therefore, remains one of the most important branches of military history.[7]

The battle history of the Cold War focuses first and foremost on the planning for the nuclear clash between NATO and the Warsaw Pact. Although between 1945 and 1989–1990 the world saw countless hot wars on the periphery of the Cold War, the "Cold World War," as Detlef Junker termed it, is best examined through the operational plans of the military alliances for what would have been World War III. To conduct such an analysis we must consider total war under nuclear conditions.[8]

Analyzing the war planning, however, is far from easy. The main difficulty lies in access to the files. The records of both the Warsaw Pact and NATO are still largely classified and therefore relatively inaccessible. Nor is access to the archives in Moscow twenty years after glasnost and perestroika at all encouraging. At the request of historians, NATO has begun to declassify some of its key documents, including Central Army Group (CENTAG) Emergency Defense Plan 1-1960. Nonetheless, the specific details of the nuclear operational planning will continue to remain inaccessible to historians for the foreseeable future. As an alternative, historians then are forced to rely on collateral documents in the various national archives or on the compilations of diverse oral history projects. The initial results of such an approach are quite encouraging, although we must caution repeatedly that the scenarios of specific war plans or military exercises are not necessarily identical to the actual operational plans developed by the general staffs of the military alliances.[9] The impact of those war plans, in turn, is reflected in the political controversies of the 1970s and 1980s over the practicality of waging a nuclear war. Many people who lived through that era still remember the slogan "Better red than dead." The impact of NATO's Dual Track Decision on the domestic policy of the Federal Republic of Germany (FRG) is described in many volumes of the literature and has been the topic of several interesting exhibitions.[10]

The North German Plain as the Key Area of NATO Defensive Planning

During the Cold War, the North German plain and the Fulda Gap were considered the most probable axes of advance for the Warsaw Pact forces to thrust into Western Europe. The region from Kassel in the south to Hamburg in the north of Germany was, therefore, of particular importance for NATO's planning staff officers.

Although the strategy evolved over the period, the operational planning in the 1960s for the defense of the Central Sector against a massive Warsaw Pact attack rested squarely on the early use of nuclear weapons. There were, however, increasing doubts, particularly among the German military, that the conduct of a combined-arms battle would be at all possible under nuclear conditions. Even the selective use of nuclear weapons on German soil could not be in the interest of the FRG. But until far into the 1970s NATO lacked the conventional ground and air forces necessary to conduct an effective forward defense without the early use of nuclear weapons.[11]

Confronted with this dilemma, German commanders had to plan the defense of their German homeland and translate those concepts into the daily training of their soldiers. The compromise in the 1960s was the development of the emergency defense plans (EDPs) with as little reliance as possible on nuclear fire on German soil. Accordingly, the German general officers and staff officers at NATO headquarters influenced NATO's nuclear target planning process along those lines.

Bundeswehr Ground Forces, 1963–1968

When NATO adopted the forward defense concept in 1963, the Bundeswehr was in its eighth year. Defense Minister Kai-Uwe von Hassel and the Bundeswehr chief of staff, General Friedrich Foertsch, led the Bundeswehr through a phase of consolidation following the turbulence of those early years, which included the Cuban missile crisis and the scandal of the "*Spiegel* Affair." Initially the alliance had tasked the German forces to be "prepared for defense only to a limited degree."[12] Despite shortages in funding, personnel, equipment, and infrastructure, German army chief of staff Lieutenant General Alfred Zerbel was able to report quite impressive results. By 1963 the army component of the Bundeswehr had grown from approximately 1,000 soldiers, first established in Andernach in 1956, to more than 270,000 soldiers. About four-fifths of the programmed active force units had been established, including seven Panzer Grenadier (mechanized infantry) divisions, two Panzer (armored) divisions, and one mountain and one airborne division, with a total of thirty brigades assigned to NATO.[13] The structure of a Bundeswehr brigade, as defined in the document *Army Structure 2,* was based on the requirements of combat under nuclear conditions. The German divisional structure was the NATO standard in the Central Region.

German ground forces had achieved a considerable degree of mechanization with forty-two armored and fifty-two mechanized infantry battalions—even if many of those mechanized infantry units still moved on wheeled vehicles. The equipment, which included 2,300 M-47 and M-48 main battle tanks and some 1,900 Hispano-Suiza 30 armored infantry fighting vehicles, compared favorably with the other allied armies. The addition of 1,500 Leopard 1 main battle tanks and 700 *Kanonenjagdpanzer* (tank destroyers) was programmed for the near future.[14]

The requirements of modern warfare resulted in a further specialization of the branches of service. Both airmobility and nuclear-capable artillery were urgent requirements. The newly established German rocket and missile artillery units were equipped with the delivery systems, while the nuclear warheads were kept in special storages facilities under tight American control. By 1963 the Bundeswehr fielded twelve MGR-1 Honest John rocket artillery battalions with a total of seventy-two launchers, and four MGM-29 Sergeant guided missile battalions with a total of eighteen launchers. The Honest Johns were division-level assets, while the Sergeants were corps level.[15] As of 1963 the Bundeswehr also had M-110 8-inch (203-mm) nuclear-capable howitzers organized in field artillery battalions. By April 1967 the Bundeswehr had a total of 472 nuclear weapon delivery systems. The army had seven Sergeant and fifty-eight Honest John launchers and seventy M-110 howitzers. The German air force's nuclear delivery systems included five F-104G fighter squadrons with thirty-six aircraft each, 153 MIM-14 Nike-Hercules air defense missile launchers, and four MGM-31 Pershing medium-range ballistic missile launchers.[16]

The War Scenario in 1963

In 1962 Major General Wolf Graf von Baudissin delivered a paper before the German Atlantic Society in Heidelberg outlining the scenario of any future war. He noted that in times of change it was particularly difficult to develop a precise picture of a possible war. The common alliance strategy had been evolving since at least the Cuban missile crisis. As the strategy of Massive Retaliation began to crumble, an appropriate response to the various forms of modern warfare seemed necessary. Baudissin in his paper distinguished four possible forms of war: cold war, subversive war, nonnuclear conventional war, and nuclear war. He further divided the latter into limited nuclear war and total nuclear war. That same year, Colonel Gerd Schmückle, the public affairs officer for Minister of Defense Franz Josef Strauss, wrote a controver-

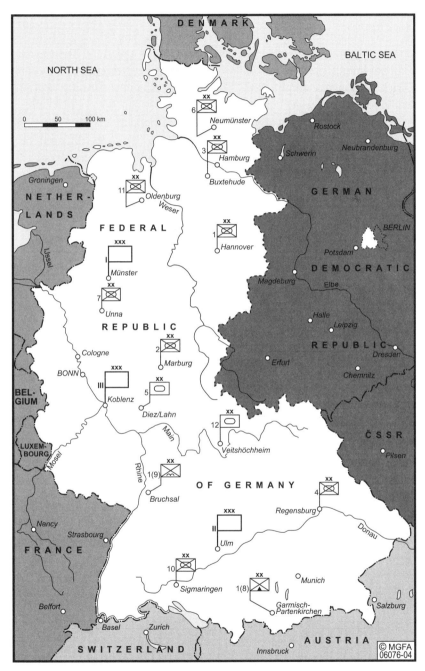

Map 10.1. German corps and divisions in the 1960s.

sial essay in which he referred to the "transformation of Apocalypse," arguing that any nuclear war could not be controlled. The primary mission of the armed forces, therefore, was deterrence and not warfare. The German national interest was the prevention of war through deterrence. As General Ulrich de Maizière emphasized, "Deterrence strategy has priority over potential warfare strategies."[17]

The German officer corps was divided. General Adolf Heusinger, the Bundeswehr's first chief of staff, identified the solution to the dilemma very early on. The German military needed both capabilities, combat-ready divisions for conventional and for nuclear warfare (*Sowohl-als-auch-Streitkräfte*).[18] Because of the tight budget, however, such a compromise meant for the Bundeswehr a balancing act between expensive modernization of the conventional forces and costly new weapons. The underlying assumption was a limited conventional attack by the Warsaw Pact, to which NATO had to be prepared to make an appropriate response, which included conventional defense as well as the selective use of nuclear weapons, and even total nuclear war. Baudissin, however, pinpointed the heart of the matter while many of the German army generals remained in denial. As Baudissin noted, "As soon as one side tries to bring about a decision, it will resort to nuclear weapons."[19]

That conclusion was consistent with the doctrine then in effect. The October 1962 edition of the German army regulation, *Command and Control of the Armed Forces HDv 100/1* (or TF-62), for the first time combined conventional and nuclear warfare. The key sentence in the section on defense was: "454. The strength of the defense lies in the deliberate and flexible use of nuclear weapons in conjunction with the conduct of offensive operations by the mechanized units."[20]

Forward Defense, 1957–1969

The urgent imperative of the German military was to conduct the defense of the alliance's territory as far to the east as possible.[21] That imperative fit in with the NATO strategic doctrine then in force, but the shortage of the necessary combat divisions required to accomplish that objective left something to be desired in the implementation. The assignment of German major units to the NATO force structure and the increasing influence of German general officers within the alliance, especially the commander, Land Forces Central Europe (COMLANDCENT), General Hans Speidel, led to important modifications in the thinking of the alliance.[22] Other senior NATO commanders, including the commander-in-chief, Allied Forces Central Europe

(CINCENT), General Jean Valluy, and the supreme allied commander, Europe (SACEUR), General Lauris Norstad, also wanted to initiate the fight up near the Inner-German Border.[23] The British and French, however, remained mostly reticent on the issue. Until 1958 the main defensive line was set at the Rhine and IJssel Rivers. Forward of that, the delaying zone reached to the Ems-Neckar line, and forward of that the initial line of resistance ran along the Weser and Lech Rivers. NATO assumed, however, that the enemy forces would cross the Ems-Neckar line after only a few days. As early as spring 1957 Brigadier General Ulrich de Maizière of the Bundeswehr armed forces staff noted: "Most of southern Germany, mainly Bavaria, is to be given up more or less without fighting. First real resistance is the Ems-Neckar line. Intervention by LANDCENT and possibly by SHAPE [Supreme Headquarters Allied Powers Europe] would be urgently required!"[24] At that time the situation in the north of Germany was not much better, since the British wanted to commit only light covering forces east of the Weser.

An initial breakthrough was achieved in July 1958 with the issuance of CINCENT's Central Europe EDP 2-58, which designated the Ems-Neckar line, rather than the Rhine-IJssel line, as the main line of defense.[25] The enemy was to be delayed starting at the Weser-Lech line. From summer 1958 onward, the Central Army Group designated four successive lines of defense to the east. The most forward line ran from Vogelsberg west of Fulda via Schweinfurt and Nuremberg to Landshut and Rosenheim. In the south the French forces would now establish initial contact with the enemy at the Lech River, rather than the Iller. In the north, however, the commander of the British Army of the Rhine, General Sir James Cassels, continued to oppose advancing the defense eastward of the Weser because of the shortage of divisions. NATO's Northern Army Group (NORTHAG) would have had nine weak divisions to cover a frontal width of 380 kilometers, meaning 42 kilometers per division. According to the doctrine in force at that time, a combat-effective division in favorable terrain was capable of defending a combat sector some 25 kilometers wide.

Despite those difficulties, SACEUR Norstad in April 1962 ordered the conduct of a mobile defense starting immediately at the Iron Curtain. The execution of such a defense was planned for multiple phases.[26] The first phase would deploy strong delaying forces, designated covering forces. As early as June 1962 COMLANDCENT Speidel issued an operational directive to his subordinate army groups that defined the conduct of the forward defense through 1966. Behind a border observation zone of 10 to 15 kilometers, the covering forces were to be positioned in such a way that they were able to initiate immediately the delaying battle with full effectiveness.[27] During a NATO exercise in spring 1962, however, it became obvious that a reinforcement of the terrain in the delaying zone, the use of atomic demolition munitions (ADM), and the early use of other tactical nuclear weapons were all necessary for the conduct of a successful forward defense.[28]

CINCENT's Central Europe EDP 1-63 issued in September 1963 marked the final acceptance of the operational concepts advocated by the German military leaders. The Ems-Neckar line as the primary line of defense was abandoned in favor of the Weser-Lech line. Unlike earlier EDPs, which were designed to defend only 50 percent of the territory of the FRG during war, the new EDP would defend some 90 percent. But the price was high. NATO's senior commanders assumed that nuclear weapons would have to be used at an early stage. As General Speidel noted in January 1963, "Considering the current strength ratio, our fight can be successful only if nuclear weapons are used. Their early release is of vital importance."[29]

In the 1960s the Warsaw Pact had more men in uniform than NATO and had a larger military force in the critical Central European region. Despite that, NATO retained a numerical and qualitative advantage in tactical nuclear forces, especially nuclear artillery.[30] NATO's clear superiority in nuclear forces constituted a deterrent against both conventional and nuclear attack by the Warsaw Pact.

German I Corps and the Defense of Northern Germany

In 1968 the mechanized forces based in the German Democratic Republic and the Czechoslovak Socialist Republic totaled no fewer than twenty-six Soviet divisions, which gave the Warsaw Pact the capability to launch a surprise attack at any time with little or no deployment preparations. The warning time for such an attack would be less than eight hours, which was not sufficient for the deployment of NATO forces.

NATO's assessments of the enemy's intentions indicated that their first operational objective was the Rhine. The Warsaw Pact forces intended to seize rapidly the critical terrain areas in order to facilitate freedom of operations for their armored units to achieve a breakthrough in the depth. In the NORTHAG sector the main thrust was expected to come from the area of Wittenberge-Stendal via the Weser crossings between Bremen and Verden, proceeding in the direction of the Rhine between Nijmegen and Wesel. Two supporting offensive wedges were anticipated. One would come from the area of Letzlinger Heath-Magdeburg on both sides of the autobahn in the direction

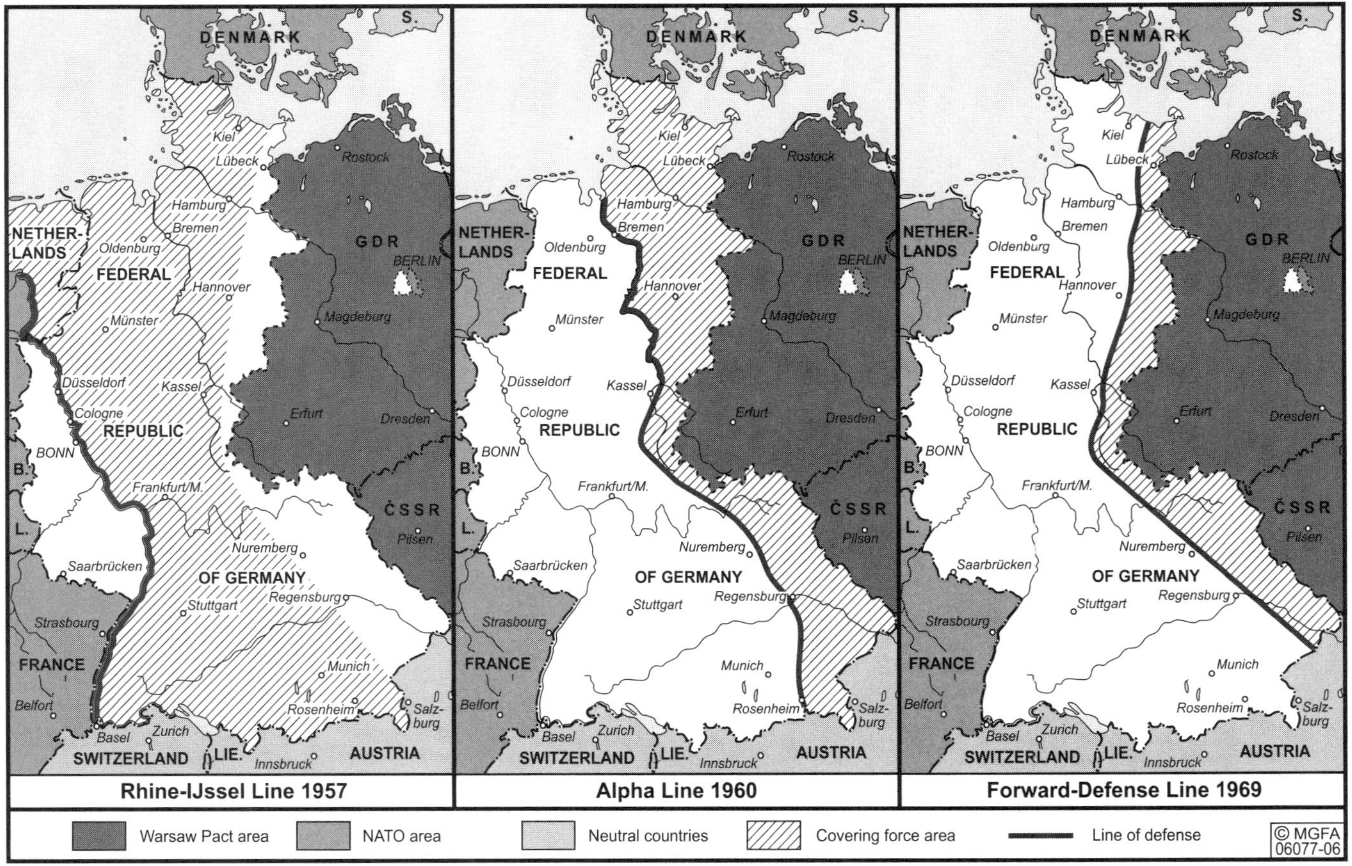
DENMARK
S.
NETHER-
LANDS
FEDERAL
REPUBLIC
OF GERMANY
GDR
BERLIN
ČSSR
B.
L.
FRANCE
SWITZERLAND
LIE.
AUSTRIA
Kiel
Lübeck
Rostock
Hamburg
Bremen
Oldenburg
Hannover
Münster
Magdeburg
Düsseldorf
Kassel
Cologne
Erfurt
Dresden
BONN
Frankfurt/M.
Pilsen
Nuremberg
Saarbrücken
Stuttgart
Regensburg
Strasbourg
Munich
Belfort
Rosenheim
Salz-
burg
Basel
Zurich
Innsbruck
Rhine-IJssel Line 1957
Alpha Line 1960
Forward-Defense Line 1969
Warsaw Pact area
NATO area
Neutral countries
Covering force area
Line of defense
© MGFA
06077-06

Map 10.2. Forward defense, 1957–1969.

of the Weser crossings on both sides of Minden and proceeding farther in the direction of the Ruhr area. The second could come from the area of Nordhausen in the direction of the Weser crossings near Hannoversch-Münden and Höxter, proceeding in the direction of Paderborn. The first assault echelon was expected to have fourteen divisions; the second, eleven divisions.

Another complicating factor was the Warsaw Pact's 4:1 superiority in conventional combat aircraft. In the late 1960s NATO assessments predicted 2,500 to 4,000 conventional sorties and a total of some 800 nuclear sorties with strike aircraft and missiles per day against targets in the Allied Forces Central Europe sector.[31] An attack in the German I Corps sector by the Third Shock Army was expected to have four tank divisions and a motorized rifle division in the first echelon, carried out by some 1,600 T-54 and T-62 main battle tanks and 1,400 armored infantry fighting vehicles, and supported by heavy artillery forces. The spearheads of the enemy attack could reach the Hoya-Minden-Hameln line at the Weser after nine to fourteen hours if launched after only a short preparation phase, and after fifteen to twenty-five hours following a more deliberate preparation.[32] Elements of the Second Guards Tank Army or of the Twentieth Guards Army with a total of eleven divisions were projected as the second echelon. Until the early 1960s NATO intelligence assessments did not expect the commitment at the beginning of the attack of Polish forces or units of the East German National People's Army (NVA), but the enemy use of nuclear and chemical weapons was anticipated at any time.

NORTHAG intended to conduct the defense with four corps abreast, the center of the main effort being in the south of its sector. Belgian I Corps, operating on the left flank of CENTAG, along with British I Corps and Netherlands I Corps had the mission of delaying the enemy advance east of the Weser and transitioning to the defense along the course of the Weser. The Second Allied Tactical Air Force (2 ATAF) was to support ground operations initially with conventional weapons and aerial reconnaissance, and, if necessary, execute the NORTHAG nuclear strike plan.

In response to a surprise attack, German I Corps had the mission to block the enemy attack as far as possible to the east while simultaneously preparing to repel the enemy with a counterattack to prevent the breakthrough to the Rhine and Ruhr. To accomplish this mission, German I Corps had two mechanized infantry divisions and an armored division, totaling some six hundred main battle tanks and seven hundred armored infantry fighting vehicles. The reinforced 7th Panzer Grenadier Division with four brigades—including the attached 33rd Panzer Brigade of the 11th Panzer Grenadier

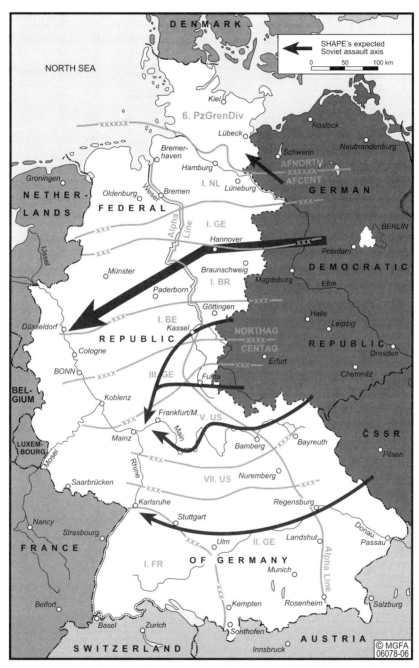

Map 10.3. Assumed Soviet/Warsaw Pact assault axis (simplified illustration).

Division—constituted along with a British infantry division the NORTHAG reserve. German I Corps planned to conduct its defense with the 3rd Panzer Division on the left, the 11th Panzer Grenadier Division in the center, and the 1st Panzer Grenadier Division on the right. The corps itself did not have a major reserve.[33] Instead, the respective divisional reserves were earmarked for the operational command of the corps.

With his eight mechanized or armored brigades in the line, the German I Corps commander had some capability to counter the enemy's mobile and armored attack forces. Nevertheless, the conduct of a fully effective mobile defense was hardly possible with the forces available, the lack of territory, and the enemy's air superiority. The German divisions had to engage the enemy far forward. Generally, each division put forward one brigade plus its armored reconnaissance battalion to operate in a small delaying zone, while the two other brigades prepared for the main defense. As the partially expended delaying force drew back behind its division's own lines, it would become the divisional reserve for counterattacks or other missions. Thus, the corps commander's freedom of action was very limited. A contemporary witness quoted the commanding general of German I Corps, Lieutenant General Wilhelm Meyer-Detring, as saying: "If the corps commits its reserves, it will hardly be able to disengage them because of the force ratio. Consequently, there will hardly be much for me to do."[34] As a limited and temporary response to this situation, *Army Structure 3* of 1970 established an armored regiment for each corps and also attached an airborne brigade.

Artillery

The commander of Artillery Command 1 was responsible for the fire support of German I Corps. His fire plan ensured the massing of the nonnuclear artillery on short notice as well as the delivery on West German soil of nuclear warheads of up to ten kilotons (KT) immediately upon the receipt from SACEUR of selective release or release.[35] (For comparison purposes, the bomb dropped on Hiroshima in 1945 had a yield of 15 KT.)

After the receipt of release, the battalions of the corps artillery were to destroy enemy masses, concentration areas, and artillery positions in the expected centers of gravity and deliver on order fires against the additional atomic fire zones.[36] The atomic fire zones consisted of multiple nuclear target groupings and, combined with the preplanned individual nuclear targets, constituted the nuclear artillery fire plan. The nuclear artillery units were to be positioned forward so that upon the receipt of release the enemy masses

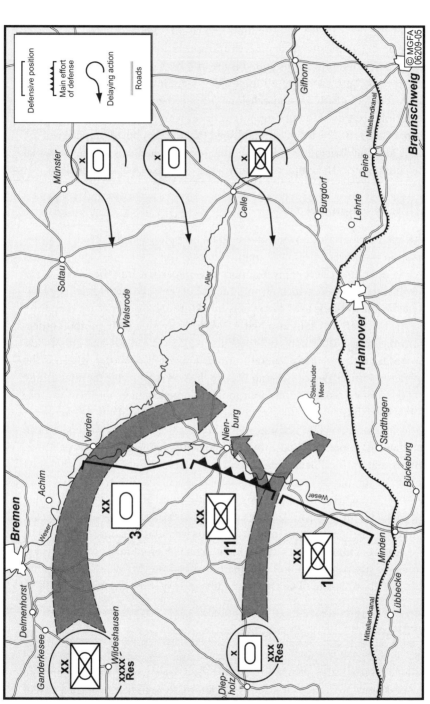

Map 10.4. German I Corps: concept of operations (EDP, 1963).

east of the fire support coordination line could be engaged and destroyed. The primary targets were significant transportation hubs and bridges, centers of and exits from towns and villages, and high ground. The nuclear fires delivered by both army and air force assets were intended to destroy the enemy's reserves of the second echelon. Despite the absence in the currently accessible records of the fire support annexes with the details on the deployment of the artillery, it can be established that the combined firepower of the corps and the divisions would have had devastating effects on any potential attacking forces. The emphasis clearly was on the use of nuclear artillery.

Military Engineers

The enemy's forward movement was to be brought to a halt through a combination of barriers, fires, and counterattacks. The preplanned and prepared barrier operations were of great importance, in particular in the terrain of the North German plain, which favored the use of tanks. Minefields laid by helicopters would also be used to stop any breakthrough by enemy armored forces. The German divisions also had ADM, which would be used upon orders from the corps. The main targets for the ADM were roads and crossroads. According to Lieutenant General (retired) Franz Uhle-Wettler, who was the operations officer G-3 of German I Corps, he was responsible for establishing ADM detonation points every four to five kilometers and coordinating those points with those of the adjacent corps. As General Uhle-Wettler remembers, the course of that ADM belt west of the Weser ran for 120 kilometers. We can estimate, therefore, that some thirty ADM were planned for the corps sector. Unfortunately, the documents currently available do not indicate the exact course of the planned ADM points. The 1963 EDPs of German III Corps, however, show an echeloned disposition with a total of ninety targets between the Inner-German Border and the corps's defensive sector. Nonetheless, at the start of combat operations German III Corps was allocated only twelve ADM. The corps commander at the time, Lieutenant General Franz Meyer-Detring, expressed his skepticism on the battlefield use of the ADM: "If this happens, then it will be the end of Germany and probably of most Germans as well."[37]

Logistics

In 1968 COMNORTHAG estimated that in the worst case, the enemy would be able to reach the defensive sector at the Weser within thirty hours. No major depots or storage tank farms, therefore, were to be established east of the Weser. German I Corps was requested to store only one or two supply increments in addition to the basic load east of the Weser. In contrast, German I Corps assumed a requirement for seven to eight basic loads. Moreover, the construction of a pipeline to the tank farms at Bredorf and Hodenhagen across the Weser was halted temporarily, even though the project had been approved previously by NATO. That was another key indicator that NORTHAG did not plan to defend east of the Weser in the 1960s.

Air

Combat aircraft of 2 ATAF were to support German I Corps with armed reconnaissance flights along the enemy's axis of attack and by providing close air support with nonnuclear weapons. Upon the receipt of nuclear release, the planned targeting package of NORTHAG's Nuclear Strike Plan and the Armed Strike Recce programs would have been flown, destroying enemy targets in depth. In 1968 four hundred combat aircraft were available to fly such missions. Nevertheless, the air force always pointed out that its resources available to support the ground forces would not be sufficient in a mobile defensive battle.[38]

The war as planned in the 1960s was a war under nuclear conditions. Mainly because of a lack of conventional armed forces, it would have been necessary to ensure forward defense with the early use of nuclear weapons. The operational plans at that time, therefore, focused on that early use. That was the only way to establish early contact with the enemy at the demarcation line and to conduct delay and defense operations in the sector of German I Corps. A 1964 report by a corps artillery commander about a nuclear targeting conference conducted by adjacent CENTAG notes: "So far the operations of the corps in the defense are firmly focused on the use of available nuclear devices. Nuclear target points and nuclear fire zones are an integral part of the combat in the defensive sector."[39] In his estimation, any new concept for a modern conventional firefight could be feasible only if the necessary forces were available.

The concerns of many German general officers that the massive use of nuclear weapons would make the control and direction of battle impossible were more than justified. But it was not easy to influence the nuclear target planning of NATO. Colonel Helmuth Groscurth describes in his memoirs how as a young major in 1966 when he became the NORTHAG G-2 staff officer for nuclear target selection he was not given any national guidance concerning his influence on the nuclear target planning process.[40] In numerous letters to various higher headquarters for years he criticized that nuclear operational planning had been to a large degree determined by a British major. In addition, Groscurth indicated that many NATO exercises committed a disproportionately high number of nuclear warheads with high KT yields. Groscurth's superiors did not feel able to help him but tried to appease him by assuring him that as long as there were no objections from Bonn, everything was fine. The first change in the nuclear targeting situation came in July 1966 when German army chief of staff Lieutenant General Ulrich de Maizière issued the national command and control directives for the use of nuclear weapons. That document, which de Maizière developed in consultation with COMLANDCENT General Adolf Graf von Kielmansegg, was designed to obligate the senior German commanders to a responsible and restrictive application of nuclear weapons.[41] De Maizière continued to acknowledge the necessity for an early use of nuclear weapons to accomplish the EDP mission during any large-scale attack by the enemy. But he also recognized that the failure of a credible and complete deterrence would result in inconceivable destruction on German territory. He therefore made the following demands on his subordinate commanders: "During the use of nuclear weapons particular attention must be paid to the effects on the population and the survival of our country. . . . By choosing the right place, type, and time for employment, it is possible both to accomplish the military requirements and to show the appropriate consideration."[42]

According to statements by former Bundeswehr general officers, EDP 1-68 did not designate any nuclear fire zones or preplanned ADM detonations. But as General de Maizière learned in a conversation with COM-NORTHAG in January 1969, the NORTHAG plan of operations nevertheless continued to focus on the canalization of the enemy's forces until they reached the defensive sector near the Weser. There the defensive battle would be decided through the selective use of at least fifty nuclear weapons.[43] The chief of staff of the German air force, Lieutenant General Johannes Steinhoff, summarized the situation that assumed a Warsaw Pact aerial superiority ratio of 4:1 as follows: "There will be neither operational mobility nor will it be possible to ensure the coherence of the defensive forces." He continued, "The Federal Republic of Germany cannot agree to the conduct of operation that inevitably turns its territory into a battlefield in depth and exposes it to nuclear devastation. The use of tactical nuclear battlefield weapons—up to 50 warheads in a nuclear strike—is an unacceptable part of a conventional defense." Steinhoff strongly urged the Bundeswehr chief of staff to counteract the "wrong interpretation of MC 14-3."[44]

The German army chief of staff, however, indicated that NORTHAG EDP 69 was based on the assumption of a "major aggression." Any assumption of a limited aggression by the Warsaw Pact was abandoned. In the event of an attack limited in space, forces, and scope, the intent would be to operate freely from a preplanned deployment. According to the German army staff, SACEUR in his EDP 69 instructed COMNORTHAG to give greater consideration to forward defense than had been the case so far. In late April 1969 German army Staff Branch II 3 referred to a revised version of Paragraph 3a (Concept of Operations) of the NORTHAG EDP: "NORTHAG intends to engage the enemy as close to the DML [line of demarcation, or Inner-German Border] as possible with main forces."[45]

The worst-case scenario, then, was based on the intention of retaining important sectors of terrain east of the Weser while also defeating the enemy east of that river—if necessary with the use of nuclear weapons. Although that in principle satisfied the German requirements for a forward defense, many units of the necessary conventional forces had yet to be established. The sword of Damocles of an early use of nuclear weapons resulting from a lack of conventional forces continued to hang above the chart tables of the NATO general officers, despite the complete shift in strategy in 1968.

Notes

1. Bernd Wegner, "Wozu Operationsgeschichte?," in *Was ist Militärgeschichte?*, ed. Thomas Kühne and Benjamin Ziemann, Krieg in der Geschichte, vol. 6 (Paderborn, 2000), 105–13, quote on p. 109.

2. Jutta Nowosadtko, *Krieg, Gewalt und Ordnung: Einführung in die Militärgeschichte*, Historische Einführungen, vol. 6 (Tübingen, 2002). Johannes Hürter, "Militärgeschichte ohne Krieg? Eine Standortbestimmung der deutschen Militärgeschichtsschreibung über das Zeitalter der Weltkriege," in *Geschichte der Politik: Alte und neue Wege*, ed. Hans-Christof Kraus and Thomas Nicklas, Beiheft HZ, vol. 44 (Munich, 2007), 287–308.

3. For example, see Georges Duby, *Der Sonntag von Bouvines 27. Juli 1214* (Berlin, 1988).

4. Gerd Krumeich, "Militärgeschichte für eine zivile Gesellschaft," in *Geschichtswissenschaften: Eine Einführung*, ed. Christoph Cornelißen (Frankfurt am Main, 2000), 178–93. In contrast, see *Schlachten der Weltgeschichte: Von Salamis bis Sinai*, ed. Stig Förster et al. (Munich, 2001).

5. Ludolf Herbst, *Komplexität und Chaos: Grundzüge einer Theorie der Geschichte* (Munich, 2004).

6. For example, Jürgen Luh, *Kriegskunst in Europa 1650–1800* (Cologne, 2004); Nikolaus Buschmann and Horst Carl (eds.), *Die Erfahrung des Krieges: Erfahrungsgeschichtliche Perspektiven von der Französischen Revolution bis zum Zweiten Weltkrieg, Krieg in der Geschichte,* vol. 9 (Paderborn, 2001). A few examples of Anglo-Saxon historians who conduct extensive analysis of military operations are John Keegan, Michael Howard, Hew Strachan, Jeremy Black, and Geoffrey Parker.

7. Stig Förster, "Operationsgeschichte heute: Eine Einführung," *Militärgeschichtliche Zeitschrift* 61, no. 2 (2002): 309–13. Sönke Neitzel, "Des Forschens noch wert? Anmerkungen zur Operationsgeschichte der Waffen-SS," *Militärgeschichtliche Zeitschrift* 61, no. 2 (2002): 403–29.

8. For the 1950s and 1960s, see Bruno Thoss, *NATO-Strategie und nationale Verteidigungsplanung: Planung und Aufbau der Bundeswehr unter den Bedingungen einer massiven atomaren Vergeltungsstrategie 1952 bis 1960,* Sicherheitspolitik und Streitkräfte der Bundesrepublik Deutschland, vol. 1 (Munich, 2006), in particular the basic comments on civil defense during the Cold War. For the quote from Detlef Junker, see "Die Internationalen Beziehungen nach dem Zweiten Weltkrieg," in *Mauerbau und Mauerfall: Ursachen—Verlauf—Auswirkungen,* ed. Hans-Hermann Hertle, Konrad H. Jarausch, and Christoph Kleßmann (Berlin: Ch.Links, 2002), 19–31, here p. 30.

9. Voitech Mastny (ed.), *War Plans and Alliances in the Cold War: Threat Perceptions in the East and the West* (London, 2006). On the initial results of the operational planning of the Warsaw Pact, see the website of the Parallel History Project on NATO and the Warsaw Pact: http://www.isn.ethz.ch/ (accessed 22 Nov. 2006). Jan Hoffenaar and Christopher Findlay (eds.), *Military Planning for European Theatre Conflict during the Cold War* (Zürich, 2007).

10. Karla Hannemann, "Der Doppelbeschluss der Nato: Genese, Motive und Determinanten einer umstrittenen bündnispolitischen Entscheidung" (diss., Munich, 1987); Herbert Dittgen, *Deutsch-amerikanische Sicherheitsbeziehungen in der Ära Helmut Schmidt: Vorgeschichte und Folgen des NATO-Doppelbeschlusses* (Munich, 1991); Stephan Layritz, *Der NATO-Doppelbeschluß und die westliche Sicherheitspolitik im Spannungsfeld von Innen-, Bündnis- und Außenpolitik* (Frankfurt am Main, 1992); Nathalie Andries (ed.), *Zerreißprobe Frieden: Baden-Württemberg und der NATO-Doppelbeschluß,* exhibition catalog, Haus der Geschichte Baden-Württemberg (Karlsruhe, 2004).

11. David Miller, *The Cold War: A Military History* (London, 1998); John Lewis Gaddis, *The Cold War: A New History* (New York, 2007); Bernd Stöver, *Der Kalte Krieg 1947–1991: Geschichte eines radikalen Zeitalters* (Munich, 2007).

12. Helmut R. Hammerich, Dieter H. Kollmer, Martin Rink, and Rudolf J. Schlaffer, *Das Heer 1950 bis 1970: Konzeption, Organisation, Aufstellung,* Sicherheitspolitik und Streitkräfte der Bundesrepublik Deutschland, vol. 3 (Munich, 2006), 270.

13. In late 1961 twelve divisions with a total of thirty-four brigades had already been established in full or in part. Martin Rink, "Strukturen brausen um die Wette:

Zur Organisation des deutschen Heeres," in *Das Heer 1950 bis 1970,* ed. Hammerich et al., 353–483.

14. Dieter H. Kollmer, "'Klotzen, nicht kleckern!' Die materielle Aufrüstung des Heeres von den Anfängen bis Ende der sechziger Jahre," in *Das Heer 1950 bis 1970,* ed. Hammerich et al., 487–614.

15. Michael Poppe, "Die Entwicklung der Artillerie in der Bundeswehr 1956–2006," *Zu Gleich: Zeitschrift der Artillerietruppe* 1 (2006): 5–14.

16. FüS III, Atomare Trägermittel der Bundeswehr, NHP-Dok. Nr. 175. Cited in Axel F. Gablik, *Strategische Planungen in der Bundesrepublik Deutschland 1955–1967: Politische Kontrolle oder militärische Notwendigkeit?,* Nuclear History Program, vol. 5 (Baden-Baden, 1996), 477.

17. Gerd Schmückle, "Die Wandlung der Apokalypse: Eine Betrachtung über das Kriegsbild in Europa," in *Christ und Welt,* 26 Jan. 1962, pp. 33–34; Ulrich de Maizière, "Zur Mitwirkung der Bundesrepublik Deutschland an der Nuklearstrategie der NATO (1955–1972)," in *Deutschland zwischen Krieg und Frieden: Beiträge zur Politik und Kultur im 20. Jahrhundert,* ed. Karl-Dietrich Bracher, Manfred Funke, and Hans-Peter Schwarz (Bonn, 1990), 277–90, quote on p. 288.

18. Georg Meyer, *Adolf Heusinger: Dienst eines deutschen Soldaten 1915–1964* (Hamburg, 2001).

19. Wolf Graf von Baudissin, "Das Kriegsbild," *Beilage zu Information für die Truppe,* no. 9 (1962): 3–19, quote on p. 17.

20. HDv 100/1, Truppenführung, Oct. 1962, 193f., Bundesarchiv-Militärarchiv Freiburg (hereinafter BA-MA), BHD 1.

21. Gablik, *Strategische Planungen in der Bundesrepublik Deutschland 1955–1967;* Christian Tuschhoff, *Deutschland, Kernwaffen und die NATO 1949–1967: Zum Zusammenhalt von und friedlichem Wandel in Bündnissen,* Nuclear History Program, vol. 30/7 (Baden-Baden, 2002); and Helga Haftendorn, *Kernwaffen und die Glaubwürdigkeit der Allianz: Die NATO-Krise von 1966/67,* Nuclear History Program, vol. 30/4 (Baden-Baden, 1994).

22. Hans Speidel, *Aus unserer Zeit: Erinnerungen* (Frankfurt am Main, 1977).

23. Robert S. Jordan, *Norstad: Cold War NATO Supreme Commander. Airman, Strategist, Diplomat* (New York, 2000).

24. DTB de Maizière, STAL FüS III, 28 May 1957, BA-MA, N 673/23.

25. Helmut R. Hammerich, "Kommiss kommt von Kompromiss: Das Heer der Bundeswehr zwischen Wehrmacht und U.S. Army 1950–1970," in *Das Heer 1950 bis 1970,* ed. Hammerich et al., 19–351, here pp. 131–54.

26. NATO Archives, SHAPE/80/62.1220/7, SACEUR Lauris Norstad and CINCENT P. E. Jaquot, 6 Apr. 1962. My thanks to Dr. Gregory Pedlow, Chief Historical Office SHAPE, Mons, for declassifying the document.

27. Militärgeschichtliches Forschungsamt, Personal Papers Speidel/82, Reference in the paper by General Dr. Speidel "Forces de couverture," 29 June 1962.

28. NATO EX HOSTAGE BRUN in June 1962. See BMVg, FüH II Erfahrungsberichte NATO-Übungen, BA-MA, BH 1/599.

29. Statements by COMLANDCENT on 17 Jan. 1963, BA-MA, BW 2/8742.

30. *The Balance of Forces in Central Europe,* CIA 1977, http://www.foia.cia.gov/.

31. Chief of Staff, Bundeswehr, to Chief of Staff, Air Force, 30 Jan. 1969, Operational planning NORTHAG/2. ATAF, BA-MA, BL 1/4050. I thank my colleague Dr. Bernd Lemke for this information.

32. FüH II 1, 17 Nov. 1961, Zeitbedarf für sowjet. Angriff von Zonengrenze bis zur Weser, BA-MA, BW 2/2552.

33. In autumn 1965 7th Panzer Grenadier Division was to become corps reserve. See Artillery Regiment 7, EDP order of 30 Nov. 1965, BA-MA, BH 2/1247.

34. Letter by Lieutenant General (ret.) Dr. Franz Uhle-Wettler to the author of 30 Jan. 2007.

35. With the declaration of S-Hour, SACEUR authorized the commanders responsible for release to use one or a number of nuclear weapons. With the declaration of R-Hour, SACEUR authorized the commanders responsible for release to use nuclear weapons with indefinitely high nuclear yields on the territory of the Soviet Union or the satellite states. On West German or neutral territories, nuclear weapons of up to 10 KT could be used if the territories were attacked by armed forces of the Soviet bloc. Another prerequisite is that their use was in consequence of military requirements. II. Korps, Anweisung für den Einsatz von Atomwaffen im Bereich des II. (GE) Korps, 15 Nov. 1963, BA-MA, BH 2/1247.

36. Honest John: range 40 km, 2–50 KT; Sergeant: range 150 km, 2–50 KT. Division Artillery 6 HJ-launcher, 12 x 175–mm, 4 x 203–mm guns. Corps Artillery 8 Sergeant-launchers, 12 x 203–mm guns. First rocket fired after 10–15 minutes! Second firing after 10 minutes (HJ), or after 1 minute (Sergeant).

37. Letter by Lieutenant General (ret.) Dr. Franz Uhle-Wettler to the author of 30 Jan. 2007.

38. Chief of Staff, Bundeswehr, to Chief of Staff, Air Force, 30 Jan. 1969, Operational planning NORTHAG/2. ATAF, BA-MA, BL 1/4050.

39. Artilleriekommandeur 2, Kurzbericht über die Atomzielkonferenz bei CEN-TAG am 17. Dez. 1964, 22 Dec. 1964, BA-MA, BH 2/1247.

40. Helmuth Groscurth, *Dienstweg: Rückblicke eines Generalstabsoffiziers der Bundeswehr* (Waiblingen, 1994), 43–46 and documents 3–8.

41. Führungsrichtlinien für den Einsatz von Atomwaffen (de Maizière), 18 July 1966, BA-MA, BH 2/ 160.

42. Ibid., p. 9.

43. Chief of Staff, Bundeswehr, to Chief of Staff, Air Force, 30 Jan. 1969, Operational planning NORTHAG/2. ATAF, BA-MA, BL 1/4050.

44. Ibid., here: comment Steinhoff, 7 Feb. 1969, BA-MA, BL 1/4050.

45. Ibid., here: comment FüH II 3, 29 Apr. 1969, BA-MA, BL 1/4050.

11

The German Democratic Republic

Torsten Diedrich

Eggesin in the north of the German Democratic Republic (GDR): Shrill alarm bells are ringing in a remote barracks complex. Units of the 9th Tank Division of the Nationale Volksarmee (National People's Army, NVA) are lined up for a large-scale division-level exercise. The soldiers are told that NATO has declared an alert and is prepared to launch an attack of aggression against the Eastern bloc. Among the attacking forces is the Netherlands 1st Division, which is based along the same latitude. It is not long before the old joke is heard among the soldiers: "Listen, can you hear the clattering of wooden clogs yet? If so, we can stay in position!"

As of this writing, access to the records of the basic operational plans of the Warsaw Pact and the NVA is much more complicated than access to the records of NATO and the West German Bundeswehr. The Russian archives are still largely inaccessible, especially for the recent military planning records, and they will probably remain so for the foreseeable future. Those archives alone hold the fundamental information on Soviet thinking about strategic and nuclear warfare, our understanding of which remains vague. That thinking, however, would have directed the military actions of the entire Warsaw Pact. As we now know, even the leading GDR general officers had not been privy to the real-time planning of Moscow's strategists.[1] When the East German NVA ceased to exist in 1990 it is probable that their most important operational documents were shipped to Moscow, and many other records were destroyed.[2] For the time being, the only option open to historians is to attempt to reconstruct the operational thinking of the Eastern bloc and the NVA by considering various exercise scenarios, the preparation of the countries for war, and structural changes in their armed forces. At the same time it is necessary to close gradually the gaps in our historical knowledge through international cooperation, especially with historians from the former Eastern bloc countries.

The Warsaw Pact's general ideas on modern warfare, its preparations for and conduct of national defense in general—that is, its common military doctrine—were based on the thinking of Moscow's military leadership, which naturally was heavily influenced by the thinking of the Soviet political leadership. Nevertheless, the individual Warsaw Pact states, including the GDR, did in fact develop their own ideas, and the general opinion that the NVA primarily served foreign interests does not hold up under closer examination.[3] The thinking of the leadership of the Sozialistische Einheitspartei Deutschlands (Social Democratic Unity Party of Germany, SED) was subject to the established principles of the Leninist understanding of the protection of the "socialist revolution," without the party's losing sight of its objective of an armed defense of the social regime. The NVA was the product of Soviet and East German security and power interests during the Cold War period. But the East German rulers did not simply tolerate the development of the state's instruments of force to support the system. Rather, they actively encouraged the arming of the GDR. Thus, they had crucial responsibility for the increasing totalization and militarization of their society.

Military Doctrine

Military doctrine is a complete system of political and military principles and views on the nature, causes, and character of wars. It includes the methods and means of warfare, military objectives, analysis of the enemy, and the derived techniques for armed defensive or offensive warfare.[4] Within the framework of Communist ideology, war was understood as the continuation of policy by other means. The Communist theoretical approach on the development of social formations conceived war as a "class conflict" in an "epoch of transition from capitalism to socialism." As a rough generalization, *just* wars were those that served to defend socialism, or could be classified as revolutionary civil wars of the "working class" against the bourgeoisie, or as wars of national liberation from foreign rule and colonialism. Consequently, *unjust* wars were all military actions of imperialism against socialism, "counterrevolutionary wars of the bourgeoisie against the working class," colonial wars and wars of aggression, and wars of the capitalist states against each other.[5] This framework served to channel the moral restraints concerning war—a strong political factor in the West—within the socialist ideology. An important imperative in Soviet thought was the quest for potential superiority, which would serve both as a deterrent from military conflict and as a means to achieve war aims. The result was supposed to be the "legitimate victory of socialism over imperialism" and not the establishment of the status quo ante.[6]

Soviet military doctrine was shaped by the deeply rooted traumas of World War II. First, there was the surprise attack of Hitler's Wehrmacht in 1941. The Soviet Union, therefore, used the reorganization of Europe after the war to protect its territory from a direct attack through a cordon sanitaire of states that were subject to dominant Soviet influence. The second trauma was the long-lasting strategic overmatch of the Red Army by the Wehrmacht. It was only in 1942–1943 that the Soviet armed forces were able to make a large-scale transition from strategic defense to the principle of offensive operations in-depth. The lessons drawn from World War II resulted in the post-1945 military-doctrinal guidelines that assumed the Soviet Union had to be superior to any potential enemy and had to initiate the strategic offensive in the early stages of any war. Thus, Soviet military strategy stressed taking any future war to the enemy's territory as soon as possible to prevent a repetition of the previous experience of millions of casualties and extensive destruction. This was especially important because the economic potential of the country and the functioning of its war industry were seen as crucial for prevailing in any military conflict.

During the initial phase of their postwar military-operational thinking, which lasted until 1953, the Soviet Union responded to the American nuclear weapons monopoly with the Red Army's capability to conquer Europe by conventional means.[7] The wartime experience underlined the exceptional importance of armored forces, heavy industry as the backbone of arms production, and the role of paramilitary units, such as those that had conducted partisan warfare in the rear areas of the conventional forces. Technical innovations, however, also led to the conclusion that while the duration of operations would shorten, the tempo would increase considerably. The Soviet political and military leadership, therefore, gave absolute priority to the complete motorization and mechanization of their forces, while simultaneously continuing efforts to break the nuclear weapons monopoly of the United States and to acquire missile technology.[8] Armored and airborne forces, aviation units, and air defense systems all became especially important. All planning centered on breaking through the enemy's tactical defensive zone in the first days of any possible conflict. The attack would be conducted in the depth, committing mobile groups with the missions of conducting classic encirclement operations and annihilating the enemy forces. Defensive operations were to be conducted only during the initial phase of the war. Permanent states of high combat readiness would largely prevent any surprise action by the enemy. In the case of war, the initiative was to be taken immediately through active warfare and extensive use of all the means of combat in coordination with all services and units.[9] The result of this line of thinking was an overestimation of the deployment phase as the decisive factor in the course of the entire military conflict.[10] This offensive approach, however, assumed a numerical superiority, which the Soviet Union knew it had on the Continent and which it aimed to maintain throughout the course of the entire arms race during the Cold War.

During the second phase of Soviet military-theoretical planning, following 1953, the nuclear strike gained in importance, not least as a result of the Soviet successes in nuclear research. From 1956 on, Khrushchev, in contrast to his general staff, focused on massive strategic nuclear warfare. The new Soviet missile forces assumed vital strategic and operational importance, although they generally were included in the plans for destroying and annihilating the enemy by all available means.[11]

Until 1987, Soviet military strategy focused on responding to an attack by launching a massive strike on all three levels of warfare: strategic, operational, and tactical. The purpose of such a strike conducted over the entire width of the front was to deprive the enemy of his nuclear strike capabilities and to weaken him considerably for the follow-on attack by the Warsaw Pact.[12] Such a strategy, however, had certain consequences for the conduct of conventional warfare. The concept of closed-formation fronts was abandoned in favor of independent actions by operational units, versatile maneuvers, and deep alternating penetrations with envelopments and bypassing operations.[13] Intensive reconnaissance, decentralized deployment, and perpetual momentum of the units would deny easy targets to NATO's increased capability to deliver nuclear fires.[14]

The short-term downsizing of the Soviet Union's conventional forces in the second half of the 1950s resulted in an increased reliance on the forces of the Warsaw Pact.[15] It was not without reason that in the late 1950s Moscow began to transform the originally rather pro forma alliance into an increasingly more effective political and military one. The principles of the military doctrine of 1960 shaped to a considerable degree the concept of warfare and the operational-strategic thinking of the Warsaw Pact states through the mid-1980s.[16] Soviet doctrine eventually permeated the military thinking of all the Warsaw Pact states and was largely adopted by the GDR military—not least because of the influence of Soviet military advisors and later by the training of the GDR's military elite at Soviet military academies. In the late 1960s, however, the GDR made attempts to develop a military doctrine tailored to its own requirements.[17] Considering the formation of its offensive military approach, the Western perception of the Warsaw Pact as aggressive was not unfounded, nor even unavoidable, especially since Soviet thinking remained unchanged until the mid-1980s.[18]

The Roles of the GDR and the NVA

Soviet military strategy divided the world into strategic regions and theaters of war. The strategic or military-geographical areas were the continents—areas of potential enemies but not areas of immediate Soviet interests. The area closer around the Soviet Union was divided into theaters of war (*Teatr Voyny* or *Teatr Voennykh Deystviy*, TVD). Europe consisted of the Scandinavian, Central European, and Southern European theaters of war—which coincided closely with NATO's concept of the Northern, Central, and Southern Regions. The Baltic and the Mediterranean were designated maritime theaters of war. Central Europe—the "Western Theater of War"—was vitally important to the Soviet strategists. They planned thrusts in three main directions: (1) along the northern coast in the direction of the Netherlands; (2) through the North German plain in the direction of the Ruhr area; and (3) in a southwestern direction to southern France via Bavaria.

Consequently the GDR, as the largest base area for Soviet troops outside their own territory and also as the initial defensive area of the Socialist bloc, was of utmost strategic importance. As an armed military buffer, the GDR was the initial defense zone of the Eastern bloc. The forces deployed there maintained a permanently high level of combat readiness (85 percent of the NVA in the 1980s) to prevent a surprise attack by the enemy. The territory of the GDR was thus the most important sector for the deployment, operation, and transit of forces for a military conflict with NATO. During the initial phase of a potential war, the NVA focused only on the Western Theater of War. The GDR's armed forces were established as an alliance army. They were never designed for an independent role and therefore did not have a national operational concept.[19] In the 1960s the NVA was the smallest military force within the Warsaw Pact, with a programmed war strength of 280,000 troops and a peacetime strength of 120,000. It was not until the 1970s and 1980s that the NVA succeeded in increasing its combat power with quality improvements. Meanwhile, great importance was placed on the preparation of the GDR's territory for war and the conduct of the planned operations. From the 1960s on, there was an increasing emphasis, as in the extensive academic military studies on the military-geographical situation of the Federal Republic of Germany and the Baltic region, on the strength and capabilities of NATO forces, on the ground combat operations of the Unified Armed Forces of the Warsaw Pact and their logistic support, and on the preparations of the GDR's territorial defense capabilities.[20]

The build-up of the GDR's armed forces started in the 1950s. Because of economic problems and the People's Uprising of 1953, it had not been immediately possible to meet Moscow's demands to establish the GDR as a "bulwark against the West" and to transform the Kasernierte Volkspolizei (Garrisoned People's Police) into an operational armed force.[21] By 1955 the Garrisoned People's Police with some hundred thousand troops still lagged far behind in its training, equipment, and readiness for war. In the event of a war at that time, they would have been integrated into the formations of the Group of Soviet Forces in Germany (GSFG) as reserves or augmentees. The Volkspolizei See (People's Sea Police), the future naval forces of the GDR, were capable of functioning at best as light security forces. The air force units, disguised as "aero clubs," still operated just for training purposes and were equipped only with training versions of combat aircraft.

The first regular East German armed forces based on the Soviet model were established in 1956. Two newly established military districts, Leipzig and Neubrandenburg, corresponded to army corps staffs or army command echelons. The regiments and battalions, as well as one armored and two motorized rifle divisions, were subordinate to the military districts. In peacetime an armored division consisted of some 7,500 troops, 300 tanks, and 200 armored infantry fighting vehicles. (The 8th Motorized Rifle Division had up to 9,000 troops, 200 tanks, and 350 armored infantry fighting vehicles.) In case of war the military districts formed territorial military subcommands under the NVA's national command, which was responsible for filling out and supplying all units as well as the proper functioning of industry and the territorial infrastructure to meet the requirements of the military. The primary task, however, was to command, control, and train the NVA units so that they would be equal to the GSFG units.

But even in 1960 the then-commander-in-chief of the Warsaw Pact Unified Armed Forces, Marshal of the Soviet Union Andrei A. Grechko, criticized the East German NVA, air forces, air defense forces, and naval forces as lacking the capabilities to organize and command and control offensive operations. Nevertheless, or specifically for that reason, the Soviets began to include the NVA systematically in war games and exercises of the Unified Armed Forces and to issue guidelines for the structure and the armament of the NVA and its mobilization.[22] Simultaneously with the establishment of missile brigades, the NVA was equipped with weapon systems capable of delivering nuclear warheads. Though the NVA itself had never possessed nuclear weapons, it would have been armed with operational-tactical nuclear warheads by the GSFG in case of war. The receipt of these weapon systems, along with the integration of NVA combat units into the Unified Armed Forces and the joint exercise activities, constituted the third prerequisite for the GDR to achieve the status of an equal partner within the alliance.[23]

The Scenario of War

The general scenario of war was based on the assumption that hostilities would start with a conventional attack by NATO after a more or less protracted phase of tensions. The Western "aggression" was to be brought to a halt by not later than the third day, whereupon the fronts (army groups) of the Unified Armed Forces would launch a general offensive. In the first strategic echelon alone, ten armies and one army corps with at least thirty-six active and five mobilized reserve divisions were to operate on the GDR's territory.[24] The Unified Armed Forces assumed that the start of a war would be conventional but that NATO would use nuclear weapons first if they suffered an operational loss of territory equaling about one hundred kilometers. Adhering to the American doctrine of Flexible Response, NATO most likely would have resorted to tactical nuclear weapons much earlier that that.

The NVA's air force and air defense forces were integrated into the Warsaw Pact's air defense system under the commander-in-chief of the Western Front. That subordination meant that the air defense assets would advance westward with the front, which in turn would leave a significant part of the GDR's territory without air cover. The 1961 command staff exercise BURYA (Storm) had demonstrated already that the GDR's air force and air defense forces alone would not be able to ensure the country's protection against NATO air attack. But such protection was necessary because the lines of communications of the Warsaw Pact's forces ran through GDR territory. The territorial defense forces were responsible for securing the infrastructure and for the economic functioning of the hinterland. Up to the final days of the GDR, no satisfactory solution was found for that problem.[25] Furthermore, exercises such as BURYA demonstrated that the GDR had to make enormous efforts to establish a working structure in the rear area of the front. The NVA's rear services organization had to establish a multitude of units and facilities to support just the GSFG. Eventually, a recognition of the high rates of personnel attrition following a nuclear confrontation made it necessary to develop a comprehensive mobilization plan to call up conscripts and to activate the supply of material from industry.

What specific ideas did the Warsaw Pact have regarding warfare in the Western Theater and the role of the GDR and its army? As noted previously, the war scenario provided for three strategic directions. In the north German direction, the Coastal Front operated under Polish supreme command with forces of the Polish People's Army, Military District V (V Army Corps) of the NVA, and elements of the Unified Baltic Fleet in coordination with the Soviet Baltic Red Banner Fleet, the Polish Naval Fleet, and the People's Navy of the GDR.[26] The Coastal Front and the Unified Baltic Fleet were considered equal-level commands, both subordinate to the commander-in-chief of the Western Theater. The Coastal Front's mission would be to advance through the Baltic and North Sea areas with two to three Polish field armies as the main force in the direction of the German-Dutch North Sea coast, with the secondary direction toward Schleswig-Holstein and Jutland-Danish main islands. Such a maneuver required close synchronization with the naval and air forces, with priority missions for their subordinate units focusing on maritime landing and airborne operations to occupy the Danish main islands. Since the Polish army units would reach the zone of operations no sooner than the second day of the war, the burden of the defense until that point rested with the three divisions of the NVA's V Army Corps. After the arrival of Polish forces, V Army Corps would come under Polish frontal supreme command and attack in the direction of Bremen-Meppen. A motorized rifle regiment from Rostock was to support the Jutland operation. In the 1980s the temporary unavailability of Polish armed forces following the Solidarity crisis of 1980–1981 resulted in Military District V being given the mission of acting as a reinforced Fifth Army and spearheading the attack in the directions of both Bremen and Jutland.[27]

The main and central strategic direction of attack of the Unified Armed Forces was the Ruhr area and Lorraine beyond. The Western Front—also often referred to in plans as the Central Front—operating along that axis consisted of units of the GSFG and the NVA main forces of Military District III, all under Soviet supreme command. Two tank armies and three combined-arms armies with at least twenty divisions were in the order of battle. The forc-

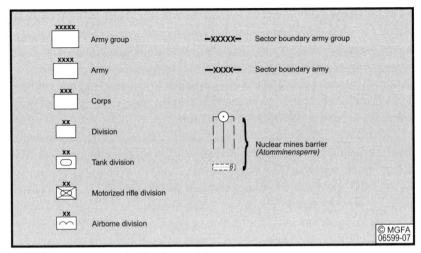

Legend for maps appearing in chapter 11.

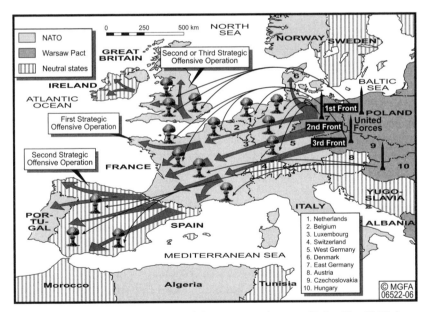

Map 11.1. Strategic offensive plan of the Western Theater of War. Harald Nielsen, *Die DDR und die Kernwaffen: Die nukleare Rolle der Nationalen Volksarmee im Warschauer Pakt* (Baden-Baden, 1998), 38.

es included the GSFG's Second Guards Tank Army, Third Combined-Arms Army, Eighth Guards Army, and First Guards Army in the first echelon. The Soviet Twentieth Guards Army and the NVA's Third Combined-Arms Army formed the second echelon. The Soviet Sixteenth Air Army, an artillery division, two frontal rocket brigades, an air assault brigade, two frontal engineer brigades, and other units were subordinate to the commander-in-chief of the front, as required by the operational mission.

The Southwestern Front, executing the third strategic direction of operations, is included in this discussion only for the sake of completeness. That attack would originate from Czechoslovakia and proceed to the area of Upper Bavaria and Lake Constance through to Lorraine. Its three directions of thrust were Karlsruhe-Strasbourg-Chaumont; Fürth-Stuttgart-Dijon; and Ulm-Freiburg-Besançon. Two armies of the Czechoslovak People's Army and units of the GSFG would operate under Czech supreme command and attack from the south of the GDR in the direction of Suhl-Darmstadt and Suhl-Bamberg.[28] After 1968 the Southwestern Front also included the Soviet forces deployed in the Czechoslovak Socialist Republic after the Prague Spring uprising. NVA units were not scheduled to be committed in this sector of the Western Theater. Supported by Soviet air armies, the lead echelon of the Southwestern Front had the mission of blocking the "imperialist" attack and establishing the conditions for the commitment of the second strategic echelon. The main forces of the Unified Command coming from Poland and the Soviet Union would enter the battle between the third and fifth days of the war with the mission of taking the area crucial for the incapacitation of the Western European NATO states. The Southwestern Front's second strategic echelon was the Soviet Carpathian Military District, while the Western Front's second strategic echelon was the Soviet Belorussian Military District.[29]

The TROJKA War Game

What did the initial phase of a war look like from the NVA perspective? The 1967 TROJKA bilateral, single-level, operational war game provides some insight into this question.[30] The war game took place from 16 to 21 January with the objective being to train the NVA staffs in the planning and conduct of an offensive operation. The NVA leadership simulated the operations of the Unified Armed Forces in the Western Front with three field armies under their command. Following the common assumptions, the "Westerners" had elevated the readiness level of their armed forces to a state of war. The United

States and Great Britain deployed their strategic reserves to the Central European theater. NATO's Northern Army Group (NORTHAG) and elements of the Baltic Approaches Command then deployed to attack with five corps, twenty divisions, and 418 nuclear warheads totaling 12.3 megatons in the direction of Hanover-Bad Freienwalde and Hildesheim-Frankfurt/Oder in order to destroy the 1st Western Front and to reach the Oder River within six to eight days.

The front line was held by the GDR's border troops, which were not part of the first strategic echelon but had the mission of acting independently and defending the border region against the NATO attack.[31] The field armies, each having their operating zones of some one hundred kilometers secured by a border brigade, had to commit covering forces from their own units into the battle to reinforce the border units. Upon alert, those main force battalions or regiments based close to the border were to assume the defense of the border for three to nine hours, operating from prepared covered areas, firing positions, and command posts. Until the main force units were operationally ready, the border force units had to defend the pre-fortified border sections, bases, and key positions. They in turn would be supported by the territorial defense forces of the Bereitschaftspolizei (alert police) and the *Kampfgruppen* (combat groups). The Polizeibereitschaften (alert police regiments) were equipped and trained for both massed domestic employment and military combat action, and in strength and armament they equaled light infantry regiments. The members of the "Combat Groups of the Working Class" were recruited from factory workers who were loyal to the SED. They were organized into *Hundertschaft* (companies) and served as an armed maneuver force for regional operations during domestic protests and riots. The light and especially the fully motorized heavy battalions of the *Kampfgruppen* were capable of operating against diverse groups and airborne forces. Both types of paramilitary formations were established in the GDR following the 1953 People's Uprising. As in other Eastern-bloc states, such organizations were the pillars of the system of power. Their commitment to combat action was rehearsed in such training exercises as TERZETT and FRÜHLING in the spring of 1969. The NVA's leadership was aware, however, that those paramilitary forces would not have had a serious chance of stopping the NATO forces and probably would have been attrited before the arrival of the regular armed forces.

As the 1st Western Front of the Unified Command deployed its forces, it initiated air defense operations. Exploiting the nuclear and air strikes—under the exercise scenario they were allocated 365 nuclear warheads totaling 13.6

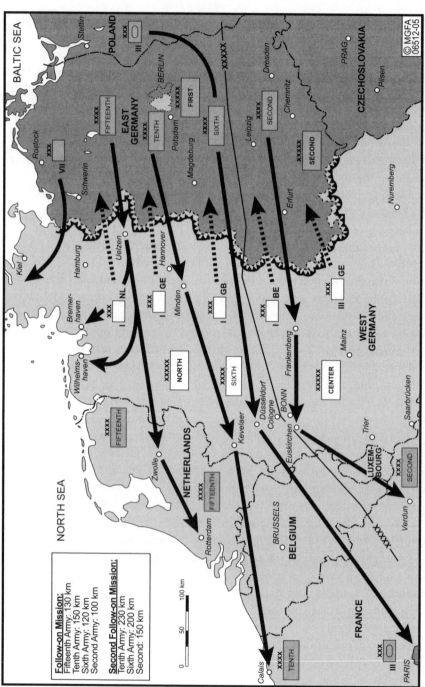

Map 11.2. Concept of the unilateral single-stage operational war game TROJKA. BA-MA, VA-01/18835, Zweiseitiges, einstufiges, operatives Kriegsspiel "Troika," 16–21 Jan. 1967, fol. 642.

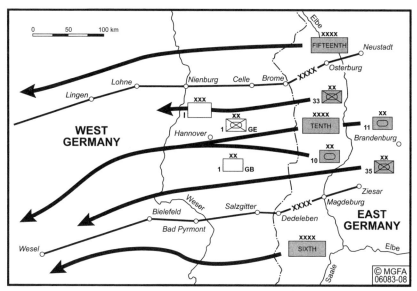

Map 11.3. Decision of the commander-in-chief of Tenth Army on the conduct of the attack operation. BA-MA, VA-01/18835, Zweiseitiges, einstufiges, operatives Kriegsspiel "Troika," 16–21 Jan. 1967, fol. 668.

megatons—they proceeded to attack on 18 January. The front's first echelon consisted of the Fifteenth, Tenth, and Sixth Combined-Arms Armies. The second echelon was formed by the Third Tank Army. Flank security—which in the exercise was only notional—was provided in the Baltic area by VII Army Corps and in the south by the Second Combined-Arms Army.

The Tenth Combined-Arms Army executed the main strike in the center sector thrusting in the direction of Magdeburg-Osnabrück-Brussels-Paris to destroy NORTHAG and elements of the Baltic Approaches Command, on a timeline to occupy the area of Arnheim-Cologne-Dortmund between the fifth to seventh days of operations. Supported by the Eighteenth Air Army, they were to destroy British I Corps as well as elements of German I Corps in the area of Celle-Hanover-Salzgitter, cross the Weser, and reach the area of Nienburg-Lübeck-Hessisch-Oldendorf on the second day. Continuing the advance, they were to cross the Rhine with the support of the 24th Airborne Division, occupy the area of Nijmegen-Venlo-Wesel on the fifth and sixth days of operations, and consolidate and prepare to continue the attack in the direction of Eindhoven-Calais. The final objective of the Western Front was to reach the northwestern coast of France on the tenth to twelfth day of operations.

Prior to going over to the offensive, the Tenth Combined-Arms Army was tasked to destroy the invading enemy. NORTHAG's German I Corps and British I Corps would be crushed in a maneuver at the boundary between the Fifteenth and Tenth Armies. In the course of the exercise scenario, an enemy attack against the right flank would be defeated with the use of nuclear strikes and the commitment of the 33rd Motorized Rifle Division. NORTHAG responded by committing the Bundeswehr's 11th Panzer Grenadier Division, but with little success. NORTHAG then brought up its operational reserves consisting of the newly formed 13th and 7th Panzer Grenadier Divisions. At that point the Western Front committed its 35th Motorized Rifle Division from the second echelon to increase the momentum of the attack, which crossed the Weser River on the bound.[32]

The Fifteenth Combined-Arms Army operated simultaneously on the Tenth Combined-Arms Army's right (northern) flank. Under this particular exercise scenario it represented the Coastal Front, but without executing the Jutland operation. Other exercises added the planned actions in the Baltic and North Sea areas, which rounded out the complete scheme of maneuver in the Western Theater.[33]

The GDR's People's Navy was tasked with the security of the western at-

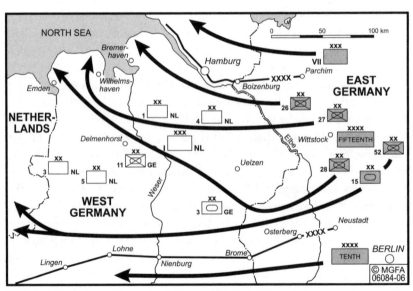

Map 11.4. Decision of the commander-in-chief of Fifteenth Army on the conduct of the attack operation. BA-MA, VA-01/18835, Zweiseitiges, einstufiges, operatives Kriegsspiel "Troika," 16–21 Jan. 1967, fol. 666.

tack until the Polish units reached their assembly areas on the second day of the war. The mission of the People's Navy was to counter the NATO naval forces—particularly the submarines and medium surface units—that had penetrated into the zone of operations. That mission also included the maintenance of naval superiority in the central sector of the Baltic Sea, the Mecklenburg Bight, and the Arkona Sea, thereby preventing enemy surface and submarine units from breaking through into the Mecklenburg Bight. People's Navy coastal artillery and antitorpedo and antisubmarine forces would be used to establish a secure anchorage at Libben for the Unified Baltic Fleet.

The main forces of the Unified Baltic Fleet and the Coastal Front were to advance on the allied northern sector via Schleswig-Holstein to the German-Dutch North Sea coast. Conducting a secondary attack, Polish and NVA units supported by landing operations advanced along the coast, to the Bay of Kiel, the Kattegat, the Skagerrak, and the German Bight, finally occupying Schleswig-Holstein, Jutland, and the Danish main islands. Significantly, the People's Navy knew from the 1960s that in any intervention against a NATO attack by the Unified Baltic Fleet and the units of the Coastal Front, 60 percent of their overall forces probably would have been destroyed in the defensive actions alone. Nonetheless, the Polish and Soviet navies were reluctant to move their units forward for the initial defense. Not until the 1980s did the Soviets finally deploy a naval unit to Swinemünde.

The NVA motorized rifle regiment in Rostock, which was specially trained for amphibious landings, was tasked with the occupation of the island of Fehmarn. Simultaneously, airborne operations on the island of Lolland and in the belt and sound zones were planned to block the southern exit of the Great Belt. Combat swimmers and engineers were to neutralize the NATO coastal battery on the island of Langeland. The People's Navy also had the mission of landing the Soviet 5th Armored Brigade in two echelons in the sector of Bülk-Friedrichsort and establishing barriers in the Kiel Fjord. The People's Navy also deployed an assault ship group of missile boats, torpedo boats, and coastal defense vessels south of Langeland to transfer a coastal battery to Laaland and to land in the Kiel Fjord.[34]

During the TROJKA exercise scenario the operations of the Coastal Front, as represented by the Fifteenth Combined-Arms Army, were to be supported by massive nuclear missile strikes on political and economic centers, troop concentrations, missile bases, and other military targets throughout the entire depth of the sector of advance. Subsequently, the Coastal Front supported by the Eighteenth Air Army would continue the attack in the direction of Wittenberge-Uelzen-Hoya, destroy Netherlands I Corps and

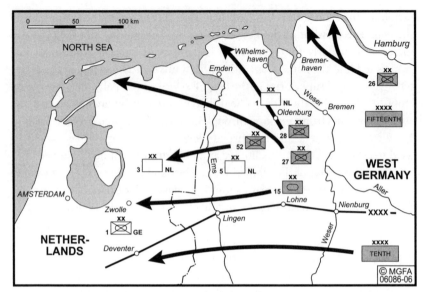

Map 11.5. Decision of the commander-in-chief of Fifteenth Army on the situation of the forces on 21 January, 0900 hrs. BA-MA, VA-01/18835, Zweiseitiges, einstufiges, operatives Kriegsspiel "Troika," 16–21 Jan. 1967, fol. 699.

elements of German I Corps in the Lüneburg-Soltau-Celle area in coordination with the Tenth Combined-Arms Army, cross the Weser, and reach the Rothenburg-Achim-Nieburg area by the second or third day of the war. The Coastal Front would then continue its advance toward Rotterdam, seizing the coastal regions around Cuxhaven, Bremerhaven, Wilhelmshaven, and Emden by the fifth or sixth day of operations. Finally, the front would advance into the section of Alkmar-Dordrecht.[35]

In the course of the exercise scenario the Fifteenth Combined-Arms Army's 15th Tank Division was repelled by the West German 3rd Panzer Division, but the 26th Motorized Rifle Division was able to advance across the Elbe with the 27th Motorized Rifle Division deployed on its right flank and then attack and destroy the Netherlands 4th and 1st Divisions in the area of Lüneburg. On the left flank the 28th Motorized Rifle Division supported by the second echelon of the 15th Tank Division was able to destroy the West German 3rd Panzer Division before the advancing West German 11th Panzer Grenadier Division succeeded in engaging in the battle. By the evening of the first day of operations, the Fifteenth Combined-Arms Army was to have destroyed major elements of Netherlands I Corps and German

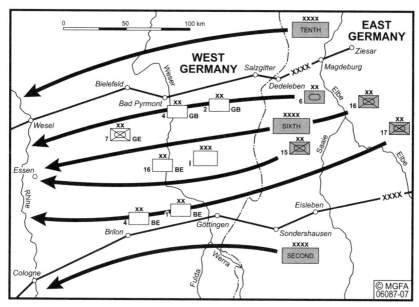

Map 11.6. Decision of the commander-in-chief of Sixth Army on the conduct of the attack operation. BA-MA, VA-01/18835, Zweiseitiges, einstufiges, operatives Kriegsspiel "Troika," 16–21 Jan. 1967, fol. 670.

I Corps, advancing sixty kilometers into the depth of enemy territory. On the second day, the 52nd Motorized Rifle Division from the reserve was to join the battle as the second echelon in the area of Salzwedel-Beetzendorf-Arendsee-Brunau. In the meantime, NATO tried to stabilize the front lines with the commitment of the Netherlands 5th Division.

According to the exercise scenario, the Sixth Combined-Arms Army operated on the southern flank of the Western Front. It engaged in the direction of Bernburg-Holzminden and was tasked with destroying in coordination with the Tenth Combined-Arms Army Belgian I Corps and elements of British I Corps in the area of Alfeld-Göttingen-Osterode. Crossing the Weser River from the march, the Sixth Combined-Arms Army was supposed to reach the area of Bad Pyrmont–Nieheim-Warburg-Hardegsen by the second day of operations, cross the Rhine, and reach the Dinslaken-Düsseldorf-Dortmund area by the fifth or sixth day of operations.[36] In the Sixth Combined-Arms Army area of operations the exercise scenario had elements of British I Corps successfully repel the 6th Tank Division at Wernigerode by using nuclear weapons. The 15th Motorized Rifle Division blocked

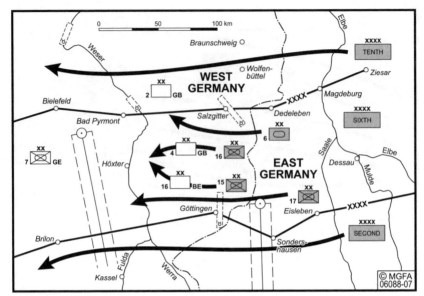

Map 11.7. Decision of the commander-in-chief of Sixth Army on the situation of forces on 19 January, 1100 hrs. BA-MA, VA-01/18835, Zweiseitiges, einstufiges, operatives Kriegsspiel "Troika," 16–21 Jan. 1967, fol. 695.

the advance by elements of Belgian I Corps. Enemy forces also were pushed back to Herzberg-Nesselröden, exploiting the success of the 2nd Western Front's 60th Motorized Rifle Division.

Since the Harz Mountains had been bypassed by the Warsaw Pact forces, the Canadian 4th Infantry Brigade was able to penetrate onto GDR territory and threaten the flank of the Sixth Combined-Arms Army. The Sixth Combined-Arms Army commander then decided to introduce the second echelon of the 6th Armored Division, supported by nuclear strikes and fighter-bomber attacks to prevent the development of an attack by the British 2nd Infantry Division and to disrupt the deployment of the second echelon of British I Corps. The newly committed 16th Motorized Rifle Division and 10th Tank Division contributed to the defeat of the enemy main forces.

NATO tried to delay the advance of the Sixth Combined-Arms Army by detonating two atomic demolition munitions zones and to delay the deployment of the 17th Motorized Rifle Division by launching a nuclear weapons strike set for a ground detonation. The commander of the Sixth Combined-Arms Army responded by ordering the destruction of the remaining elements of the British 2nd and 4th Infantry Divisions with the support of the

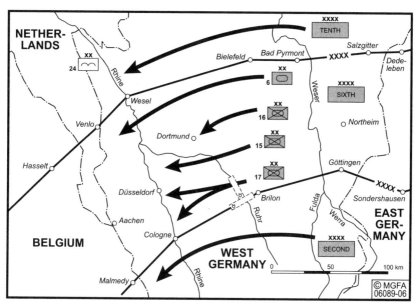

Map 11.8. Decision of the commander-in-chief of Sixth Army on the situation of forces on 21 January, 0900 hrs. BA-MA, VA-01/18835, Zweiseitiges, einstufiges, operatives Kriegsspiel "Troika," 16–21 Jan. 1967, fol. 705.

6th Tank Division and the bypassing of the nuclear detonation zones by the 16th and 17th Motorized Rifle Divisions. The engaged NVA staffs had to plan the operations by considering the locations of the existing nuclear minefields and the procedures to breach them. The basic assumption was that the mine zones had been established thirty to fifty kilometers behind the border. The NVA planners thought it would be possible to clear the minefields in the sectors of Fallersleben-Schöningen, Northeim-Göttingen, and Rothenburg-Fulda-Gersfeld. But they also anticipated additional barriers along the Weser and the Rhine. This was the first time that the problem of the NATO nuclear minefields was addressed in an exercise. As the planners were faced with major tactical and technical problems, it became obvious that clearing and bypassing a nuclear minefield under combat conditions would be much more difficult than had been assumed at the start of the exercise.[37]

During the initial phase of the exercise the field armies had expended some 30 percent of their nuclear weapons, thereby meeting the Warsaw Pact requirement of retaining the majority of their nuclear weapons for future operational requirements.[38] According to NVA projections, by the third day of operations on the enemy's soil NATO would attempt to establish a defensive position in front of the Rhine. The exercise scenario did not restrict the Unified Armed Forces from crossing the Rhine and Ems Rivers from the march by using nuclear strikes and airborne units, nor from continuing the advance into France. The TROJKA exercise thus served to validate the Warsaw Pact's thinking on the course of a military conflict with NATO in the Western Theater.

Although an operation against West Berlin was not part of the TROJKA exercise, it was a key element in the military planning for the Western Theater. The exercise staff for the BUYRA exercise had been closely connected with the erection of the Wall in 1961.[39] The BUYRA exercise scenario was based on the assumption that NATO would make an aggressive attempt to break through to Berlin with forces of up to a division in strength, as had actually been intended during the LIVE OAK deliberations. After the first Berlin crisis in 1948 the Soviets had developed plans for a military "solution of the Berlin problem." In the subsequent years, units of the border troops, the NVA, the GSFG, and the various paramilitary formations of the alert police and combat groups had been concentrated around Berlin. In the 1980s the order of battle of the forces designated for the Berlin operation included some thirty-five thousand troops, more than four hundred tanks, one thousand armored infantry fighting vehicles, artillery, and antitank weapons. Following the establishment of the NVA, the forces in and around Berlin included the 1st Motorized Rifle Division, Intelligence Battalion 40, Guard and Support Battalion 40, two assault engineer battalions of Engineer Brigade 2, and later elements of Air Assault Regiment 40. They were augmented by units of the Border Command Center and Border Regiment 5 of Border Command North, as well as by the 6th Independent Motorized Rifle Brigade and the 40th Artillery Brigade of the GSFG. Plans also provided for the commitment of the Berlin combat group battalions, Battalions I to IV from Potsdam, and the 18th and 19th Police Alert Forces from Basdorf.[40]

The operations plan divided West Berlin into two sectors. The southwestern sector with the British and American garrisons was to be occupied by the 1st Motorized Rifle Division and units of the Border Command Center. The thrust in the center in the direction of the Tiergarten was to be carried out by the 6th Motorized Rifle Brigade of GSFG, flanked by the 18th Police Alert Regiment and Border Regiment 33. The 1st Regiment of the 1st Motorized Rifle Division and Border Regiments 38 and 40 were to invade West Berlin from the north, while Border Regiments 35, 39, and 42 were to penetrate into the city from the southeast. The plan called for the neutralization of Tempelhof and Tegel airport with airborne troops of Air Assault Regiment 40 and Helicopter Transport Squadron 34. Security Battalion 40, the 19th Police Alert Regiment, and the four combat group battalions were held in reserve.[41] It is important to remember, however, that these were contingency plans in the case of war and were not actual preparations for an attack. The Warsaw Pact states, as well the GDR knew, that the violation of the status quo of the "free city" would presumably have resulted in a nuclear conflict between the two blocs.

The Impact of Nuclear Weapons

The apparent simplicity of the East German–Soviet war scenario in the exercises might seem astonishing. The conduct of NATO's planned delaying operations up to the Weser River did not play any role in the war games under consideration. The conventional warfare aspects obviously included elements typical of the final stages of the fighting in World War II, albeit with consideration for increased mobility and the existence of nuclear arms. The consequences of the use of nuclear arms, however—in terms of both the strategic nuclear arms potential of NATO and the United States and the effects that a battlefield devastated by nuclear detonations would have on the psyche and morale of the attacking forces—were apparently neglected. For decades the Warsaw Pact acknowledged the destructiveness of nuclear weapons. There was, nevertheless, a considerable gap between the assumed effects of their own strikes and those of NATO. The troop deployments and attacks of their own forces were conducted as if the strikes had hardly any impact. At most, the exercise scenarios tested the breaching or bypassing of nuclear minefield belts, reconnaissance of contaminated areas, or damage repair by engineers. The direct impact on the forces and the loss of entire units was rarely the subject of study, or was considered only to a limited extent during the 1960s. During the BURYA exercise in 1961, for example, NATO nuclear weapons strikes against the front resulted in the loss of only seven companies, forty tanks, and one missile launcher by the six regiments in the target area.[42]

Obviously, the impact of nuclear weapons on the territory, the population, and above all, the troops was deliberately downplayed. In 1964 the chief of the General Staff Academy, Marshal Matvei V. Zakharov, even insisted that the low-contaminated zones were particularly to be used for attack routes since a second strike would not be expected in those areas. A Soviet instructional film from the 1950s showed the actions of troops under the real effects of nuclear weapons. It suggested the possibility of continuing combat operations after a decontamination pause. In the early 1970s a transportation exercise in the area of Dresden was based on the assumption that the city had suffered a nuclear weapons strike. The main train station, located only five hundred meters from ground zero, was to resume operations after only twelve hours. As late as the 1980s the NVA Military Academy in Dresden continued to teach the conduct of an uninterrupted attack through radioactively contaminated areas, despite the growing criticism of such a doctrine. It appears obvious that such thinking was based on the fact that the Soviet Union's offensive concept was not challenged as long as the military considered it feasible. It was not until the new military doctrine of 1987 and after the reactor disaster at Chernobyl that a more realistic approach to the actual consequences of a nuclear war won recognition.

Defense Preparations

For the GDR, as mentioned previously, the preparation of its territory for defense was a substantial component of its economic and general social obligations within the Warsaw Pact. The Soviet attack strategy required extensive provisions of personnel, fuel, supplies, ammunition, and maintenance, combined with a well-developed system of transportation, stockpiles, production and maintenance bases, medical support, and the continuation of operations under any constraint of modern warfare. It was a fundamental assumption that in the case of war, NATO would launch massive strikes to disrupt the transport and support systems. In the 1960s Warsaw Pact planners assumed NATO would conduct barrier strikes against the Elbe-Saale and Oder-Neisse lines. Thus all necessary preparations for the reconstruction of destroyed transportation lines and war-essential facilities had to be put in place in peacetime. The GDR was especially affected as a military operational and transit zone. Although a comprehensive comparison of the various Warsaw Pact national defense systems has yet to be made, it seems that over the course of the years, of all the Eastern bloc nations, the GDR developed the most sophisticated network of logistics preparations for the state of war. That also includes an almost complete integration and cross-linking of governmental institutions and social organizations into the system of national defense.

The general term of "logistics" as understood by NATO meant two cooperating but nevertheless separate fields for the GDR—the *Rückwärtige Dienste* (rear services) of the armed forces on the one hand, and territorial defense on the other. The NVA rear services were responsible for direct combat support, including supporting the operations of the Unified Armed Forces. The preparation of the territory included the general mobilization of the state, industry, and society to support the functioning of the GDR's zone of operations.

The GDR's national defense systems developed in three stages. The preliminary phase from 1953 to 1961 was dominated by the establishment of the NVA and its support structures. The second phase from 1961 to 1970 was characterized by standardization and centered on the build-up of the support systems for the troops and the national-specific aspects of territorial defense. From 1970 on, the emphasis was on the further development of the system according to the plan.

It is the second phase that is most relevant to this discussion. In March 1961 the Warsaw Pact decided to standardize the mobilization preparations of the member states. The mobile military national defense components (the army and the border troops) and the territorial defense components, which included the internal security system forces (police forces, combat groups, the State Security Service, the Air Raid Protection Service, and the Society for Sports and Technology) were increasingly integrated into the national defense preparations. A striking aspect of the territorial security forces was that they were intended for operations not only against NATO airborne and special forces troops but also against anticipated "counterrevolutionary" actions by the people of the GDR. The combat groups, alert police, and other armed elements were to be committed to such a role in addition to their tasks of ensuring the safety and restoration of production, traffic, and civilian social functions. These latter tasks would be executed in coordination with the Air Raid Protection Service, civil defense, the German Red Cross, the fire protection services, the Society for Sports and Technology, and other organizations.

In 1964 the commander-in-chief of the Warsaw Pact Unified Armed Forces, Andrei Grechko, demanded that the GDR improve its road system and rail network in the east-west direction while bypassing the towns to better prepare the territory for war. The routes Szczecin-to-Wittenberge, Halle-to-Halberstadt, Dresden-to-Leipzig, and Děčin-to-Gotha were to be extended to the West German border. In addition, twelve bridges across the Oder, Havel, Mulde, and Saale Rivers were to be doubled for rail and vehicle traffic. Grechko also requested an undersea cable between Kaliningrad and Rostock and the further extension of existing communications nodes.[43]

The structural development plan for the road, railway, and intelligence systems for the period from 1962 to 1965 included the additional investment of 560 million East German marks, which amounted to 7 percent of the total investments in the transport, post, and communications systems.[44] The demand for a railway transloading facility from Russian broad gauge to German standard gauge met with strong resistance. Further billions would have been required for that. The rear services had to provide hospitals with a capacity of thirty thousand beds for the Unified Armed Forces; seventy thousand beds for the NVA, which was 30 percent of its wartime strength; and twenty-five ambulance trains in case of war. In addition, banked blood urgently required by the GDR health service was to be stockpiled, and blood transfusion stations were to be established.

Soviet control of the GDR's armaments was exercised through compulsory treaty provisions. The Protocol of 17 May 1967, for example, specified a peacetime strength for the NVA of 120,000 troops, increasing to 280,000 troops in the case of war. The protocol laid down the numbers and types of units of all three military services and how they were to be equipped. An annex to the protocol listed new weapon systems that had to be procured, with details of the purchasing arrangements being set forth in bilateral agreements. In 1967 the equipment of an NVA tank division was specified as three launchers for Luna M missiles; at least three hundred T-54 and T-55 tanks; six combat vehicles with antitank guided missiles; and a 100 percent fill-out for armored personnel carriers.

The NVA and the Warsaw Pact Unified Armed Forces were required to maintain stocks of ammunition, fuel, and food for at least thirty days of combat. The result was an enormous stockpile of supplies, and even then the norm was never met. In the event of war the NVA also had to support the GSFG with thirty transport battalions, four medical transport companies, and four hundred vehicles with drivers.

The GDR built on the illusion that in the case of war, a rapid transition to the attack would enable them to limit the damage on their own territory. The national defense system was gradually perfected, and in the process, GDR society was increasingly militarized, becoming an instrument of military operations. In the end that served the purpose of facilitating the Warsaw Pact's ability to conduct war. Up through the 1980s the potential consequences of a nuclear war were kept out of discussions within the military and the public. But the voices of the peace movement were becoming louder, and discussions started within the military about the implications of waging nuclear war. It was only the internal reforms in the Soviet Union, however, that permitted the emergence in 1987 of a military doctrinal concept of sufficient defense.

Notes

1. Joachim Schunke, "Militärpolitische und strategische Vorstellungen der Führung der NVA in der Zeit der Blockkonfrontation," in *Was war die NVA? Studien— Analysen—Berichte: Zur Geschichte der Nationalen Volksarmee* (Berlin, 2001), 81.

2. Document KK 4566, "Militärische Planungen des Warschauer Pakte in Zentraleuropa. Eine Studie," in *Des Dokumentations- und Fachinformationszentrums der Bundeswehr (DOKFIZBw)*, Bundesministerium der Verteidigung (Bonn, 1992), 3.

3. Peter Joachim Lapp, "Die NVA 1956–1990," in *Aufarbeitung von Geschichte und Folgen der SED-Diktatur in Deutschland,* vol. II.3, *Macht, Entscheidung, Verantwortung,* Enquete-Kommission (Baden-Baden, 1995), 1901.

4. See *Sowjetische Militärenzyklopädie* 12 ([East] Berlin, n.d.), 12; *Militärlexikon,* 2nd ed. ([East] Berlin, 1973), 232–33.

5. Ulrich Berger and Wolfgang Wünsche, *Jugendlexikon Militärwesen* ([East] Berlin, 1984), 134.

6. Manfred Backerra, "Zur sowjetischen Militärdoktrin seit 1945," *Beiträge zur Konfliktforschung* 13, no. 1 (1983): 50–51.

7. Peer H. Lange, "Militärpolitik," in *Pipers Wörterbuch zur Politik,* ed. Dieter Nolen, vol. 4, *Sozialistische Systeme: Politik-Wirtschaft-Gesellschaft,* ed. Klaus Ziemer (Munich, 1986), 283.

8. Ulrich Albrecht, Andreas Heinemann-Grüder, and Arend Wellmann, *Die Spezialisten: Deutsche Naturwissenschaftler und Techniker in der Sowjetunion nach 1945* (Berlin, 1992).

9. *Sowjetische Militärenzyklopädie* 18 ([East] Berlin, n.d.), 102–3.

10. See Bundesarchiv-Militärarchiv Freiburg (hereinafter BA-MA), DVW 1/39 489, fols. 10–25, Informationen des Ministeriums für Nationale Verteidigung über "Maßnahmen der weiteren Erhöhung der Verteidigungsbereitschaft der Mitgliedsstaaten des Warschauer Vertrages," Annex to the NVR protocol of 27 June 1968.

11. Ibid.

12. Harald Nielsen, *Die DDR und die Kernwaffen: Die nukleare Rolle der Nationalen Volksarmee im Warschauer Pakt,* Internationale Politik und Sicherheit, vol. 30/6 (Baden-Baden, 1998), 50.

13. *Sowjetische Militärenzyklopädie* 18, 103–4.

14. Autorenkollektiv, *Streitkräfte der UdSSR* ([East] Berlin, 1974), 598–99; Autorenkollektiv, *NATO, Tatsachen und Dokumente* (Brussels, 1976), 12.

15. Frank Umbach, *Das rote Bündnis: Entwicklung und Zerfall des Warschauer Paktes 1955–1991,* Militärgeschichte der DDR, ed. Militärgeschichtlichen Forschungsamt Potsdam, vol. 10 (Berlin, 2005), 575–80.

16. Heinz Hoffmann, "Grundfragen der Militärpolitik der Sozialistischen Einheitspartei Deutschlands," in *Sozialistische Landesverteidigung: Aus Reden und Aufsätzen 1963 bis Februar 1970,* part 1 ([East] Berlin, 1971), 116–44, here pp. 133–38.

17. Armin Wagner, *Walter Ulbricht und die geheime Sicherheitspolitik der SED:*

Der Nationale Verteidigungsrat der DDR und seine Vorgeschichte (1953–1971), Militärgeschichte der DDR, ed. Militärgeschichtliches Forschungsamt Potsdam, vol. 4 (Berlin, 2002), 196–97.

18. Nielsen, *Die DDR und die Kernwaffen,* n. 12, 178–79; Matthias Uhl, "Storming on to Paris: The 1961 Buria Exercise and the Planned Solution of the Berlin Crisis," in *War Plans and Alliances in the Cold War: Threat Perceptions in the East and West,* ed. Vojtech Mastny, Sven G. Holtsmark, and Andreas Wenger (London, 2006), 47–48.

19. Horst-Henning Basler, "Das operative Denken der NVA," in *NVA: Anspruch und Wirklichkeit nach ausgewählten Dokumenten,* ed. Klaus Naumann (Berlin, 1993), 180.

20. See BA-MA, Bestand DVW 2-2/ . . . Dissertationen und Studien der MAK Dresden. See, for example, Klaus-Peter Brandes, "Die Planung, Organisation und Durchführung der materiellen Sicherstellung der Truppen in der Angriffsoperation einer Armee im Kampf um ein Ballungsgebiet" (Dresden, 1985); Hermann Dietrich, "Die Möglichkeiten zur logistischen Unterstützung angespannter, langanhaltender Kampfhandlungen der NATO-Landstreitkräfte auf dem Zentraleuropäischen Kriegsschauplatz 1980–1990" (Dresden, 1983); Klaus Hannemann, "Militärgeographische Untersuchungen der Cimbrischen Halbinsel in der jütländischen Operationsrichtung und die sich daraus ergebenden Schlußfolgerungen für den Einsatz der taktischen Verbände der Landstreitkräfte" (Dresden, 1970).

21. In April 1952 Stalin had demanded that the GDR leadership establish an army of 300,000 troops, an extensive defense industry, a military defense of the borders with the Federal Republic, and a developed system to support both their own armed forces and the Soviet occupation forces. On this, see Torsten Diedrich and Rüdiger Wenzke, *Die getarnte Armee* (Berlin, 2001).

22. BA-MA, AZN 32594, fols. 40–75, Letter from Grechko to Hoffmann of 8 Nov. 1960 and minutes of the Beratung des Vereinten Kommandos of 1–2 Dec. 1960.

23. In August 1957 the NVA conducted the large coordination exercise with GSFG. *Zeittafel zur Militärgeschichte der Deutschen Demokratischen Republik 1949–1988* ([East] Berlin, 1989), 85–86.

24. The NORTHAG Defense Plan 1969 assumed a similar force concentration. BA-MA, BL 1/4050, o.B., Aufzeichnungen des Generalinspekteurs der Bundeswehr bei der NORTHAG, 28 Jan. 1969. See also Helmut Hammerich's chapter in this volume.

25. See Schunke, "Militärpolitische und strategische Vorstellungen," 84–85.

26. In this context, a front is not understood in the Western sense as battle line but as an army group. Contrary to the situation in the West, the commander-in-chief of the front had all the services necessary for the operations of his front at his disposal. Other than the supreme command in the theater of war, the front staff was the national staff of the subordinate army that had the strongest contingent of troops in the front. The other allied armies were involved in the staff with "operational groups." Thus, in addition to the Soviet fronts, there were the Coastal Front under the Poles and the Southwest Front under Czechoslovak supreme command.

27. Friedrich Engels, *Die Jütländische Operation*. Instructional material of the Military Academy. See BA-MA, VA-04/37779.

28. Parallel History Projekt on NATO and the Warsaw Pact (PHP), Tschecho-slowakischer Kriegsplan 1963. See http://www.isn.ethz.ch/php/documents/collection _1/docs/warplan1-engl.htm.

29. BA-MA, AZN 32614, fols. 99f. These fronts were played in a secret bilateral strategic operational war game in three stages of the Supreme Command of the Unified Armed Forces from 8 to 18 May 1963.

30. See BA-MA, VA-01/18835, Zweiseitiges, einstufiges, operatives Kriegsspiel "Troika," 16–21 Jan. 1967.

31. Kurt Röhr and Günter Broschat, "Die Heranführung der Truppen einer Armee an die Staatsgrenze zu Beginn eines Krieges, die Deckung der Heranführung und Entfaltung bei gleichzeitiger Sicherung der Staatsgrenze im Handlungsstreifen der Armee" (diss., Dresden, 1969), 24.

32. BA-MA, VA-01/18835, fols. 693f.

33. See BA-MA, DVH 17/25480, Kommandostabsübung "Barriere-S," 1969; VA-01/188809, Kriegsspiel der Schulungsgruppe des Ministers 1962; and DVM 10/37779, *Lektion*, "Die Aufgaben der Seestreitkräfte zur Unterstützung der Küstenfront bei ihren Kampfhandlungen in der Jütländischen und Norddeutsch-Niederländischen Operationsrichtung im Rahmen der ersten Angriffsoperation," 1967.

34. Günther Pöschel, "Die Volksmarine als Teil der Vereinten Ostseeflotte," *Marineforum* 11 (1992): 388–90.

35. BA-MA, VA-01/18835, fols. 793f.

36. BA-MA, VA-01/18835, fols. 646f.

37. BA-MA, VA-01/18835, fols. 649–69.

38. BA-MA, VA-01/18835, fol. 679.

39. BA-MA, VA-01/6302 and VA-01/6289.

40. Helmut Göpel, "Die Berlin-Operation," in *NVA: Anspruch und Wirklichkeit*, ed. Naumann, 285–99.

41. On this see Exercise "Bordkante 85" in BA-MA, VA-10, 20750, as well as "Bordkante 86" in VA-10, 22942.

42. The subjects of study were command and staff exercise (KSÜ) military district (MD) V 1958; operational-strategic war game of the Unified Armed Forces BURYA, 1961; minister training war game, January 1962; Oktobersturm, 1965; Moldau, 1966; TROJKA, 1967; Bulgaria, 1967; and Barriere-S, 1969. BA-MA, DVH 17/25480, VA-01/18805, VA-01/18809, and BStU MfS, GH 8/68.

43. BA-MA, DVW 1/22120, Consultation between Commander-in-Chief of the Unified Forces and Ministry of National Defense, 17–21 Mar. 1964.

44. *Statistisches Jahrbuch der DDR* 1965 ([East] Berlin, 1965), 44.

12

The British Army of the Rhine and Defense Plans for Germany, 1945–1955

Robert Evans

Early British defense planning for a Soviet invasion of Germany is a subject that has received little scholarly attention. During the research for this essay I found that little primary planning material has survived. The records that remain originate mostly from the higher levels, and although these provide some idea of the operational plans, they represent brief glimpses rather than a comprehensive view. One reason for this absence of planning material was the British security system, which in this instance appears to have been particularly effective. Every year the corps-level plans for Germany were renewed and distributed to the relevant subordinate headquarters; on receipt of the new plans, these headquarters destroyed the obsolete plans. Year on year changes were normally relatively minor, but over a long period and combined with some major changes in NATO defense policy, it is impossible to track the planning rationale backward. I have looked for operational plans up to 1968, but none appear to have survived in the UK's archives. More material has survived from the earlier part of this period—that is, before the formation of the NATO command structure where British planning was done on a largely national basis. Even so, operational detail is in short supply. After 1954 the number of available records reduces dramatically, and it may therefore be that the surviving planning material was sent to NATO's archives rather than the UK's, even when it concerned British I Corps.

BAOR's Military Weakness

During the majority of this early period Britain provided the bulk of forces available for the defense of northern Germany, and until the early 1950s this was a responsibility it exercised on a national basis. In practice this remained the case until German rearmament and the establishment of viable Dutch and Belgian forces. The assumption by the commander-in-chief of the British Army of the Rhine (BAOR) of the role of commander, Northern Army Group (COMNORTHAG), therefore, had little immediate effect on the nature and reality of British operational plans.

At the end of World War II in Europe Britain had approximately seventy-five thousand troops in Germany, most of whom were attached to the Second Army and the 21st Army Group. In July 1945 these two combat formations were abolished and a new headquarters titled the British Army of the Rhine was established. BAOR was not intended to be a combat headquarters; rather, it was an administrative headquarters with two primary functions. First, it was responsible for military support to the civilian authority within the British zone of occupation. With the exception of a small U.S. enclave around Bremen, the British zone constituted all of Germany north of a line running roughly from Düsseldorf to Gottingen, including Schleswig-Holstein. Second, and in support of a wider government objective to transition the British war economy back to a peacetime footing as quickly as possible, BAOR was responsible for the rapid demobilization of conscripted troops.

Prior to the increase of East-West tensions during the Berlin crisis, the British assessed that there would be no major war in Europe for at least five years.[1] This view did not alter until mid-1948, when the change in the international situation led to urgent reevaluation of the military position in Germany and the combat readiness of BAOR. The conclusion was that BAOR was incapable of defending the British zone against an attack from the Soviet Union. This remained the prevailing view among Britain's senior military officers until the early 1950s.[2]

Since June 1945 the British had been demobilizing men, most of whom were well trained and experienced, at a rate of approximately twenty thousand per month.[3] By 1948 BAOR's total strength was about fifty thousand men assigned to roughly eight brigades that were deployed evenly throughout the British zone in an internal security posture. BAOR headquarters was not capable of conducting combat operations, and its brigades lacked mobility as they were dependent on static facilities and German civilian labor.

All of the brigades were below war establishment, and roughly half of the total personnel were national servicemen who lacked training. The regular personnel were largely engaged in providing basic military training to the conscripts, and consequently overall effectiveness was reduced further. Of the eight brigades, only one, 16 Independent Parachute Brigade, was composed exclusively of regular troops. There were also significant shortcomings in the availability of materiel. Military planners estimated that equipment and ammunition stocks were sufficient for only about eight weeks of operations. These shortages were more acute for some of the key munitions, such as .303-caliber small arms ammunition, 6-pounder antitank shells, and 2-inch mortar bombs, where it was assessed that stocks were adequate for only about fifteen days' worth of fighting. BAOR's military weakness was exacerbated by a lack of any coordinated allied planning or common command and control structures. It also lacked a subordinate corps-level headquarters to command the national combat formations.

The poor correlation of forces in Germany led to a strategic acceptance that the defense of Germany was essentially a lost cause and that no attempt would be made to reinforce BAOR should a war break out. Instead the military priority was the defense of the UK base and the empire, in particular the Middle East, which would receive all of the available reinforcements. Faced with a Soviet attack, BAOR would withdraw northwestward to the United Kingdom. It was decided that reinforcement of BAOR would not be considered until there was a reasonable chance of conducting a successful defense on the west bank of the Rhine River. In 1948 it was assessed that this would not be possible before 1953.[4]

Montgomery, now chief of the Imperial General Staff, proposed a series of measures that included a halt to demobilization, remobilization of reservists, the regearing of industry back toward a war footing, and the establishment of a properly structured allied high command. All but the latter were unaffordable and therefore politically unacceptable to the British government. It is interesting to see that Montgomery's views and suggestions are firmly rooted in his experience of total war and his proposals were not grounded in the political and economic realities of the day. His views about the military capabilities of Britain's European allies were similarly uncompromising and blunt.

Contingency Planning

Despite the poor strategic prognosis for BAOR, contingency plans were drawn up for a withdrawal to a line on the west bank of the Rhine. These plans were collectively known as CONGREVE and assumed that the Soviet

Union was capable of mounting a surprise attack against BAOR from forces based in Soviet-occupied Germany. Planners estimated that the Soviet forces would outnumber allied forces by about three to one. This numerical advantage would be enhanced by the fact that Soviet forces were perceived to be more homogeneous, better trained, and on the whole better equipped than the available allied forces. In the British zone these included Norwegians and Danes; the Dutch and to a lesser extent Belgian forces were deemed to be of little military value until such time as they could reequip and reform. Berlin was considered to be a first-class military liability that could not be defended.[5]

In the event of a Soviet attack, CONGREVE planned for an immediate withdrawal of BAOR's forces to the west bank of the Rhine. Unfortunately the internal security disposition of many of the brigades militated against the success of this westward move. Planners predicted that if the Soviets mounted a surprise attack, as much as 35 percent of BAOR's forces would be isolated by the speed of the Soviet advance and would be unable to reach the Rhine. The outlook for the forces in Hamburg and Schleswig-Holstein was particularly gloomy as geography dictated that in all but the most favorable circumstances they would be cut off. Only the 2nd Infantry Division, which was based close to the Rhine around Düsseldorf, was expected to be able to take up its war positions with any degree of ease. For the remaining forces the timings necessary for successful British withdrawal, compared against the expected speed of Soviet advance, were challenging. Soviet troops potentially could reach Bremen within nine hours, and British troops from Hamburg could reach it in seven hours. Similarly, a withdrawal from Hamburg to Deventer would take British forces twenty-two hours, with Soviet troops potentially able to reach the same point in twenty-six hours. As previously noted, the administrative components of these units were static and would therefore be quickly overrun, which in turn would reduce their operational mobility and combat endurance.

To have some prospect of a viable withdrawal, three armored car regiments (roughly of battalion size) and 7th Armoured Brigade provided a covering force that was expected to delay the Soviet advance by four to five days, using the Weser River as its main defensive line. The difficulty for the planners was that although the covering force had to buy time to allow BAOR's withdrawal to the Rhine, it was hardly sufficient for the task and would inevitably suffer heavy casualties in the process. Such losses would make a defense of the Rhine unviable. In addition, the covering forces were garrisoned to the east of their intended defensive positions and would struggle to occupy them before substantial Soviet forces arrived. Should they have been fortunate enough to establish a viable defensive line, there was little prospect of holding it for the required four to five days given the lack of support elements.[6]

In the unlikely event of a successful withdrawal to the Rhine, BAOR planned to defend a line from the coast, along the line of the IJssel-Rhine to a point opposite Düsseldorf. Planners anticipated that a British brigade would probably have to cover the line of the IJssel until Dutch forces were available. BAOR lacked antiaircraft artillery, and the threat of a Soviet airborne assault to seize the Rhine crossings was considered high. Any such assault would impede the withdrawal and reduce the chances of a successful defense. The senior army officer in Germany assessed that if the Soviets obtained a bridgehead across the Rhine and were in a position to commence mobile operations, further effective resistance would be impossible.[7] It was the Rhine or nothing, with the prospects of holding the Rhine being poor.[8]

British I Corps

Although Britain accepted that the defense of Western Europe was untenable in all but the most positive scenarios, the withdrawal policy was forced by military reality rather than choice. Economic constraints and other more pressing defense commitments had to take priority to Germany, but that defense of a line at least as far east as the Rhine was critical to the security of Britain's interests.[9] Plans were therefore instituted to enhance BAOR's men, equipment, and dispositions so that it would be capable of conducting a mobile defense, within an alliance framework, with a reasonable prospect of success. That took about eight years to complete and was impeded by the continuing shortage of resources and the persistent demands of the empire. British policy makers also acknowledged that the plan to abandon Germany east of the Rhine was not one that was desirable or sustainable in the longer term. In 1950 the British Chiefs of Staff concluded that "the present military vacuum between the Rhine and the Elbe cannot endure and that continued planning for defense of the Rhine line will lead West Germany to conclude that, since they are to be abandoned by the west in the event of war, they must reinsure with the east."[10]

Between 1949 and 1955, force levels in BAOR were gradually increased so that by 1954 it comprised three armored divisions, one infantry division, and one Canadian brigade, for a total of ten brigades. At the same time a corps-level headquarters, British I Corps, was formed to assume operational control of British forces in the event of hostilities. The center of gravity of garrison positions was adjusted so that they were more suited to war deployments and were less susceptible to overrun or isolation. These relocations were expensive and had to be undertaken incrementally because of the lack of funds. They were not completed until 1954. Map 12.1 shows the rough garrison positions of the formations available to the British corps commander.

It is easy to forget that during this period the British army was not the all-professional force that it has been since 1963. Roughly 50 percent of the army's strength was composed of national servicemen, who were essentially conscripts who served for eighteen to twenty-four months. This means that the apparent numerical strength of the British army in general, and BAOR in particular, is quite misleading and did not translate into real combat effectiveness. Army units in the UK and Germany bore the brunt of the overhead for the conscripts' training, which took place at the expense of regular personnel, and ultimately reduced the military capabilities of the units providing it. The emphasis on conscript training also reduced the strategic mobility of army units. The extent of this inflexibility became clear when Britain needed to rapidly deploy modest expeditionary forces to Korea and Suez. In each case forces could be generated only by the mobilization of reservists to bring units up to war fighting strength and capability. Map 12.2 illustrates the extent of the British army's global commitments in 1954.

By 1952 some progress had been made. But the BAOR commander-in-chief was still primarily concerned with bringing his forces up to an acceptable level of military efficiency and readiness. He anticipated that by the end of the year, BAOR headquarters would in the event of war be fit for its new task as the headquarters of the Northern Army Group (NORTHAG). Enhancements to British I Corps were taking effect, and the corps's ability to conduct mobile operations greatly improved. The demands of imperial defense, however, meant that many individuals with key skills, such as staff officers and signalers, were being deployed overseas, undermining the improved provision of equipment.

The British corps was still short in a number of areas. Artillery allocation was only a quarter of the required total, and there was a critical shortage of engineers to facilitate friendly movement and counter the mobility of the enemy. The corps was still overly reliant on the German Service Order and the Mixed Service Organisation for provision of the service units required to sustain the army in war. Neither organization was subject to exacting discipline, and they were staffed by locally employed civilians who "had no inherent loyalty to the British Army." The Belgian and Dutch forces on either side

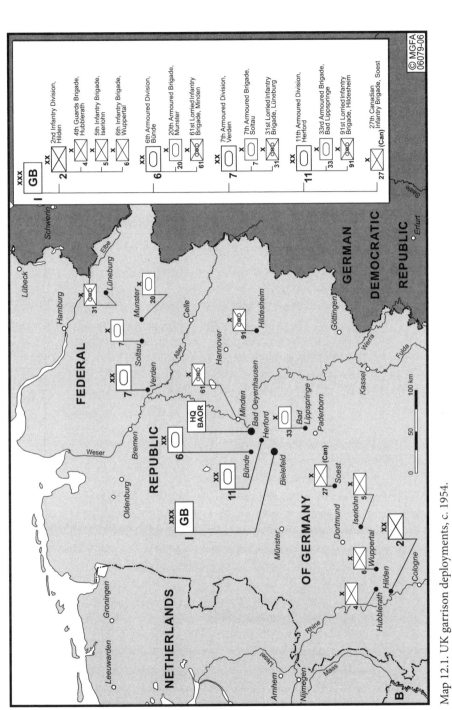

Map 12.1. UK garrison deployments, c. 1954.

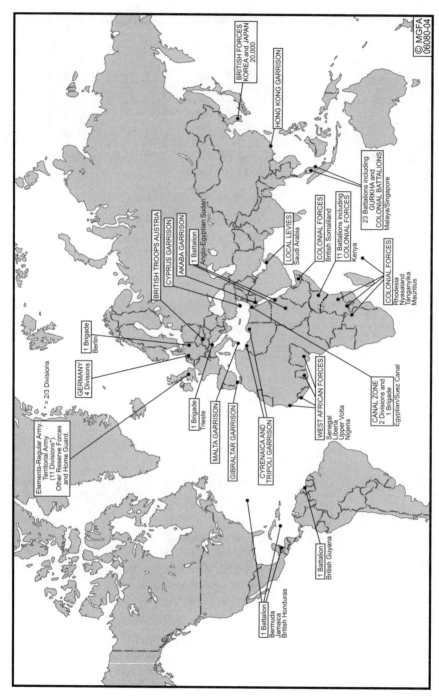

Map 12.2. Disposition of British and colonial forces, January 1954.

of British I Corps needed more training, and coordinated planning between the three nations required great improvement.[11]

The plan still remained as a withdrawal to the Rhine, but much had been done to increase the strength and capacity of the forces available to take the first shock of attack. These forces were now considered fit for defensive mobile operations. Nevertheless, the operational plan still relied on a quick withdrawal to the Rhine, and the problem for the commander of British I Corps remained the time, space, and casualty trade-offs. Although the covering force could delay long enough to enable a withdrawal to the Rhine, it needed to complete this task and still remain combat effective. If the covering force was too badly degraded then the force correlation at the Rhine became very unfavorable.

By 1954 BAOR had continued to improve its combat readiness, and garrison positions had been readjusted to better complement operational war plans (see map 12.1). The availability of nuclear weapons added a complicating factor to British I Corps's withdrawal plans. It now had to aid the Royal Air Force (RAF) by holding key navigational and bombing beacons located in West Germany for twenty-four hours. Once that mission was completed, the corps would make a clean break to the Rhine, and presumably the employment of nuclear bombs would make that possible. The BAOR commander-in-chief believed that the corps must not become embroiled in a running fight as it moved west and that it may have problems coordinating the move with allied forces to the south if they attempted a fighting withdrawal. The correlation of forces in the north was so close that any significant combat losses before the assumption of the Rhine position would probably compromise the corps's ability to hold it.

Map 12.3 illustrates the corps's anticipated defensive positions on the Rhine-IJssel line at about D+5. The corps area constituted the west bank of the Rhine from Dusseldorf in the south to the vicinity of Nijmegen in the north. The covering force formations, 11th Armoured Division and the Canadian Brigade, reconstituted in the south while 6th Armoured and 2nd Infantry Divisions manned the majority of the line. The planners accepted that these forces were insufficient to cover the entire line and that it would probably be impossible to prevent localized Soviet crossings. Consequently, 7th Armoured Division was assigned the role of corps reserve to provide a small counter-penetration force, comprising one armored and one infantry brigade.[12] The Royal Navy Rhine Flotilla would conduct interdiction operations on the river to obstruct Soviet crossings. If necessary, one brigade was ready to move north to reinforce Dutch forces. Over the next fourteen days,

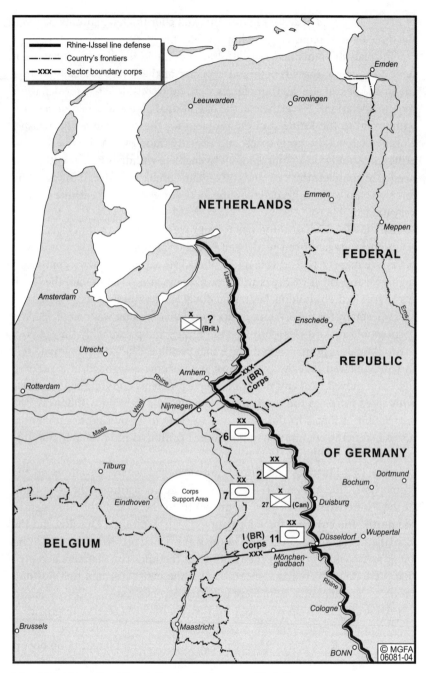

Map 12.3. Rhine-IJssel line defensive deployments D+5–7.

BAOR would receive thirty thousand individual replacements to bring its units up to war strength. By D+20 the corps would receive an additional division from the UK. Between D+20 and D+40 the corps expected to receive the main Soviet assaults on the river line. Toward the end of this phase, BAOR would receive another two reinforcing divisions and a second corps headquarters would be formed. By D+60 another division would arrive and BAOR would attain its maximum strength of three armored divisions and five infantry divisions. At that point an army-level headquarters, First British Army, would be established.

Nuclear Bombing

By 1955 the RAF believed that nuclear bombing would halt a Soviet attack almost before it crossed into West Germany. The British army was skeptical about this claim but adjusted its plans accordingly. It still anticipated a clean break back to the Rhine, but that would now be initiated by Soviet pressure rather than the outbreak of hostilities. At the same time, the army began to rethink its operational-level doctrine focusing on brigade groups capable of operating with a degree of self-sufficiency on a nuclear battlefield. Division-level assets, such as artillery and engineers, were allocated permanently to each brigade to make them capable of operating independently.

General Sir Richard Gale, the BAOR commander-in-chief and COM-NORTHAG, reaffirmed the shortage of engineer and administrative support units within I British Corps. In addition, he confirmed that the corps still required twenty-six thousand personnel to reach war establishment, twelve thousand of which were key staff who were reservists not on the active strength of the army in the UK. A nuclear battlefield would significantly delay the arrival of these reinforcements and in fact might make it impossible.

By 1955 the plan of the supreme allied commander, Europe, relied on the full use of the United States strategic bomber force, and that in turn relied on navigation and bombing aids located in Germany. Consequently, NORTHAG now had to deploy sufficient troops to defend those installations for the period required for the conduct of the air offensive—forty-eight hours. After that period, if the enemy were still capable of a westward advance, I British Corps would fall back and make a clean break to the Rhine-IJssel line. The key change here was the necessity to hold some positions for forty-eight hours and then a triggered withdrawal, rather than an automatic retreat west.

The British army remained skeptical about the ability of the nuclear bomber force to halt the enemy offensive. The slim margin of available conventional forces meant that the forces committed to the defense of the bombing control stations had to be extricated without significant losses. If they could not, then it was likely that there would be insufficient force for the Rhine battle. The British corps and the army group, therefore, had to avoid a running fight. This caused a problem, as COMNORTHAG believed that the Central Army Group's (CENTAG) intention, aided by the terrain, was to conduct a running battle as it withdrew to the west. He believed that CENTAG's was a high-risk strategy that could lead to defeat in detail or envelopment before it reached the Rhine—and that, of course, would render the NORTHAG Rhine position untenable. This weakness was exacerbated by the French corps that covered the boundary of the two army groups. COMNORTHAG believed that it was dangerously understrength and lacked sufficient reserves.

COMNORTHAG considered that the entry of Germany into NATO would lead to an evolution in operational plans that would require the increasing committal of forces to a more protracted delaying action east of the Rhine. He held a far more favorable view of the capabilities of the Belgian and Dutch forces within his command, believing that they were up to the tasks assigned to them. He did, however, comment that the continental armies were developing a strong tendency to favor small, cheaper, but consequently weaker divisions, which lacked depth and endurance. In respect of the Soviet forces he concluded: "It is of interest to note that the deployment of Russian forces, particularly air forces, radar, and anti-aircraft weapons, indicates a defensive posture prepared to meet an Allied attack rather than the reverse. My assessment of the situation as it is at present is that deterrents are being effective."[13]

In conclusion, then, it can be seen that Britain's operational plans for northern Germany up to 1955 were inextricably linked to the wider political and economic situation that the country found itself in at the end of World War II. British commanders frequently complained, with good reason, that the government consistently refused to balance its military commitments to the available resources. From 1945 to 1950 BAOR came off second best in the competition for scarce resources, resulting in an operational plan that was based on immediate withdrawal to the most easily defended position—the west bank of the Rhine. The phrase "most easily defended" is, of course, a relative statement, and in real terms the military professionals of the day accepted that this defensive line had little prospect of holding a Soviet attack. As Britain's strategic situation changed, the immediate withdrawal became politically untenable; forces were therefore built up to allow some degree of conventional defense, and war reserves were allocated to BAOR. This represented a modest increase in force levels that was undermined by large-scale individual abstractions to imperial postings. Ultimately, the defense of Germany depended on airpower and nuclear bombing.

Notes

1. CIGS/BM/30/2235, "Plans for Emergency Measures and Mobilisation," 1 May 1948, National Archives (hereinafter NA), WO 216/254.

2. "Memo Tabled by Field Marshal Montgomery for His Meeting with WUCOS," 20 June 1950, NA, PREM 8/1845.

3. CIGS/BM/31/2524, "The Situation in Western Europe and British Army Problems Arising Therein," 1 July 1948, NA, WO 216/688.

4. CIGS/BM/30/2235, "Plans for Emergency Measures and Mobilisation."

5. CIGS/BM/31/2524, "The Situation in Western Europe and British Army Problems Arising Therein."

6. COS 1096/2/7/8, "The Emergency Plan," 5 July 1948, NA, AIR 20/10513.

7. Letter from General Robertson to the Chiefs of Staff Committee, 1 July 1948, NA, AIR 20/10513.

8. COS (50) 244, "Preparation of the Short-Term Plan in the Western Union," 17 May 1950, NA, AIR 20/10138.

9. "Memo Tabled by Field Marshal Montgomery for His Meeting with WUCOS."

10. Chiefs of Staff to the Cabinet—DO(50)67, Aug. 1950, NA, DEFE 11/27.

11. General Harding's "Appreciation of the Situation," Jan. 1952, NA, WO 106/6051.

12. "Vulnerability of the L of C of Northern Army Group (British element)," Operational Research Report 11/53, NA, WO 291/2387.

13. General Gale's "Appreciation of the Situation," 29 Sept. 1955, NA, WO 216/888.

13

The Dutch Contribution to the Defense of the Central Sector

Jan Hoffenaar

From 1951 until the end of the 1960s and following a period of reticence, the Netherlands was fully committed to making a meaningful military contribution to the NATO defense of the Central Sector in Europe.[1] Since 1945, it had been quite obvious to most of those involved that the defense of the Netherlands could be guaranteed only within the context of an alliance and that such a defense had to be established as far forward as possible.[2]

The initial hesitation resulted from two political prerequisites. First, in the second half of the 1940s the Dutch armed forces were focused almost entirely on deployment to the Dutch East Indies (present-day Indonesia). This was the top priority at that time. Over 150,000 young men—out of a population of approximately 10 million—were hurriedly prepared for duty and deployed overseas. There they mainly experienced guerrilla and counterguerrilla warfare. That was very different from participating in regular operations in a much larger context, which was what would be required from them in Western Europe. The Dutch armed forces were chiefly oriented toward satisfying short-term needs. The development of armed forces that were better suited to operations in Europe as expected in the long term was therefore neglected.[3]

The second factor preventing the Netherlands from devoting all its efforts to the rapid development of an extensive allied defensive force in Europe was the fact that particularly the Social Democrats, who for a number of years led successive governments together with the Catholics, did not perceive the Soviet Union as an acute military threat. They wished to mark time following the Dutch military withdrawal from Indonesia in 1950. Greater importance was given to economic reconstruction: more money to stimulate the economy and less for defense. In their view, that was the best way to keep the influence of Communism within manageable proportions. They considered the armed forces mainly as an insurance premium that was due in order to guarantee American involvement in the security of Europe.[4]

I do not intend to suggest that in the late 1940s Dutch politicians and soldiers were not concerned about the defense of their country. There were, however, other issues that were given higher priority. After all, a guilder could be spent only once.

The Initial Plans

Before 1 July 1949 the Netherlands had in the event of a land attack only emergency plans to evacuate the members of the Dutch Royal Family, together with approximately ten thousand other prominent citizens, to Suriname and the Netherlands Antilles.[5] The most important task of the operational troops not deployed to the Dutch East Indies was to cover that evacuation. Virtually all attention was focused on the military deployment in the Dutch East Indies. In addition, the British officers from the British Military Mission to the Netherlands Government who assisted in the reestablishment of the Dutch army (initially with a view to a Dutch contribution to the occupation of Germany) were particularly unimpressed by the quality of their Dutch comrades. They had been on the sidelines for too long, either as prisoners of war or in Great Britain, and so had little or no experience of modern warfare.[6]

From 1 July 1949 onward, automatic evacuation was no longer part of the emergency defense provisions. Three months earlier, the short-term plan of the Western Union Defense Organization had entered into force. This plan provided the framework for the Dutch plan LION, according to which the Dutch troops would maintain a static defensive line on the IJssel River, so as to protect the economic and political heart of the country situated in its western parts.[7] However, while most of the troops were being sent to the Dutch East Indies, this plan would exist primarily only on paper. There was some coordination with plan ABIGAIL of the British occupying force in Germany, the British Army of the Rhine (BAOR).[8] In an emergency, the commander of BAOR would make available two divisional regiments of his armored corps.[9] The alert procedure for the Dutch troops was linked to that of the British occupation zone.[10] Initially the British also played a leading role in the development of the air defense system.[11] Until the late 1950s the Netherlands would have major shortcomings in that area, as in fact did the allied air defense in general.[12]

NATO

The North Korean invasion of South Korea in June 1950 eventually led the Netherlands to increase its defense efforts considerably to ensure the security of Western Europe. In all NATO member countries, frantic efforts were made to set up some meaningful form of allied defense. In addition to the supreme allied commander, Europe (SACEUR), General Dwight D. Eisenhower, his deputy, Field Marshal Sir Bernard L. Montgomery, was the greatest driving force behind this build-up. He assumed that if Stalin wanted to attack Western Europe, he would do so soon, as the NATO defense was still weak.[13]

At that time, the NATO operational planners believed—and the Dutch analysts and planners agreed with them—that the Soviet Union would prefer a coordinated offensive with a short preparation time to a complete surprise attack. Thus the West would have some advance warning. The planners assumed that a northern advance route—from Berlin via Hanover toward Brussels—would be the most likely one and also posed the greatest threat. The southern part of the Netherlands—the area south of the major rivers—was situated on this axis of advance. The north of the country was part of the flank zone. Operations aimed at the north of the Netherlands would be intended primarily to provide cover for the main advance route. The military assumed that two or three Soviet mechanized divisions would advance to the IJssel River. Once they had broken through the front there, they would attempt to establish a number of bridgeheads over the major rivers. In addition, the planners allowed for members of a fifth column (whose numbers and strength were estimated as fairly low) and airborne troops, who would endeavor to disrupt the mobilization and concentration of the Dutch armed forces and to take control of important objectives such as river crossings and airfields without inflicting any damage on them. Nuclear bombs, they assumed, would not be dropped on the territory of the Netherlands. Such weapons were scarce, and the Netherlands was on the sidelines. Moreover, the occupiers would try to take control of the Dutch economic centers with as little damage as possible. The darkest scenario was that of at most a single nuclear bomb dropped on the Netherlands, aimed primarily at breaking the morale of the population.[14]

The allies tried to establish a strong defense against this threat as quickly as possible. The Dutch army had difficulties in keeping up with the pace of the build-up, not establishing a complete army corps until the mid-1950s. It consisted of one combat-ready division and eventually three mobilizable divisions. In time of war this corps would operate under the commander of the

Northern Army Group (NORTHAG), a position held by the commander of BAOR. An almost equal number of territorial troops were to be raised. This plan, in fact, ran counter to American wishes in particular. They wanted the Dutch to concentrate all efforts on the combined forces in the front line. But the Dutch still had very vivid memories of the German airborne invasion of May 1940.[15] Other points of criticism concerned the low percentage of regular military personnel, the relatively high ratio of mobilizable reserve troops, and their infrequent refresher training exercises.[16] During the early years the Dutch performance in military exercises came under heavy criticism from allied observers. According to Montgomery, the Dutch army was "unfit to fight anybody."[17] At his insistence, a military mission from Supreme Headquarters Allied Powers Europe (SHAPE) was sent to the Netherlands and for six years provided assistance in the build-up and training of military units.[18]

Persuading NATO to include the IJssel River in its plans from the outset took a lot of effort by Dutch politicians and military officers. The French in particular were opposed to the idea. They wanted a defensive line located entirely behind the Rhine.[19] What many people did not know at the time was that the Americans simultaneously had adopted a peripheral strategy, under which the allies would withdraw behind the Pyrenees.[20] The fact that the IJssel River was eventually included in the defense plans resulted from British interests and especially from Dutch practical preparations that managed to turn the IJssel into a formidable water obstacle. In case of an enemy attack, two large floating barriers would be moved into the Rhine and Waal Rivers. In this way the water from the Rhine would flow into the IJssel, which in conjunction with a third barrier to be placed in that river would cause the IJssel to flood. No fewer than four hundred thousand civilians would have had to be evacuated. Full flooding would have taken six to seven days to complete. That was roughly the same time as the Soviet units were expected to need to reach the river line. The allied military leaders quickly became confident in the huge water barrier.[21]

All efforts were focused on the implementation of the operational plan of the Dutch army corps, which became official in mid-November 1952.[22] That plan was based on the higher-level allied plans that had been introduced during the course of the year.[23] Thus it was part of the collective allied response to a potential attack by the Soviet Union. The territory of the Netherlands was divided into the operational area (the combat zone) and the rear areas, the National Sector (zone of the interior) where the defense of the territory would take place and the Rhine-IJssel defense would be supported. The

National Sector was also considered to be a staging area (communications zone), from where supplies would be moved up to the troops in the combat zone and to which casualties would be evacuated. The combat zone on Dutch territory was organized from north to south as follows: (1) the area with the three most northeasterly provinces, under the command of the territorial commander north;[24] (2) the area covering roughly the provinces of Overijssel, Utrecht, Gelderland, and part of North Brabant, which in wartime would be under the command of the commander of Netherlands I Corps; (3) the area including the eastern part of North Brabant and the northern and central parts of the province of Limburg, which would be under the command of the commander of British I Corps; and (4) the area of South Limburg, which would be under the command of the Belgian corps. Allied operational plans stated that as soon as enemy units reached the Rhine-IJssel line, the whole of the Netherlands would be included in the combat zone.

In the initial draft plans, the boundary between the Dutch and the British corps was farther north, along the Waal River. Increasing allied confidence in the IJssel line was one reason for moving the border farther south. The result was that one Dutch reserve division would have to be mobilized in order to operate to the south of the major rivers. That in turn would allow British units to concentrate on dealing with the expected major thrust of the enemy attack. If the attack had taken place in the Dutch sector, after all, support would have been provided by the British 7th Armoured Division.[25]

According to this operational plan, the Dutch corps would have operated as follows.[26] Prior to or at the very latest upon receiving the NATO simple alert, telegram N would be issued, whereupon a number of strategic security measures would be initiated. Platoons from the Royal Netherlands Military Constabulary (Koninklijke Marechaussee) would step up border controls. Security units, made up of conscripts who had completed four to eight months of military service, would occupy major intersections, communications centers, and other key points. In addition, surveillance and demolition troops would be sent to bridges, locks, and ferries. At the same time, a combat-ready infantry regiment would move forward to the Dortmund-Ems Canal to prepare demolitions between Rheine and Haren.[27] A reconnaissance squadron and transport and engineer troops also would move to that area. The defense of the three floating barriers, which were already under permanent protection during peacetime, would increase rapidly to one infantry battalion per position plus air defense artillery.

At that stage preparations would start as unobtrusively as possible for the flooding and the evacuation of the population in the IJssel area. The evacuation of a limited number of Dutch and allied nationals from the occupied zones of the Federal Republic of Germany (FRG) to the Netherlands, Britain, and the United States also would begin. A start would also be made on removing boats from the Rhine. As well as avoiding material loss, that measure would deprive the enemy of the use of those boats to cross the river and, in the event of the area being occupied, would limit the opportunities for transporting ores to and coal from the Ruhr area. The majority of troops in training depots would move westward. Plans to move certain training units to other countries in order to pursue their training and continue the battle were abandoned because of objections by the proposed host countries.

As soon as possible after the simple alert, the mobilization telegrams P and Q would go out. At that stage, measures to cover general mobilization would be implemented. The units providing security would be replaced by or augmented with mobilized so-called Q units. Six Q-companies would move to the border in order to control the flow of expected "panicking refugees"—estimates of numbers were as high as one million—from the FRG. It would be necessary to keep the refugees out of the corps area of operations as far as possible. Holding camps would be set up in the northern provinces. Any refugees who managed to cross the IJssel and those who entered the Netherlands to the south of the major rivers would be taken to Belgium as quickly as possible.

The second phase of the preparations would begin once the reinforced alert was issued. Mobilization telegrams B and C would be issued in quick succession, after which there would be effective general mobilization. If the enemy actually attacked, a general alert would be announced, which would initiate the third phase. Only then could the order to flood completely be issued. As a consequence, around 225,000 inhabitants from the eastern bank of the IJssel were to be evacuated to the north and the east and another 185,000 from the western bank to the west. That operation would be completed within two days, before the great tide of panicking refugees reached the Netherlands. The order to flood would mean that it was no longer possible for boats to leave the Rhine, which is why that withdrawal operation had to be completed before the general alert. Further, it is likely that once the signal was given, a number of prominent Dutch citizens would have left the country. That number would be limited to avoid creating the impression that the defense was a hopeless cause.

The defense also consisted of a dynamic phase and a static phase. The first—dynamic—phase involved withdrawing to behind the Rhine-IJssel line, carrying out as much demolition as possible along the way in order to delay the enemy advance. Own losses were to be kept as low as possible. The demolitions would be carried out by the regiment on the Dortmund-Ems Canal and by demolitions troops stationed along a number of other demolition lines.[28] In the Rheine-Zutphen-Rees triangle the reconnaissance squadron was to remain in contact with the British corps located to the south of the Dutch corps. If the British corps or the forward infantry regiment had to withdraw, that squadron would be responsible for identifying in good time any threat from either the north or the south. During withdrawal it would be necessary to ensure that the bridges were not destroyed before the allied units crossed them. The Royal Netherlands Military Constabulary would have to keep certain routes clear of refugees. Obviously, those troops would have to cross the IJssel before flooding was completed.

In the static phase of the defense, the 1st Division, and from 1955 on also the 5th Division (both mobilizable reserve units), would take up the defense behind the IJssel. Since that would have been an insufficient force, territorial regiments were also earmarked for the IJssel defense. The area of operations of the mobilizable 3rd Division was below the Waal, behind the Rhine. The combat-ready 4th Division would be held on the Veluwe as the corps reserve and a counterattack force. The regiment that withdrew from the Dortmund-Ems Canal and the reconnaissance squadron and the battalions that initially had been stationed at the barriers would also move to that sector. According to the plans, the defensive operations would be supported by the Dutch navy's IJsselmeer and Wadden Sea Flotillas and, after completion of their mission in the German Bight, by the Royal Naval Elbe Squadron and the U.S. Navy Weser River Patrol Squadron.

Over the course of the first half of the 1950s the allies gradually grew more confident. This is reflected, for example, in the objectives of the major international exercises conducted during those years. Exercise COUNTERTHRUST in 1951 was an exercise in withdrawal. HOLD FAST one year later centered on persistent defense. GRAND REPULSE in 1953 involved the rehearsal of a rapid counterstrike by an independent corps. In that exercise one British armored division and a Canadian brigade were put under the command of the Dutch corps commander—a clear sign of confidence in the progress that had been made in the build-up of the Dutch army. The last large-scale allied exercise to be held for some time, BATTLE ROYAL in 1954, was actually a ground offensive exercise. There were, however, major operational concerns remaining in the areas of air defense and supply.[29]

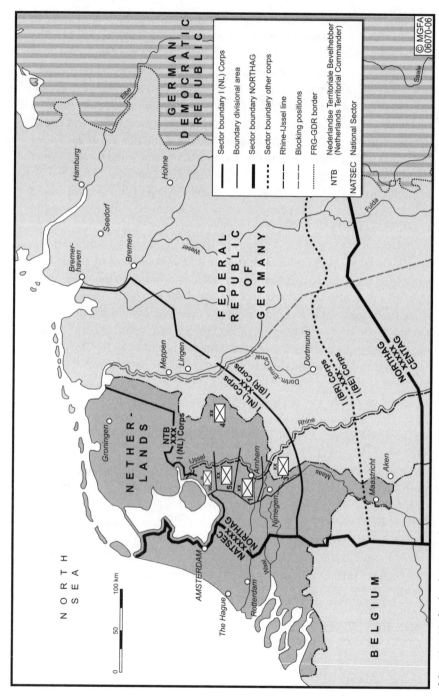

Map 13.1. Netherlands I Corps's area of operations, early 1955–July 1958.

Toward the Weser

Nonetheless, on 1 July 1958 NATO's main defensive line was moved forward considerably to the Weser and Fulda Rivers.[30] That shift was possible because the FRG, having joined NATO in 1955, had been able to commit its initial divisions to the allied defensive system. Additionally, allied armed forces had an ever increasing number of tactical nuclear weapons at their disposal, which made NATO a great deal stronger and enhanced its power and deterrence. Under the NATO strategy of Massive Retaliation, member states were firmly resolved to counter any form of enemy attack using all means at their disposal.[31] The Dutch corps was assigned the northernmost sector in the NORTHAG area of operations, next to the sector of German I Corps.

For the Dutch army the new operational tasks entailed a number of substantial challenges. In peacetime the Dutch units were based far away from their deployment zones. At first, concerns about this so-called maldeployment were aggravated because there were no sound agreements on the crossing of borders by Dutch troops. Although the 1956 events in Hungary did result in the modification of allied alert procedures, no solution to this problem was ever found.[32] It was not until 1967 that better arrangements were established.[33]

The forward defensive line required a larger number of combat-ready troops capable of responding rapidly. Another complicating factor was that the SACEUR at the time, American general Lauris Norstad, doubted whether NATO, and ultimately the president of the United States, would respond to any kind of aggression with the immediate use of nuclear weapons, considering the devastating effects such an action would have.[34] For a number of years SHAPE had been urging the Netherlands to establish a second combat-ready division.[35] But for many years such an action had not been possible because of the sheer size of a division and its necessary supporting units.

The establishment of a second combat-ready division became feasible only after the size of divisions was decreased. That happened when all the NATO member countries began adapting their armies to the conditions of nuclear warfare. Initially the Netherlands developed its own version, an infantry divisional structure known as Atom. The key characteristic of this divisional organization was the disbanding of the infantry regiments and the establishment of tactical battle group staffs that, depending on the operational situation, would be assigned a number of attachable divisional units. The core of the combat power came from seven infantry battalions and two tank battalions, all of which were capable of operating with a fairly high degree of autonomy. However, when the commander of Allied Land Forces Central Europe in 1959 presented a new divisional organization, the so-called LANDCENT Division, the Netherlands also adapted that organization. The new divisional structure, notable for its self-contained brigades, was the answer to the enemy's expected rapid, large-scale offensive with mechanized units. All units in the NATO Central Sector had to be capable of conducting defensive operations while maintaining optimal mobility. With the support of antiarmor defenses, the counterattack then could be launched. The enemy units had to be forced into concentrations that would make them vulnerable to attack with nuclear weapons. Artificial terrain obstacles and tactical air forces would be used to support the ground forces.[36]

In order to meet the modified requirements, the Dutch corps was completely reorganized and equipped with a large amount of new materiel. As of 1959 the corps officially had two combat-ready divisions, the 1st and the 4th Divisions, although it would take until 1968 before the last of the total of six brigades was finally combat ready. Those divisions were assigned to the front line of the corps area of operations, while the mobilizable 5th Division was positioned in the rear combat zone as a reserve force. The rear boundary of the rear combat zone was the Dortmund-Ems Canal. This meant that the roles of the combat-ready and mobilizable divisions were now reversed. During the 1960s the combat-ready units were fully mechanized and motorized. They were equipped with French AMX tracked armored vehicles, Dutch (DAF) YP 408 wheeled armored vehicles, and tracked amphibious vehicles of the American M-113 family. The mobilizable units for the time being had to manage with the old equipment released by the combat-ready units.[37] During the first half of the 1960s the Dutch corps was allocated tactical nuclear weapons, including the MGR-1 Honest John rocket, nuclear-capable M-110 8-inch howitzers, and atomic demolition munitions (ADM).[38]

The full deployment of all assigned units would have been a major undertaking, partly because of the great distance to the combat zone. Assuming that there would first have been a period of tensions, during which all the preparations established in the formal alert system could have been carried out, such a deployment would have transpired as follows.[39] As soon as the NATO preliminary military vigilance alert was given, the covering forces would assemble in the east of the Netherlands. Following discussions between the chief of the Dutch General Staff, the commander of NORTHAG, and the German government in Bonn, the covering force would move to the Weser. As of 15 December 1960 the main body of this force was the 121st Light Brigade, consisting of two reconnaissance battalions, three companies

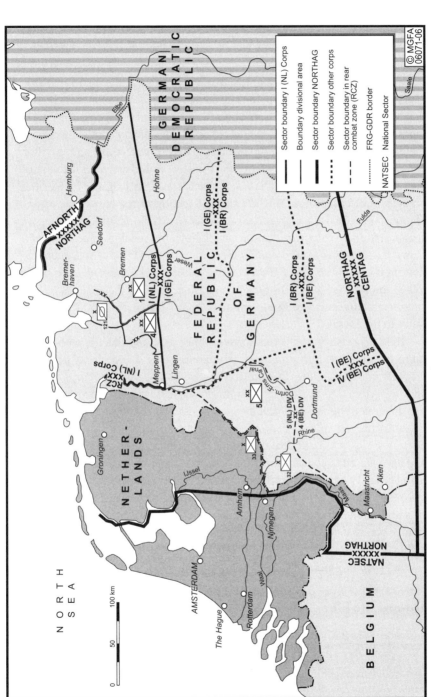

Map 13.2. Netherlands I Corps's sector within NORTHAG's area of operations, summer 1961.

of commandos, and a mobile security company.[40] The rest of the corps would assemble a few hours later but would not be allowed to cross the border straight away. That would happen only once the simple alert was issued.

Upon arrival in the Dutch corps area of operations, the 121st Light Brigade would assume the tasks of the German 3rd Panzer Division, which until that time was responsible for screening the advance of the corps. The covering force would make the preparations for the flooding, complete work for the demolitions that had already been prepared in peacetime, and monitor key points. As soon as possible the 1st Division would arrive in the area of operations and take over the tasks of the 121st Light Brigade. Part of the brigade would then move to the northern section of the corps area of operations, a sector with a great deal of water in which no attacks by enemy armored units were expected and where light troops would suffice. However, many of the covering troops would remain in the 1st Division area of operations in the southern sector of the corps area. The 4th Division would quickly follow the 1st Division to the area of operations. Only if the enemy attacked completely unexpectedly would the tank-heavy 1st Division be the first to move to the Weser.

The 1st Division would conduct a mobile aggressive defense with maximum fire support, including nuclear weapons, over a wide front with two brigades in the front line. The 4th Division would deploy as the corps reserve and be prepared to execute counterattacks against large enemy units entering the area of operations. The key to success was the importance of waiting until the last minute before launching a counterattack so that a single nuclear strike could eliminate as many as possible of the enemy units that had been forced to concentrate. After 1962 the plan provided for the 7th German Panzer Grenadier Brigade to be placed under the operational command of Netherlands I Corps, once the brigade had carried out its covering mission and upon order of the commander of NORTHAG. One reason for this change was that two combat-ready infantry battalions from the 4th Division had been sent to Dutch New Guinea in response to the threat of a military conflict with Indonesia.

Toward the Elbe

For years SHAPE had been calling for the stationing of Dutch troops in the FRG, preferably an entire division.[41] The negotiations between the German and Dutch governments eventually led to an agreement without financial considerations. As of 1963 a reinforced Dutch armored brigade was stationed

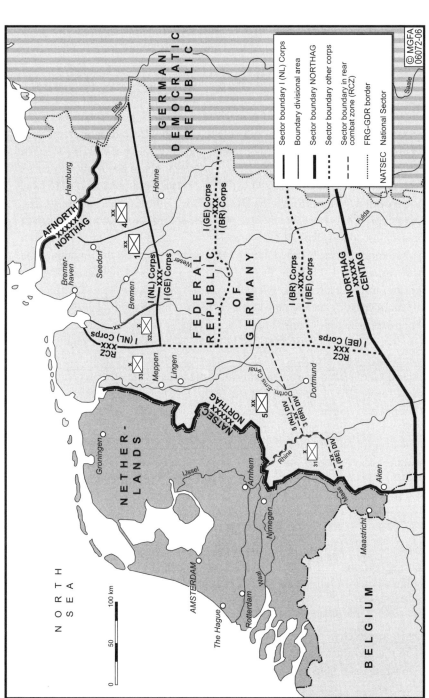

Map 13.3. Netherlands I Corps's sector within NORTHAG's area of operations, fall 1963.

in Seedorf, while a German air force training unit was based in the army camp near Budel in the south of the Netherlands. Those were the first German troops to be permanently stationed abroad since World War II.[42]

Seedorf is situated east of the Weser River. The fact that the Dutch brigade was stationed there had its origin in the last major shift forward of the allied defensive line. From September 1963 NATO's objective was to stop the Warsaw Pact forces as close as possible to the Elbe River, or in more general terms, as close as possible to the Inner-German Border between the western FRG and the eastern German Democratic Republic.[43] Naturally, the corps sectors were moved farther eastward as well. The main enemy offensive was not expected to run through the Dutch sector, with its many waterways. The Dutch corps, therefore, would face the enemy forces only at a later stage of operations, coming from the German sector located to the south.[44] The Dutch 41st Armored Brigade based in Seedorf generally assumed the mission of the now-disbanded 121st Light Brigade. Reinforced by a reconnaissance battalion and units sent from the Netherlands, the 41st was tasked with securing the main crossings of the Elbe in the corps area in the event of a simple alert. An engineer battalion immediately would begin preparing the demolitions. On order of the commander of NORTHAG, German I Corps would be responsible for the Dutch sector until the commander of the Dutch corps was able to take it over. In contrast to the earlier plans, the 4th Division would move to the area of operations ahead of the 1st Division. Its brigades were to conduct delaying actions in close coordination with the German 3rd Panzer Division, operating to the south of the area. The Aue River was the main line of resistance, which could be abandoned only on order of the corps commander. There, two Honest John rocket sections would support the corps and the ADM would be deployed. The bulk of the 1st Division would follow the 4th Division to the area of operations, where it would conduct operations on both sides of the Weser.

Deployment according to the plan was based on having a period of at least seventy-two hours in which the combat-ready units could move to their battle positions. If that were not the case—and that would be decided at the point when the reinforced alert was declared—a contingency plan would take effect. The 41st Armored Brigade would act as a screening force between the Elbe and the Weser and would then withdraw behind the Weser. The 1st Division, which in that case would move to the area of operations first, would as in the pre-1963 plan conduct the defense behind the river. The 4th Division would assemble to the west and the east of the Hunte and, acting as the corps reserve, prepare to counterattack. The objective of this plan was to hold the Weser for at least forty-eight hours to enable allied radar and navigation stations to remain operational for long enough for the allied air forces to execute the SACEUR interdiction plan. That plan involved the elimination of enemy airfields and bases of operations by aerial bombing raids and missile attacks. At the same time, SACEUR would defend NATO's own nuclear forces from air attack with Nike and Hawk surface-to-air guided missiles, which were based in belts throughout the FRG. Dutch units were components of this system.

The 1 September 1963 operational plans were provisional. A new plan took effect on 1 April 1966 that superseded the contingency plan. All defense was to be conducted as far to the east as possible. Again, this concept was based on a minimum warning time of seventy-two hours after the declaration of simple alert. Under the new plan, the 4th Division would no longer conduct a delaying battle, but a defensive one. The 41st Armored Brigade, with a reconnaissance battalion under its operational control, would monitor the Elbe and then conduct delaying actions. That would be followed by a mobile defense intended to engage the enemy with its strong armored capability in a battle of attrition, to bring it to a halt, and to destroy it. To achieve this would require the brigades to coordinate closely with the German 8th Panzer Brigade. The decisive battle again would take place in the area of the smaller Aue and Seeve Rivers.

In accordance with the doctrine of Flexible Response, officially adopted by NATO in 1967, nuclear weapons would be committed by the 1st Division only if the enemy were to break through the Aue-Seeve defense. After that the division would conduct a robust defense along the Weser. Among other things, that would allow the 4th Division to withdraw. In the meantime, the mobilized 5th Division, if it remained under the command of the Dutch corps commander during wartime, would continue to train the mobilizable units in the rear area, support operations in the Dutch and German corps areas, and on the order of the commander of NORTHAG, support operations in the rear area.

In 1969 the NORTHAG defense assumed the form it was to maintain with a few minor changes for the following two decades. In an effort to sustain the defense by conventional means for a longer period, one British and one German division were withdrawn from the front line to form a powerful counterattack reserve force. That change meant that the Dutch corps area of responsibility was extended southward and became about forty kilometers wider. Another consequence was that the Dutch units would possibly face the main enemy attack directly during the initial phase of combat rather than

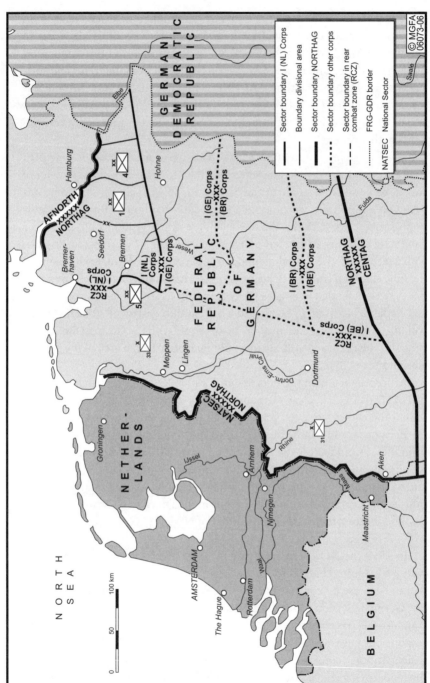

Map 13.4. Netherlands I Corps's sector within NORTHAG's area of operations, summer 1966.

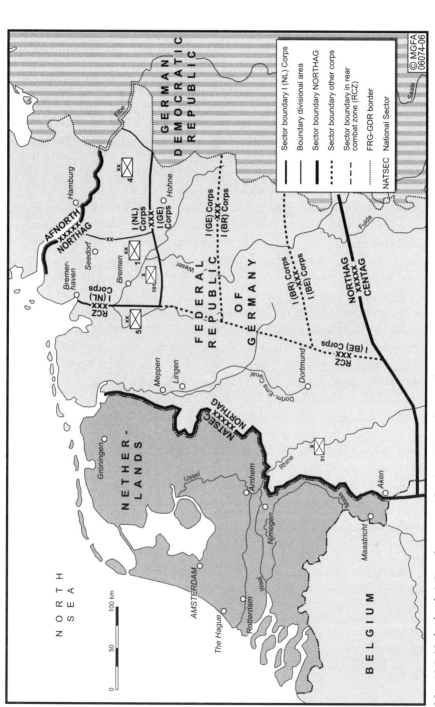

Map 13.5. Netherlands I Corps's sector within NORTHAG's area of operations, spring 1969.

at a later stage, with the attack coming from the more southerly German area of operations.[45]

The commander of NORTHAG assumed a very short warning time. The Dutch corps now had to be able to reach its area of operations within forty-eight hours of the reinforced alert without prior warning. It would now move directly from its peacetime bases to its wartime positions without first concentrating forces in the east of the Netherlands. The expected warning time, however, was too short to complete the full deployment of the corps, including the logistics build-up. There thus was an increased risk of the corps not being ready on time. In that case support would be provided by the German 3rd Panzer Division, which would then be in danger of being unable to fulfill satisfactorily its mission as the reserve for the German I Corps. Given the expected conventional superiority of the Warsaw Pact, the new operational plan for the Netherlands I Corps that took effect on 1 April 1969 included the early use of nuclear weapons in order to destroy any enemy units that broke through the defenses.

By the end of the 1960s the Netherlands was contributing substantially to NATO's forward defense. It had come a long way since the beginning of the 1950s. In international exercises and various competitions, such as the Canadian Army Trophy, Dutch military personnel were putting up a good or even a very good performance. There were still major concerns, however. The overall crisis confronting NATO, and the fact that the alliance, despite its flexible strategy, would still have to resort to the use of nuclear weapons at a very early stage, quite naturally troubled the Netherlands. A direct cause of concern for the Dutch armed forces was whether or not the nation would be prepared and able to bear in the long run the increasing burden of an effective defense. This issue, which all the member countries faced, put the Netherlands by the 1970s in an awkward position within the alliance.[46] Finally, there remained the persistent operational problem concerning the maldeployment of the Dutch corps. Even the construction of advanced depots and improvements in the transportation of units and materiel to the area of operations could never entirely eliminate the fear that the Dutch units would not manage to reach the war in time.

Notes

1. This essay is concerned mainly with preprepared land operations. To date no detailed study has been made of the Dutch contributions to allied air operations. It is expected that this will be done in the near future.

2. J. Hoffenaar, "Inleiding op de memoires van M. R. H. Calmeyer," in M. R. H. Calmeyer, *Herinneringen: Memoires van een christen, militair en politicus* (The Hague: Sdu Uitgevers, 1997), 159–60.

3. P. M. H. Groen, *Marsroutes en dwaalsporen: Het militair-strategische beleid in Indonesië* (The Hague: Sdu Uitgevers, 1991); and J. Hoffenaar and B. Schoenmaker, *Met de blik naar het Oosten: De koninklijke Landmacht 1945–1990* (The Hague: Sdu Uitgevers, 1994), 25–39.

4. J. W. L. Brouwer and C. M. Megens, "Het debat in de ministerraad over de Nederlandse militaire bijdrage aan de NAVO, 1949–1951," *Bijdragen en Mededelingen betreffende de Geschiedenis der Nederlanden* 107 (1992): 486–500.

5. For the various evacuation plans after 1945, see G. Teitler, "Evacuatie, vlucht en opvang: Voorbereiding op een Sovjetaanval," in *De Koude Oorlog: Maatschappij en Krijgsmacht in de jaren '50*, ed. J. Hoffenaar and G. Teitler (The Hague: Sdu Uitgeverij Koninginnegracht, 1992), 102–17.

6. One example is the exasperation expressed by the first commander of the British Mission, Brigadier H. P. Gardham, early in 1946. He found the army build-up a "disappointingly slow business" and the prewar officers "incredibly bad." This criticism persisted for several years. National Archives, Kew, England, archive Foreign Office 371/60218, letter from Gardham, 23 Jan. 1946.

7. For more information about the build-up of the Dutch armed forces and the first operational plans, see J. Hoffenaar, "'Hannibal ante portas': The Soviet Military Threat and the Build-Up of the Dutch Armed Forces, 1948–1958," *Journal of Military History* 66 (2002): 163–91.

8. Central Archives Depot Ministry of Defense (CAD), archive NL Detachment HQ NORTHAG, box 1, file 1, Report of a BAOR exercise on 9 Sept. 1949, written by the NL liaison officer to BAOR Col. A. D. C. van der Voort van Zijp. See also Robert Evans's chapter in this volume.

9. CAD, archive HKGS, file 1 ZG (Lion Plan), HKGS, section G3, Bureau E, no. Lion Litt 21c, "Voorlopige operatieve aanwijzingen voor de CSV," 22 Dec. 1949.

10. CAD, archive HKGS, file 1 ZG (Lion Plan), HKGS, section G1, no. 170P ZG, "Gebruik troepen in verband met short-term plan 1949," 31 Jan. 1949.

11. This topic is currently the subject of a dissertation. In autumn 1947 there was already a plan for the air defense of the Netherlands, drafted in cooperation with officers from the Royal Air Force. CAD, archive Minister of War ZG, box 7, folder 371, plan for air defence of the Netherlands, 25 Oct. 1947. This cooperation continued within the Western Union.

12. See Dieter Krüger, "Die Entstehung der NATO-Luftverteidigung und die Integration der Luftwaffe," in *Die Luftwaffe 1950 bis 1970: Konzeption, Aufbau, Integration,* Bernd Lemke, Dieter Krüger, Heinz Rebhan, and Wolfgang Schmidt (Munich: Oldenbourg Verlag, 2006), 485–556.

13. See Hoffenaar, "Hannibal ante portas," 165–66, and Jan Hoffenaar, "'To Defend or Not to Defend': Drawing the Line in the Netherlands," in *War Plans and Al-*

liances in the Cold War: Threat Perceptions in the East and West, ed. Vojtech Mastny, Sven G. Holtsmark, and Andreas Wenger (London: Routledge, 2006), 270–71.

14. Hoffenaar and Schoenmaker, Met de blik naar het Oosten, 107–8.

15. See Hoffenaar, "'Hannibal ante portas,'" 180–81.

16. See Annual Reviews (The Netherlands) 1951 and following years, NATO Archives, Brussels.

17. This opinion was mentioned during a report of a discussion with Montgomery in the National Council of Military Affairs (Raad Militaire Aangelegenheden van het Koninkrijk, RMAK) on 1 December 1951. Ministry of General Affairs, semi-static archive, box RMAK II, minutes RMAK, 1 Dec. 1951.

18. Besides the Netherlands, Portugal and Luxembourg had a similar mission. SHAPE, Mons, Historical Section, 12C R-1 L-14, "A Narrative Summary of the Progress in Training NATO Forces during 1951, 1952 and 1953."

19. For an extensive analysis of the conflict of the possible place of the IJssel in allied operational plans, see Hoffenaar, "'To Defend or Not to Defend.'"

20. Ibid., 270.

21. Hoffenaar and Schoenmaker, Met de blik naar het Oosten, 113–14. J. R. Beekhuis, "De gevolgen van de inundaties," in Drijvende stuwen voor de landsverdediging: Een geschiedenis van de IJssellinie, ed. J. R. Beekmans and C. Schilt (Utrecht: Walburg Pers, 1997), 169–82.

22. CAD, archive I Corps 1952 t/m 1957 (1 LK), box 107, file 78, Operational Instruction no. 1, 20 Nov. 1952.

23. See Bruno Thoss's chapter in this volume.

24. In 1955 the most northerly part of the province of North Holland was added.

25. Semi-static archive, Royal Netherlands Army (RNLA), archive MPA HKGS 1948–1955, file 1561, letter Gen. Sir John Harding (C-C BAOR) to Lt.-Gen. Hasselman (C-C RNLA), 22 Aug. 1952, no. BAOR 1053 C in C.

26. Hoffenaar and Schoenmaker, Met de blik naar het Oosten, 116–26.

27. After 1956 the regiment would have been the whole combat-ready 4th Division.

28. Hoffenaar and Schoenmaker, Met de blik naar het Oosten, 116–26.

29. See Herman Roozenbeek's chapter in this volume and Krüger, "Die Entstehung der NATO-Luftverteidigung."

30. See Bruno Thoss's chapter in this volume.

31. Given the developments in the years that followed, it is important to realize that the document detailing the strategy of Massive Retaliation—the "Overall Strategic Concept for the Defense of the NATO Area" (MC 14/2)—also states that NATO must be capable of responding to infiltration, local attacks, and so on, without having to resort immediately to the use of nuclear weapons.

32. Netherlands Institute of Military History (NIMH), Department of Public Information and Collection Management (PI&C), Jaarverslag Koninklijke Landmacht 1957, 47.

33. NIMH, PI&C, G3 contribution to Annual Report RNLA 1967.

34. Hoffenaar and Schoenmaker, *Met de blik naar het Oosten,* 145.

35. Ibid., 147.

36. Ministry of Defense, semi-static archives section, archive Organisation RNLA, file 000149, Report of Exercise Finem Respice (20 June 1961), III "Enemy development."

37. Hoffenaar and Schoenmaker, *Met de blik naar het Oosten,* 190–98.

38. Ibid., 157–62.

39. Ibid., 166–69.

40. In autumn 1961, as a result of the Berlin crisis, the 121st Light Brigade was temporarily stationed at the NATO firing range in Bergen-Hohne, Germany.

41. Defense White Paper 1964, 21. It is worth noting that in the early 1950s negotiations were already taking place regarding the stationing of troops on the front line, near Lingen. That was never implemented. CAD, archive NL Detachment NORTHAG, box 3, file "Onderwerpen algemene aard."

42. W. Klinkert, "Het paradepaard van de vrije wereld: Nederland en de Berlijnse crisis," in *In de schaduw van de Muur: Maatschappij en Krijgsmacht rond 1960,* ed. B. Schoenmaker and J. A. M. M. Janssen (The Hague: Sdu Uitgevers, 1997), 9–33.

43. See Bruno Thoss's chapter in this volume.

44. Hoffenaar and Schoenmaker, *Met de blik naar het Oosten,* 170–74.

45. Ibid., 230–32.

46. J. Hoffenaar, "'De baby is er!' De Defensienota 1974 en het gevecht over de toekomst van de krijgsmacht," in *Confrontatie en ontspanning: Maatschappij en krijgsmacht in de Koude Oorlog 1966–1989,* ed. Jan Hoffenaar, Jan van der Meulen, and Rolf de Winter (The Hague: Sdu Uitgevers, 2004), 37–58.

14

Concluding Remarks

Warfare in the Central Sector

Gregory W. Pedlow

More than two decades have passed since the end of the Cold War, and for younger readers the subject of this publication must seem like ancient history, and a history that fortunately never happened. But I know that for me and anyone else over the age of fifty, the Cold War was deadly serious and had a major impact on our lives, even if we were not professional soldiers. I don't know what it was like in Europe during the 1950s, but I certainly recall taking part in atomic bomb attack drills during elementary school in the United States, as we hid under our desks and covered our heads. As a high school student in the early 1960s, I prepared plans for converting our basement into an emergency fallout shelter and hoped that when—not if—the Soviet nuclear attack came, it would be when I was at home with my parents, not at school. During high school and later at university I was an active war gamer, playing historical simulations of the great battles of history. But we also looked at battles yet to come—between NATO and the Warsaw Pact—in some very detailed war games published in the 1960s and 1970s. To us this seemed like "future history"—something that would eventually happen but had just not yet arrived.

Our preparations for a war between NATO and the Warsaw Pact were not limited to sitting around a table and playing war games while drinking beer and eating pretzels. During the 1960s compulsory military service was a reality for almost all of us in Europe and the United States, and I suspect that many if not most of us over the age of fifty spent some time in uniform. I know that in my case I was beginning my third year of the United States Reserve Officers Training Corps program in 1968, and two years later I was commissioned as a second lieutenant. Training as an infantry officer and then as a military intelligence officer followed, and in those days I was very well acquainted with Soviet military tactics and equipment. Although I served only two years on active duty, I spent another twenty-six years as a reserve officer and participated in a number of major exercises in Europe during the late 1970s and early 1980s, preparing for the big war between NATO and the Warsaw Pact that never came, thank heavens! So for me, and I suspect for many readers, this subject is not just dry academic speculation about something that never happened but a discussion about a period that had a major impact on our lives.

Let's look now at what we have learned from these contributions about the planning and preparations for this war that never happened. First of all I am struck by the centrality of the debate over the use of nuclear weapons for both sides in the Cold War. Lawrence Kaplan has described NATO's growing reliance on nuclear weapons in the 1950s to make up for the alliance's failure to achieve anything near to the very ambitious force goal of fifty divisions set at the Lisbon Conference of 1952. Later in the 1950s there was a growing demand on the part of the Europeans to acquire their own nuclear weapons, a goal that Supreme Allied Commander, Europe (SACEUR), General Lauris Norstad attempted to head off with his proposal to make NATO a nuclear power. The United States soon watered down this proposal by converting it into the Multilateral Force (MLF)—a naval force with Polaris missiles, but with control of the nuclear warheads remaining in U.S. hands—and this halfway measure never came into effect as NATO grew increasingly disenchanted with the doctrine of Massive Retaliation and replaced it with Flexible Response in 1967.

What strikes me here is the growing move away from a massive early use of nuclear weapons in the United States during the Kennedy and Johnson administrations, a trend that had begun even earlier in NATO under SACEUR Norstad, while at the same time the Warsaw Pact was changing its doctrine in favor of a massive initial nuclear strike, as Matthias Uhl has shown. I must admit that my hair stood on end when I read of Warsaw Pact exercises that envisioned the use of 2,200 nuclear weapons in a war against NATO! I feel great sympathy for Admiral Derevyanko's very legitimate concerns that a nuclear war would destroy and contaminate not only Western Europe but also much of the Soviet Union, because of the prevailing winds.[1] And such contamination would not have stopped at the eastern borders of the Soviet Union.

Viktor Gavrilov's contribution examined the strategic nuclear balance between the superpowers, where the Soviet Union was for a long time at a disadvantage. He showed how the increasing reliance on nuclear weapons by the Soviet Union allowed it to reduce the size of its armed forces, a process that was somewhat similar to Western thinking during the 1950s, the difference being that the Soviet Union already had large ground forces and gradually reduced them, whereas the West began relying on nuclear weapons to make up for the fact that they would never be able to reach the force goals set in the early 1950s. What I find interesting is Gavrilov's emphasis on the Cuban missile crisis as a turning point in strategic thinking, with both sides realizing that a nuclear war was unwinnable and henceforth acquiring nuclear weapons only as a deterrent. But I find this hard to reconcile with Matthias Uhl's reporting on Warsaw Pact exercises, which apparently ruled out a conventional war in Europe even as late as 1968.

The idea of the primary purpose of armed forces being deterrence, not warfare, was also mentioned in Helmut Hammerich's contribution, citing Colonel—later General and the first German Deputy SACEUR—Gerd Schmückle. But during this period of the early 1960s, senior German officers holding high-level NATO military posts believed that nuclear weapons would have to be used if Germany was to be defended successfully. Nuclear weapons were also one of the important themes discussed by Bruno Thoss in his examination of NATO planning. Not surprisingly, the Germans were very uneasy about the use of nuclear weapons to defend their country, which reminds me of the infamous Vietnam War statement, "We had to destroy the village in order to save it."

Planning for the use of nuclear weapons in a war in Central Europe was a major theme for the collection as well. Richard Aldrich's contribution on the British Army of the Rhine (BAOR) continued the discussion of the controversies surrounding the possible use of atomic demolition munitions (ADM) in Germany, a topic begun by Bruno Thoss. Donald Carter showed how the U.S. Army sought to change its divisional structure in order to take into account operations on a nuclear battlefield. Then in the 1960s this unpopular "Pentomic" division was replaced by a new structure that most World War II generals would have recognized, as the army once again emphasized conventional warfare as part of the new doctrine of Flexible Response.

Nuclear planning also featured in Torsten Diedrich's contribution on the East German Nationale Volksarmee (NVA). But Warsaw Pact assumptions during exercises do not seem very realistic, with Diedrich showing that in the BURYA exercises of 1961, Warsaw Pact losses from nuclear strikes against an entire front were only seven companies, forty tanks, and one missile launcher.

Another common theme was NATO's gradual move to forward defense, beginning with a defense of the Rhine-IJssel line, later the Weser River, and finally the Inner-German Border. But as Robert Evans has shown, there were some disconnects during the move to this strategy. Thus up to the mid-1950s BAOR was still thinking in terms of falling back to the Rhine River, whereas the U.S. and French forces planned to defend farther forward. Had the British actually fallen back to the Rhine during a war, the flank of the American and French forces would have been left hanging in the air. And Evans has also shown that there were disconnects within the British armed forces themselves, with the army planning to avoid becoming decisively engaged while falling back to the Rhine, though the Royal Air Force needed to have its navigational and bombing aids in Germany protected for the first forty-eight hours of conflict so that nuclear strikes could be carried out. Thoss also discussed the gradual move of NATO's defenses east of the Rhine, with an interesting early strategy variant being the "gap" theory—to channelize Warsaw Pact forces in order to create more lucrative nuclear targets.

Forward defense also featured prominently in Helmut Hammerich's contribution, and Jan Hoffenaar showed the difficulties that the Dutch armed forces had in actually implementing forward defense because most of their forces were stationed too far to the rear. But the 1963 basing of a reinforced Dutch armored brigade in Seedorf—east of the Weser River—was an important symbol of NATO's commitment to defending Western Europe along the Inner-German Border.

Now that so much time has passed since German unification, it is sometimes hard to remember that a war between NATO and the Warsaw Pact would have pitted German against German from the German Federal Republic and the German Democratic Republic. This subject has been explained to us by Hammerich's and Diedrich's contributions.

Two other important areas were intelligence and logistics. I am fascinated by Richard Aldrich's "Sleeping Beauty" analogy for BAOR headquarters, with intelligence warning having the role of the handsome prince. As a former military intelligence officer myself, I find that characterization quite flattering! Also very interesting is his description of the intelligence-gathering resources available to the commander of the Northern Army Group, in marked contrast to NATO's need to rely on shared national intelligence at higher levels of command and at NATO headquarters. And Jan Hoffenaar has shown us that the NVA took a long time to build up an effective intelligence-gathering and analysis structure.

As for logistics, I am fascinated by Herman Roozenbeek's description of the efforts to develop multinational logistical facilities within NATO. This is a debate and effort that continues to this day. Dimitri Filippovych's contribution on Warsaw Pact logistics showed us the greatly increased logistical requirements of Soviet armies—for example, a tenfold increase in fuel consumption from 1946 to the mid-1950s—and the corresponding increase in the number and size of field trains to meet these logistical demands.

All in all, the contributions to this volume examine a limited but key part of the Cold War in great detail, unlike many previous studies on the Cold War that have focused on high-level political-military planning and decision making. We can only hope that there will be additional such detailed examinations of regional aspects of the Cold War in the future.

In conclusion, I would like to say that during my more than twenty-three-years as the head of NATO's history program, I have had the great fortune to serve from the final days of planning and preparation for a confrontation between NATO and the Warsaw Pact in Europe to a new era featuring cooperation in many areas and the end of the division of Europe into competing blocs. One of my most memorable experiences as the SHAPE historian was to sit at a table inside the headquarters in October 1990 with SACEUR General John R. Galvin and NATO's top generals on one side, and General M. A. Moiseyev, chief of the Soviet General Staff, and other Soviet generals on the other side during this historic first meeting of NATO and Warsaw Pact general officers at SHAPE. Since then we have seen the end of the Warsaw Pact and of the Soviet Union itself, and constantly increasing ties between NATO and Russia and other former members of the Warsaw Pact, with most of them now either members of NATO or participants in NATO's Partnership for Peace framework. We have even seen Russian participation in NATO-led operations, beginning with Bosnia and now most recently in operation ACTIVE ENDEAVOUR in the Mediterranean. While some journalists have talked about a possible new Cold War as the result of various remarks and actions by Russian president Vladimir Putin, I believe that in the long run, Russia and the West have too many common interests to return to the confrontational days of the Cold War.[2]

Notes

The views expressed in this chapter are those of the author and do not necessarily represent the views of the NATO Alliance or the Supreme Headquarters Allied Powers Europe. The contents of this essay are essentially unchanged from when it was delivered in 2007 at the conference in Münster, but I have changed a few time references to reflect the passage of five years since then.

1. Matthias Uhl's chapter cites a letter by Rear Admiral Derevyanko to Soviet premier Nikita Khrushchev in 1961 cautioning against attempting to achieve victory through unlimited nuclear warfare by asking, "Which planet do these people intend to live on in the future, and to which earth do they plan to send their troops to conquer territories? What use would it be to us in this condition?" Interestingly, a Soviet army colonel also named Derevyanko expressed similar views four years later; I do not know if the two men were related. P. M. Derevyanko, *Problemy revolyutsii v voennom dele* (Moscow, 1965), 111–12, cited in James M. McConnell, *The Soviet Shift in Emphasis from Nuclear to Conventional,* Center for Naval Analyses Research Contribution 490 (Alexandria, Va., 1983), 5.

2. When I made this remark—which reflected views I had developed during the mid-1990s, when NATO-Russian cooperation was at its high point and Russian troops were serving in NATO's peacekeeping force in Bosnia—at the 2007 conference in Münster, I was already having doubts about Russian membership in NATO occurring any time soon but decided to go ahead and include the statement as a friendly gesture toward the Russian participants present. Writing now in 2012, I believe that Russian membership in NATO is still a long way off, but I stand by my remark as a long-term goal for both NATO and Russia.

Contributors

RICHARD J. ALDRICH is professor of international security at the University of Warwick and author of several books, including *The Hidden Hand: Britain, America, and Cold War Secret Intelligence* (2001) and *GCHQ: The Uncensored Story of Britain's Most Secret Intelligence Agency* (2010). Since 2008, he has been leading a project funded by the Arts and Humanities Research Council titled "Landscapes of Secrecy: The Central Intelligence Agency and the Contested Record of U.S. Foreign Policy."

DONALD A. CARTER is a historian at the U.S. Army Center of Military History. His publications include "Eisenhower vs. the Generals," *Journal of Military History* (2007).

TORSTEN DIEDRICH is head of exhibition management at the Military History Research Institute (MGFA), Potsdam. He is the author of *Paulus—das Trauma von Stalingrad: Eine Biographie* (2009) and coauthor of *Die getarnte Armee: Geschichte der Kasernierten Volkspolizei 1952–1956* (2001).

ROBERT EVANS is head of the Army Historical Branch, which is a part of the UK Ministry of Defence. His previous publications include "The Origins and Brief History of the Commander in Chief and the Chief of the General Staff of the British Army," *British Army Review* (2011).

CAPTAIN (NAVAL) DIMITRI N. FILIPPOVYCH is professor of history at the Military University Moscow. He is a coeditor of *Vor dem Abgrund: Die Rolle der Streitkräfte der USA und der UdSSR sowie ihrer deutschen Bündnispartner in der Kubakrise* (with Matthias Uhl, 2005) and *Kto byl kto v Sovetskoj Voennoj Administracii v Germanii: 1945–1949; kratkij spravočnik* (with Manfred Heinemann, 1999).

COLONEL (RET.) VIKTOR GAVRILOV is leading research fellow at the Institute of Military History of the Russian Defense Ministry, Moscow. He is the author of *Voennaya razvedka informiruet: Dokumenty Razvedupravleniya Krasnoy Armii. Yanvar' 1939–iyun' 1941* (2008) and coauthor of *Balkanskiy tupik? Istoricheskaya sud'ba Yugoslavii v XX veke* (with Nina V. Vasil'evna, 2000).

LIEUTENANT COLONEL HELMUT HAMMERICH is a historian at the MGFA, Potsdam. He is currently writing about the implementation of NATO Strategy Flexible Response in the 1970s and 1980s. His previous publications include *Jeder für sich und Amerika gegen alle? Die Lastenteilung der NATO am Beispiel des Temporary Council Committee, 1949–1954* (2003).

JAN HOFFENAAR is head of the research division at the Netherlands Institute of Military History, The Hague, and professor of military history at Utrecht University. His main research topics are the Dutch military contribution to NATO and the Royal Netherlands Army during the Cold War. His publications include *Met de blik naar het Oosten: De Koninklijke Landmacht 1945–1990* (with Ben Schoenmaker, 1994); "'To Defend or Not Defend': Drawing the Line in the Netherlands," in *War Plans and Alliances in the Cold War* (edited by Vojtech Mastny, Sven G. Holstmark, and Andreas Wenger, 2006); and *Insurgency and Counterinsurgency: Irregular Warfare from 1800 to the Present* (edited with Thijs Brocades Zaalberg and Alan Lemmers, 2011).

LAWRENCE S. KAPLAN is a professorial lecturer in history at Georgetown University. His publications include *NATO and the UN: A Peculiar Relationship* (2010) and *NATO 1948: The Birth of the Transatlantic Alliance* (2007).

DIETER KRÜGER is associate professor (Privatdozent) of contemporary history at the Martin Luther University of Halle–Wittenberg and a historian at MGFA, Potsdam. He is the author of *Sicherheit durch Integration? Die wirtschaftliche und politische Zusammenarbeit Westeuropas 1947 bis 1957/58* (2003) and *Brennender Enzian: Die Operationsplanung der NATO für Österreich und Norditalien 1951 bis 1960* (2010).

GREGORY W. PEDLOW has been chief of the Historical Office at NATO's Supreme Headquarters Allied Powers Europe since 1989. He is the editor of *NATO Strategy Documents, 1949–1969*, and coeditor of *On Waterloo: Clausewitz, Wellington, and the Campaign of 1815* (2010).

HERMAN ROOZENBEEK is a senior researcher at the Netherlands Institute of Military History. He has written extensively on the history of the Royal Netherlands Army during the Cold War. His publications include *Vredesmacht in Libanon: De Nederlandse deelname aan UNIFIL 1979–1985* (with Ben Schoenmaker, 2004) and *De geest in de fles: De omgang van de Nederlandse defensieorganisatie met chemische strijdmiddelen 1915–1997* (with Jeoffrey van Woensel, 2010).

BRUNO THOSS is the former director of scholarship and currently acting head of the research department at MGFA, Potsdam. His publications include *Die NATO als Militärallianz: Strategie, Organisation und nukleare Kontrolle im Bündnis 1949–1959* (2003) and *NATO-Strategie und nationale Verteidigungsplanung: Planung und Aufbau der Bundeswehr unter den Bedingungen einer massiven atomaren Vergeltungsstrategie 1952 bis 1960* (2006).

MATTHIAS UHL is a senior researcher at the German Historical Institute Moscow. He is author of *Krieg um Berlin? Die sowjetische Militär- und Sicherheitspolitik in der zweiten Berlin-Krise 1958 bis 1962* (2008) and coauthor of *BND contra Sowjetarmee: Westdeutsche Militärspionage in der DDR* (with Armin Wagner, 2007).

MAJOR GENERAL DAVID T. ZABECKI, AUS (RET.), is the author of *The German 1918 Offensive: A Case Study in the Operational Level of War* and editor emeritus of *Vietnam* magazine. In 2012, he held the Shifrin Distinguished Chair in Military and Naval History at the United States Naval Academy, and he is also an honorary senior research fellow in the War Studies Programme at the University of Birmingham (United Kingdom).

Index

NVA analysts, 87; deployment of army corps and divisions of (1960s), 159 (map); as a "junior partner" in NATO, 11; media of, 78. *See also* Bundeswehr, the (West German Army)
White, Dick, 60
Wilson, Charles F., 142
WINTERSHIELD military exercise, 147
WINTEX military exercise, 83
Working Group on Intelligence and Other Data Exchange (NATO Special Committee), 67
World War II, 112, 135; destruction of the German Sixth Army in, 155

Yalta agreement (1948), 6
Yom Kippur War (1973), 69

Zakharov, Matvei V., 195
Zapad-69 command staff exercise, 47–48
Zerbel, Alfred, 157